Animating
Space

ANIMATING SPACE

From
MICKEY
to
WALL-E

J. P. TELOTTE

THE UNIVERSITY PRESS OF KENTUCKY

Earlier versions of several chapters previously appeared in the following forms: "Winsor McCay's Warped Spaces" in *Screen* 48.4 (2007): 463–74; "Ub Iwerks' (Multi)Plain Cinema" in *Animation* 1.1 (2006): 9–24; "The Stereoscopic Mickey: Space, Animation, and the Mouse" in *Journal of Popular Film and Television* 36.3 (2008): 133–40; "The Changing Space of Animation: Disney's Hybrid Films of the 1940s" in *Animation* 2.3 (2007): 245–58; "Man and Superman: The Fleischer Studio Negotiates the Real" in *Quarterly Review of Film and Video* (forthcoming).

The University Press of Kentucky

Scholarly publisher for the Commonwealth,
serving Bellarmine University, Berea College, Centre College of Kentucky, Eastern Kentucky University, The Filson Historical Society, Georgetown College, Kentucky Historical Society, Kentucky State University, Morehead State University, Murray State University, Northern Kentucky University, Transylvania University, University of Kentucky, University of Louisville, and Western Kentucky University.
All rights reserved.

Editorial and Sales Offices: The University Press of Kentucky
663 South Limestone Street, Lexington, Kentucky 40508-4008
www.kentuckypress.com

14 13 12 11 10   5 4 3 2 1

Library of Congress Cataloging-in-Publication Data

Telotte, J. P., 1949-
    Animating space : from Mickey to WALL-E / J.P. Telotte.
        p. cm.
    Includes bibliographical references and index.
    ISBN 978-0-8131-2586-2 (hardcover : alk. paper)
    1. Animated films—United States—History and criticism. 2. Space and time in art. I. Title.
    NC1766.U5T45 2010
    791.43'34—dc22   2009053155

 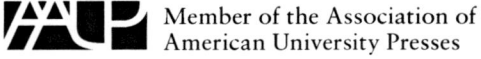 Member of the Association of American University Presses

CONTENTS

ACKNOWLEDGMENTS

A great many people have contributed to the creation of this book and deserve special mention. Foremost among them are my family members, Leigh and Gabby, who not only watched a great deal of animation with me, but did so with some apparent relish and were willing to talk about what we had seen. My fellow Georgia Tech faculty members, especially Carol Senf and Shannon Dobranski, were willing sounding boards for my thoughts on various shorts and features, and my dean, Ken Knoespel, was, as always, highly supportive, passing along films he had come upon and letting me ramble on about various animation topics over numerous lunch meetings. Deserving of special thanks are my students at Tech, especially those who have taken my courses on animation and on Disney. They brought an enthusiasm and an always surprising level of sophistication to classroom discussions that helped educate me about animation and, in the process, made this a better book. Among that group of students I would especially like to acknowledge Ben Callner, Mike Corrigan, Joshua Cuneo, Emily Mask, Stephanie Sellers, and Brad Tucker.

I also owe a debt to the editorial and production team at the University Press of Kentucky, who contributed at every stage to making this book a reality. My former editor, Leila Salisbury, encouraged this project at a very early stage and acquired it for the press. Anne Dean Watkins, who took over the project, was enthusiastic and showed remarkable patience when I neglected my correspondence and argued over the title and cover art. She was simply gracious and supportive throughout the process. David L. Cobb oversaw the editing and production process and, as with my previous UPK book, was very accessible and kept the project on schedule. My copyeditor, Ann Twombly, was thorough, professional, and—for the most part—willing to humor me on what I argued were effective rhetorical flourishes. Ashley Runyon helped create first-rate catalog copy and publicity announcements for the book. This sense of a group effort is one of the main reasons I was happy to continue my publishing relationship with UPK.

INTRODUCTION

Animating Space

The focus of this book is on animation and space—not the sort of wondrous space that we have historically looked up at and all too glibly talked about conquering, but rather another kind of space that in its own way has proven to be just as challenging and that similarly holds great attraction for us, what I term *animating space*. Within that phrase I want to bind up two things that I believe are essential to describing the work of animation properly. On the one hand, I am referring to the space within which animators work, the space of paper, cel, film frame, or computer screen that stands blankly before them, and within which they then must craft their art. And on the other, I want to describe the result of that confrontation, how that space comes alive, becomes what Henri Lefebvre terms "representational space" (43), as the work of the animator infuses it and all that seems to be within it (indeed, the space and all within it are really of the same stuff) with life or spirit (the *anima* of *animation*). I begin with this dual focus—or dual designation—in part because it seems that we often confuse these two elements, especially as we tend to focus attention on the typically amusing and often intriguing characters who are the product of that animating, but also because I believe their relationship is essential to thinking about animation. It allows us to account for what we see in the animated film as well as for its manifest appeal, which lies, from the time of Winsor McCay and his dinosaur brought to life, Gertie, to today in that seemingly magical ability of the form to generate life or vitality, to take a step in the direction of what André Bazin reminds us is one of humanity's oldest and most compelling

1

myths, that of the artistic reproduction of life, or what he terms "the myth of total cinema" (22).

This concern with space and the manifestly lively figures inhabiting it, however, comes not so much from a desire to further trace out Bazin's trajectory, to comment on another *cinematic* element and its relation to the real world—or simply to gaze from a different angle at what Alan Cholodenko ironically refers to as "the step-child of cinema" ("Introduction" 9). Rather, I want to join in an investigation of what Cholodenko and others have termed "animatics" from the vantage— primarily—of the historically dominant American animation industry. After noting that our histories and theories of film have predominantly focused on the cinematic apparatus, on the recording and presentation of "the life within objects," Philip Brophy has chronicled how, for want of more specific models, that practice has most often guided how we think about animation, leading many to view it as simply one more category—or subcategory—within this field (70). The result, he suggests, is that much of animation's key thrust, its *construction* of motion and life, has been overlooked or downplayed. Thus, in an effort to theorize animation further, Brophy insists that we might start thinking in terms of what he calls the "animatic apparatus," that which emphasizes the "dynamism" inherent in animation, or all that is involved in "engineering, producing and orchestrating rhythms in order to *make action happen*" (71). This approach shifts attention to the "engineering," to the construction of the full image in motion, to a concern that encompasses not only the animated characters, who often seem quite alive (or, by analogy, to their animator-creators), but also that challenging space I earlier described—or put more simply, to the force that through the pencil, pen, or electronic stylus works in and on this space. With this slightly shifted focus, Brophy suggests, we might gain not only a different sense of the relationship of animation to live-action film, but also some insight into the changing ways in which animators have tried to meet this different sort of challenge, this bringing to life of both figures and a world that those figures must inhabit.

What follows, then, is not quite a history of animation, although I have arranged the elements of this discussion historically and sketched out part of animation's historical trajectory, while examining many of the "usual suspects" involved in most studies of the form. Nor is this study a truly comprehensive treatment of what we might term spatial-figural relationships throughout the range of animated film. What I hope to provide, through a series of chronologically arranged case studies, is a limited investigation into the aesthetic development of animation that is focused largely but not entirely on what is often described as classic American animation, since that body of work has produced a number of the key developments in the form, has for much of its history dominated the international animation scene, and, for better or worse, has colonized the consciousness of both audiences and animators worldwide. For it is the case not only that figures like Mickey Mouse, Bugs Bunny, Popeye, and Shrek are recognized throughout the world, but also that the nature and style of their cartoon narratives have often provided paradigms for those elsewhere who want to make cartoons and for those who distribute and sell animation to an eager worldwide audience.[1]

So while not a history in the strictest sense, this study is driven by a desire to place that body of animation within a historical line of development, particularly since I want to emphasize a key shift in the form's treatment of both space and figure. Within this roughly chronological examination, then, this book aims for a balance between its treatment of the feature-length animated films on which traditional film criticism has most often focused (in part because of the very success and cultural influence of the features produced by the Walt Disney Company), and the shorter cartoons that helped shape the form's early development, largely because for a long time they dominated animation production and provided a readily available testing ground for new ideas in the form. The selection of the specific texts considered here represents an effort at balancing the treatment of particularly canonical films with other, often neglected works that together can help us isolate certain signal moments in (largely American) animation when the challenge of animating space—in both senses of the term—seems to have been particularly foregrounded and to have brought forth most telling responses from some of the key players in the field, such as Winsor McCay, the Fleischer brothers, the Walt Disney Company, Warner Bros., Pixar Animation, and others. And I shall try to describe these developments so as to clarify the legacy of these people and studios in light of the current turn toward digital animation and effects—of an emerging cinema where, indeed, animation increasingly seems to be crowding out live action, promising to turn relationships a bit topsy-turvy, perhaps even to transform conventional live-action cinema into tomorrow's "stepchild."

In order to frame the following discussion of animating space, this study draws on two key theoretical perspectives, both of them tied to specific historical eras that provide the end points for our examination. The first perspective emerged in the late nineteenth and early twentieth centuries and encompassed the notion, as Stephen Kern describes it, that "space is a form of understanding and not an objective reality" (134), that it is not only a basic category of human existence but a way of thinking about that existence. This view naturally grew out of a variety of developments in the physical and natural sciences, such as Einstein's theory of relativity, which effectively redefined space as a relativistic, perspective-determined phenomenon, and the theoretical biologist Jakob von Uexküll's discovery, neatly summed up by Kern, that "there are complete worlds with distinctive spatial orientations scattered all along the phylogenetic scale" (137). These and other developments, including Spengler's recognition that "different cultures had a unique sense of space" (Kern 138), would result not only in the emergence of new spatial sensibilities, but even in a new valuation of dimensionality.

More specifically, I want to anchor the aesthetic implications of this emerging mind-set in the work of the architect and art historian (and film critic) Anthony Vidler, who has attempted to describe late modernism—a time that saw the first efforts in both film and animation—precisely in terms of this shifting attitude toward space. In fact, Vidler holds that "the invention of a new space conception was the leitmotiv of modernity itself" (*Warped* 4). In support of this view, he points to the way that new spatial ideas at the beginning of the twentieth century began to challenge a conventional point of view, including that normally implicated in most live-action cinema, and in the process "put the assumed stabilities of the viewing subject into question" (10). Behind that challenge Vidler identifies a new psychological interpretation of space that also followed from what seemed to be specifically modern psychological complaints, such as those of agoraphobia and claustrophobia, which signaled both a heightened sense of alienation from and within the modern urban environment, and a new, psychologically loaded relationship that was emerging between the individual and lived space. Efforts to understand these complaints began to assume that our very conception of space was bound up with "the spatial dimensions of social order," was fundamentally fluid, and was constantly subject to shifting interpretation. The aesthetic response to this situation, as Vidler has chronicled, was the production of unique forms of what he terms "spatial warping" (*Warped* 10) in the graphic arts, architecture, film, and other spatially oriented media, as they sought to accommodate, evoke, and even capitalize on this fluidity.[2]

Thus, as Vidler describes, architecture for the first time began to be conceived of "as comprised of 'space,' rather than of built elements like walls and columns" (*Warped* 143). Structure dissolved into the constructed relationship between the individual and space. And in its own correlative to this shift, the cinema readily absorbed into its conventionalized sense of reality a new spatial dynamism by way of the fragmentations and constructed geography that were fundamental to practices like montage, glance-object editing, and lap dissolves. Painting, as Kern notes, "abandoned the homogeneous space of linear perspective" in favor of "painted objects in a multiplicity of spaces from multiple perspectives" (143). It is an approach that shows most clearly in a work like Duchamp's *Nude Descending a Staircase*, which seeks to spatialize our experiences of time and motion, as literally *steps* in a process of descent—the sequential presence on different parts of a staircase—were depicted, overlapped, and (cinematically) dissolved into each other. And graphic advertisements freely adopted the language of cinematic montage, casting "conflicting" images into spatial proximity, as if a dynamic interaction had simply been frozen in time. All were tapping into the possibilities of what Vidler has termed the "uncanny" nature of space, a space that, "in lived experience, has taken on an almost palpable existence" (*Architectural* 167) and a psychological complexity, as the notion of a single and objective sense of space comes to seem almost irrelevant. It is a vantage that, I would suggest, resonates loudly as we look at early animation, which provides a variety of examples that are concerned with exploring and exploiting such spatial potentials.

The second perspective ultimately relies on a number of sources as well, including the work of Fredric Jameson, who identifies the postmodern in part through its peculiar "flatness or depthlessness, a new kind of superficiality in the most literal sense" (9). That characteristic leads Jameson to see the postmodern world as marked by a singular development: the domination of "our daily life, our psychic experience, our cultural languages . . . by categories of space" (16). Working in a similar vein—and with a similar emphasis on capitalism's influence on space—David Harvey has described that spatial development as part of an ongoing and "intense . . . time-space compression" that has resulted in a widespread cultural sense of "volatility and ephemerality" (284, 285), one that inevitably "exacts its toll on our capacity to grapple with the realities unfolding around us" (306). Both that sense of flatness and the emphasis on spatial compression seem to find their ultimate extrapolation in the work of Jean Baudrillard, particularly in his suggestion that in the contemporary world, or what he terms "the age of simulation," the "real" has essentially disappeared (167). Or to be more precise, it is simply produced and reproduced at will, leaving us in a "hyperreal" realm (146) where simulacra seductively disguise the absence of reality. All of these conceptions—of flatness, compression, or disappearance—suggest that we have come to a different place, one marked by a very different sense of space from that envisioned by the late modernists, and one that has inevitably inflected more recent work in animation.

Yet in order to shift emphasis from the political thrust of Jameson's and Harvey's work (or what they both term the "geopolitical") and to avoid the abstraction to which Baudrillard's analysis is prey, I want to use the work of the architect and technology theorist Paul Virilio as the primary anchor for this second perspective. Though he has staked out similar territory in his studies of the postmodern period, his focus is more explicitly on the media and narrative consequences of these developments, as he explores what he too almost alarmingly describes as a "crisis in the conceptualization of dimension" in the contemporary world, one that, he argues, has found its reflection in a "crisis in the conceptualization of narrative" (*Lost* 25). Virilio focuses not on that modernist discovery of a new and uncanny sense of space that so intrigues Vidler, then, but rather on an absence, what he terms a "lost dimension" in the contemporary world—a world that increasingly seems to be flattened out, to have been effectively transformed by the various media technologies that surround all aspects of contemporary life, but especially film, and that largely condition and control how we view our world. In fact, he suggests that our world and our very lives have effectively become "cinematized" or "mediatized"—an effect with a disturbing fallout. For, as he offers, in the process "depth of space . . . vanishes" and our sense of reality increasingly becomes confused with a pervasive "reality effect" (*Lost* 34).

More specifically, Virilio notes that all those who work in the visual arts today seem plagued by a general diminishing of their "capacity to say, describe, and inscribe reality" (*Lost* 24), a problem compounded by the apparent elusiveness of reality itself in the contemporary cultural landscape. What he is suggesting is not, as Baudrillard has a bit more famously pronounced, that reality has simply disappeared and been replaced by simulacra. Rather, he wants to call attention to a kind of abdication that marks the postmodern world: how we have increasingly *allowed* that "reality effect" to stand in for the real, ceding primacy to what we have constructed rather than to the models for that construction, in the process rendering our sense of reference problematic, as if we were trying to animate a figure or scene with only the vaguest memory of the original as a model.

As a consequence of this cultural and aesthetic turn, he suggests, we increasingly seem to inhabit an environment in which the experience of "cinematic representation," along with its attendant sense of an illusive and elusive world, "has . . . displaced the reality of the effective presence, the real presence of people and things" (*Lost* 99). And though such a "cinematic" world might seem to make no real or immediate demands on us, and indeed might even seem rather attractive, it can, he suggests, ultimately impoverish the human experience, including our art. In Virilio's account we might see a forecast of the effects that many have ascribed to the most recent developments in digital animation, wherein live action is traced—by means of computer-driven rotoscoping or motion capture—and then placed in another tracing of the real world, a reality effect essentially constructed within the computer. And such developments, for all their promise, also resonate with another cultural fear that many people share (and that Disney anticipated in its live-action/animated hybrid film *Tron*, 1982), that of becoming swallowed up by the digital space of the computer, animated by our own technology.

In the historical space between these two descriptions, between these two periods, and between these two senses of space, this study finds both its reason and a logical starting point for constructing an animatics of the last century. I want to examine animation from the time of what Vidler terms "warped space" to today's "lost" space, as Virilio puts it, offering this shift, disappearance, or what we might more accurately think of as a transformation, as a trope that will help us describe and better understand some of those key developments in the history of animating space. In the process I hope to suggest as well a level on which the development of animation affords a useful account of certain cultural shifts: a mirror every bit as revealing, despite the fact that its images are not reflections but our own creations, as is that offered by the historically more highly valued live-action cinema.

I shall do so by emphasizing a gradual shift in the development of animation aesthetics, particularly as it implicates notions of realism. Film animation, almost from its inception, has constantly been viewed against the backdrop of the real: at times as approaching too near the real (as too imitative of live-action cinema and thus as too heedless of its own unique possibilities) and at others as drawing its very identity and value from its difference from the real (and from live-action film). In following this shift I shall give particular attention to a number of key technologies that have pushed the boundaries of animation—and here we might note just a few such developments, the rotoscope and rotograph, the various sorts of multiplane cameras developed throughout the 1930s, computer-assisted printing and coloring, computer-generated imagery, and motion and performance capture—often impelling the form to more closely approach and mimic the real, or to create various versions of what Virilio terms "reality effects." Interestingly enough, these same effects have proven crucial to producing the sense of wonder that has always been part of animation's attraction, even as they have, in various ways, also caused the form to rub against the hopes of those who have seen in animation an alternative to live-action cinema and its predominantly realistic thrust, the hope for a truly abstract form of cinematic presentation.

This study, then, attempts to chronicle the drama of what I have termed animating space by exploring the development of a spatial aesthetics primarily from the vantage of American cartooning. It begins by trying to establish a necessary historical grounding—a view of the early animated cinema's development of figural-spatial relationships in the context of that cinema's quite varied approaches to animation. It then looks at key moments in our cartooning when the real has been foregrounded, developed, and explored with an eye to revealing that unfolding story, particularly as modernist attitudes toward space develop and gradually shift into postmodernist ones, and as the various movements in the direction of a realist space constantly produce something else—a growing awareness of a "lost dimension" and of the fantastic character of that space we typically describe as the real. It is a shift that has finally come to the fore today with the capability provided by the digital regime to reproduce essentially anything we might imagine, to take animation to the point where the distinction between live action and animation often seems to have disappeared, and the *fantastic* element of the everyday, the clearly constructed nature of what we would still label the "real," becomes unmistakable.

Before outlining the full trajectory of this chronicle, I need to step back and briefly suggest the critical context against which we shall examine the development of animating space, particularly some of those attitudes toward the real that inform our thinking about animating space. Central to this study is the recognition that a conflicted attitude toward spatial representation has always been a part of our animated films. Their essential flatness has consistently evoked the specter of depth and spatial presence—or underscored, even capitalized on, the almost necessary absence of those characteristics. And in the process it has also inspired a consistent debate about their relationship to our traditions of realistic representation, and thus about the proper aim and province of animation and cartooning.

Early film animation, as presented in the works of such figures as J. Stuart Blackton, Emile Cohl, and Winsor McCay, drew much of its appeal from its presentation as a kind of ephemeral spectacle, in keeping with the nature of early cinema; it was a ready part of what the film historian Tom Gunning has evocatively described as a "cinema of attractions" ("Cinema" 63). Often done as filmed versions of "lightning sketches" or vaudeville chalkboard presentations,[3] these early efforts were characterized by their speed of presentation (and subsequent, equally speedy erasure), by the remarkable, even exciting transforma-

The Enchanted Drawing (1900): J. Stuart Blackton interacts with his lightning sketch subject.

tions in shape and reference they offered to audiences, and by their ability to exploit their basic nature as drawings, that is, their fundamental flatness, which helped license all manner of exaggerations, of departures from the real. And given the common practice in these films of what Donald Crafton terms "self-figuration," that is, the "tendency of the filmmaker to interject himself into his film" (11), as a kind of magician who could evoke these line-drawn images out of thin air, or as a surrogate figure who could work such magic, filmmakers invariably underscored the importance of a central figure for the cartoon, while they also staked out a modernist reflexive territory for themselves, as we see when Earl Hurd interacts with his Bobby Bumps character or Max Fleischer calls forth his first creation, KoKo the Clown, from "Out of the Inkwell." That reflexive element poked holes in one of the early cinema's basic attractions, its reality illusion, and it thus all the more pointedly differentiated those animated efforts from so many of the conventionally realistic films of that formative period, adding to the special appeal of early animation.

One result of such self-conscious presentation is that animated films of this period were at times seen as more nearly allied to the world of avant-garde art and its modernist spirit than they were to normal narrative cinema. Emphasizing that apparent alliance, Esther Leslie observes that their action typically seemed to be "set inside a universe of transformation, overturning and provisionality" (vi), rather than in the world of conventional experience, with its impressions of stability and solidity,

10

One of the amazing transformations found in early animation: Felix the Cat combines the moon with a palm tree to produce a banjo in *Arabiantics* (1928).

as well as its sense of a three-dimensional space. In this different space, with its different ruling laws, almost anything seemed possible, as Felix the Cat's easy transformation of word balloons, parts of the scenery, or his tail into physical props repeatedly attested. Simply put, early animated films conjured up a very different, indeed challenging sort of space that they mined for unconventional and often wildly unexpected effects. As a consequence, many examples were readily embraced by avant-garde artists of the era, who frequently incorporated various forms of animation into their own work, as Fernand Léger's surrealist *Ballet mécanique* (1924), with its pixilated figures and moving cutouts, well illustrates.

At the same time, and almost from its inception, animation has, through a variety of tactics and technical developments, also sought to claim its own sort of kinship with the real. As the animation historian Michael Barrier observes, the form has repeatedly tried to establish "a foundation in fact that would permit audiences . . . to accept the reality of what was happening in the cartoon they were watching" (3). This effort, to produce an adequate or acceptable model of an outside reality, would, in fact, increasingly form the basis of popular appreciation of the form, as well as a conventional measure of its sophistication or technical achievement. In sketching the early development of animation, for example, Conrad Smith has shown how a series of patents filed between 1914 and 1917 (particularly those by Earl Hurd and John R. Bray) opened the door to new techniques for naturalistic shading, for smoother character movement, for removing reflections that undercut the reality illusion, and for realistically registering movement in space in relation to shifting panoramic backgrounds (5–8). A number of the key studios in the 1930s—Fleischer brothers', Disney's, Ub Iwerks's—would further advance this agenda by designing new technologies for producing such naturalistic 3-D effects. And in singling out the products of the Walt Disney Studio as the new gold standard of animation in the 1930s, the noted film critic Otis Ferguson would repeatedly emphasize the realism of its product, how its films typically proceeded from a "solid basis in observation" or "from a firm basis in reality."[4]

If audiences and reviewers seemed more taken by the realistic stylings of Disney and the Fleischer brothers in the 1930s and early 1940s—as is evidenced especially by the former's *Bambi* (1942) and the latter's Superman cartoons (1941–1943), both of which aimed, at least in part, at a heightened realism that distinguished them from earlier efforts in the form and much of the cartoon competition at that time—some commentators would demur. That reaction was based on what might well be described as an increasingly essentialist approach to the animated film. In 1936 the critic and playwright William Kozlenko offered a commentary that characterizes this shifting attitude, as he announced that "the uniqueness of the animated cartoon lies in the fact that, of all film forms, it is the only one that has freed itself almost entirely from the restrictions of an oppressive reality" (246). In this same vein, one of the key theorists of film realism, Siegfried Kracauer, registered a surprising reservation about our increasingly popular animated cartoons, taking them to task for their "growing tendency toward camera reality" (*Theory* 90). In fact, his review of Disney's effort *Dumbo* (1941) flatly announced that animated films should not "draw a reality that can better be photographed" ("*Dumbo*"). For these critics that disturbingly realistic dimension did not function as another, valuable source for what Walter Benjamin had only recently described as the "exhibition value" of art (224), that is, for its ability to lay bare our world and the systems by which it operates, but rather marked a surrender to conventional film narrative—a surrender that involved the betrayal of what they saw as animation's most important properties, especially of its flat and manifestly different world.

Leslie suggests that this reaction was largely a response to the rapid technological developments occurring throughout the film industry: in the 1930s and early 1940s "film succumbs . . . to the victory of technology over technique" (136). In effect, the increasing ability to do in animation what photography and live-action film had long and seemingly effortlessly offered, that is, to reflect a vision of the real by evoking a sense of three-dimensional characters operating in a three-dimensional space, she theorizes, worked to "constrain" animators' techniques by yoking their efforts to the same sort of illusionism that characterized conventional narrative cinema. From this vantage, for example, the Fleischers' turntable and rotoscoping techniques and Disney's multiplane camera developments (all of which will be discussed in later chapters) might be interpreted as actually undermining animation's potential, especially its ability to mine its very difference to serve as a socially and aesthetically subversive art form.

That is an intriguing explanation, implying as it does that we view technology as almost having a will of its own, or at least that we see at work what Leslie terms a dominant "technical consciousness" driving film development and informing—or possessing—its workers. This consciousness, she argues, typically "constrains film" to produce a vision of the real (136), and by implication it worked to constrain the very imaginations of many animators. Of course, if that is the case, it is an element of constraint that little troubled the avant-garde animations of a Hans Richter, the expressionist-influenced films of Lotte Reiniger, or Len Lye's "direct animation" in this era, all of which explored very different veins from those that conventional live-action cinema did. And in a narrative mode, it produced only a mocking response from Felix the Cat, whose adventures typically snubbed a nose—or at least that infinitely mutable tail—at every limitation imposed by everyday reality.

It would seem that politics—or, more accurately, the changing nature of political consciousness—is somewhat responsible for these different perspectives. For realism itself was, in the early modern period, typically seen as a key aesthetic value for the way in which it dispelled what Benjamin termed the "aura" surrounding earlier art by confronting audiences with stark reflections of the social status quo, in effect, for the way in which it not only made possible but almost seemed to *compel* what he termed a "political" perspective by confronting audiences with the images of their world, allowing them to see that world clearly, as if for the first time (224). Yet a rising skepticism about mass culture and its effects, particularly as elaborated by Theodor Adorno and Max Hork-heimer, would increasingly call this function into question and inflect animation criticism. Under the imperative of mass culture and its seductive products, or as Leslie interprets it, "mimesis turns bad," realism began to be seen as a kind of naive proposition, and even cartoons could be viewed as working to "accustom audiences to a violence which civilization will mete out to them, and hopes they will mete . . . out in turn" (Leslie 117). Thus, for Adorno and Horkheimer even the laughter that our cartoons typically evoke through their assaults on a recognizably real world loses its normally subversive power and becomes nothing more than what they describe as "the echo of power as something inescapable" (140).

And yet despite these theoretical disagreements, in practice realism has seldom been the true aim of animation. The dean of Warner Bros. animation, Chuck Jones, has in numerous interviews sought to emphasize this point. He notes that the best animation has never tried to be like live-action filmmaking; it is "not an imitation. It should go where live action can't go" (Furniss, *Chuck Jones* 40). Rather, he suggests, "the basic thing in animation is that you're talking about believability. You see, I was dealing with the idea of realism first, but then I realized that believability was much more important" (Furniss, *Chuck Jones* 94). As a result, Jones began to emphasize—and to prize—what he saw as the true "triumph" of his art: "the feeling that people really believe these characters live, just like we do" (Furniss, *Chuck Jones* 166). That effect helps explain why even highly stylized characters, such as Jones's Roadrunner and Coyote and his later versions of Bugs Bunny, are so effective—and funny. It is not because they either closely approach or radically distance themselves from the real, from the world in which their audiences live, but because they seem to be alive, and living within a kind of parallel universe that has its own curious design and operates according to its own laws, even if that universe roughly resembles and thus inevitably manages to comment on our own.

Given this vantage, it seems that both of those critical perspectives outlined above, that which sees animated film as finding its aesthetic maturity in an increasingly realistic, three-dimensional vision and that which comes to see this vision as working against the subversive potential of its essential flatness, have at their base a certain mistaking of the animated world based in their attitudes toward the real. They funda-

14

mentally proceed from a vision that wants to simplify the complex space—and potential—of animation, on the one hand by offering a model of historical evolution, one in which, for example, greater depth equals better animation, and on the other by resorting to an essentialist view, wherein real animation equals flatness. The world our animated films have come to conjure up, however, is ultimately neither flat nor three-dimensional. As Kozlenko also recognized early on, the cartoon's strength does not lie simply in its ability to convincingly construct a real world, even if part of its appeal, as he does not seem to acknowledge, lies in its phenomenological ability to, as Chuck Jones suggests, *approach* or *point to* reality, to the world we inhabit, which it does indeed hold up for our amusement. And though its invariably fantastic aspect, along with the subversive thrust that always attaches to our fantasy visions, has made possible appealingly alternative visions of the everyday world, those visions gain their bite only because of resemblance, because they are able to evoke the very reality on which they conduct their assault. As numerous commentators on fantasy have pointed out, the fantastic cannot exist apart from the real world that it seems to find so frustratingly finite—or in the world of cartoons, so humorously finite. The result of these simultaneously centrifugal and centripetal thrusts, as we might term them, is an animating space that always seems to point in the direction of both a real space and a fantastic space (or dimensional and flat worlds), but which is neither.

Seen from this largely spatial vantage, our animated cartoons (both shorts and features) might well provide us with an interesting insight into the cinema's own passage from modernist to postmodernist representation, a track of that geometrical-narrative "crisis" that Virilio has tried to map out, and with which the visual arts have throughout the last century wrestled. But more significantly, by considering the development of, shifts in, and deployment of the sort of aesthetic geometry on which animation depends—those spaces variously marked by displacement, warping, compression, even a sense of loss—we might gain a new perspective on the history of the animated film, or at least on what are often considered to be some of the key events in that history.

We shall begin to follow this pattern of development, this ongoing "animating," by concentrating, in chapter 1, on those efforts of the early cinema that most insistently call our attention to the space in which they operate. Specifically, we shall look at both the variety of forms that early film animation took and some of the spatial possibilities that characterized these works. Any discussion about animation, after all, might well take in a variety of forms—cel drawing, puppet or doll animation, Claymation, silhouette films, collage work, pinboard animation, and so on—all of which share certain characteristics that also help us define the very term. As part of the framework for discussing animation's early historical context and varied forms, we shall view the evolving spatial developments of these first films alongside what Donald Crafton terms their dominant "figural" impulse, as the figure of the animator—or the animator's onscreen stand-in, the humorous character—implicates an increasingly complex animated world, one consistent with the modernist sense of space as relational, or as Vidler puts it, always informed by "the relations of space to bodies, psyches, and objects" (*Warped* 10).

Following this historical context is a series of case studies, arranged in a roughly chronological fashion and focused on the problems and potentials of animating space. It begins with a detailed look at the work of one of those pioneer animators, in fact arguably the most influential of that early period, Winsor McCay. Starting with what is certainly his most famous—and probably most studied—film, *Gertie the Dinosaur* (1914), chapter 2 frames the achievements it represents in the context of several of his other key efforts, most notably *The Sinking of the Lusitania* (1918), a film that represents his most realistic style, and two of his films that work in a very different, more fantastic register, *Bug Vaudeville* and *The Flying House* (both 1921). These films suggest the stylistic range that McCay explored in just over a decade of activity (1911–1921) and offer probably the best examples of his concern not only with bringing things to life—appropriately exemplified by the artist's promise to bring an extinct creature to life—but with exploring the strange sort of space that is implicated by the animated world, a space that is very much in keeping with emerging modernist attitudes toward space. In these efforts we can see McCay's limited canon opening an important door for the development of animation by suggesting the very pliability and constructed nature of space, and indeed hinting at a level on which all of our spaces are constructed.

Jumping ahead of several other significant developments in animation history, chapter 3 examines the appeal of one of the most successful and enduring animated figures, Disney's Mickey Mouse. Mickey's emergence has historically been linked to the studio's groundbreaking application of sound to his narrative antics, but that linkage has resulted in a tendency to overlook much of what actually goes on in such films as *Steamboat Willie, Plane Crazy,* and *The Gallopin' Gaucho* (all 1928), particularly in terms of the figural-spatial relationships that mark these early Disney efforts. What this chapter will demonstrate is that this figure owes much of his early success not simply to the new technology of sound, but also to the sort of multidimensional world that was created for him—to a vision that is at once both "warped," as Vidler would propose, and marked by new reality effects that include sound and an attention to dimensional design. The mouse, as we shall see, was a character who seems to have been designed with a mind to his functioning within a more complex, "stereoscopic" world.

Chapter 4 steps back in time and then forward to examine the work of the Fleischer brothers, who would introduce a new level of realism into animation style with their development of such technologies as the rotoscope, rotograph, and turntable camera (later described as their "Stereoptical Apparatus"). These technologies, especially the rotoscope, were in part designed to facilitate the animation process by allowing the animators to trace real motion, to place their animated figures, such as KoKo the Clown, in what seemed to be real-world contexts—as an early form of what is termed hybrid animation—and to produce three-dimensional worlds in which characters like Popeye, Betty Boop, Hoppity, and Superman might play out their adventures. Those developments also opened the way for additional narrative effects that the Fleischers only gradually discovered, as we see especially in the Superman shorts of the 1940s. For in dealing with a more realistic subject matter—the contemporary settings and figures of Superman films—the Fleischer Studio (and later Famous Studios) actually began to use those realistic animation technologies in more metaphoric ways, suggesting in the process some of both the potentials and the limits of the reality effect to which their animation had essentially contributed.

Working in a somewhat similar vein was a nearly legendary figure of animation history, although he is one who is today often relegated to brief footnotes in that history, Ub Iwerks, the focus of chapter 5. Known

Felix turns his infinitely mutable tail into a flute for snake charming in *Outdoor Indore* (1928).

early in his career as one of the fastest animators in the industry and later renowned for his contributions to the creation of Mickey Mouse and for a range of inventions and technological contributions for both his own and the Disney studio, Iwerks also created a viable multiplane camera setup for his company, as he tried to fashion a more complex sense of space for his cartoon creations, and ultimately a more realistic style of animation that could compete with the emerging Disney "illusion-of-life" style. Used especially in his ComiColor fairy tales and Willie Whopper cartoons, the multiplane camera was part of a concerted effort at producing an effective reality illusion, but one that finally met with only mixed success, as Iwerks never quite managed to turn the new sense of space he had evoked to satisfying narrative account—or, for that matter, to create sufficiently attractive or fascinating characters to enliven that space. But in the rather stylish work produced by his short-lived studio, we can see one of the clearest demonstrations of how those realistic effects came into conflict with the flat, almost surreal world of another strain of animation, that often identified with one of the most popular cartoon creations, Pat Sullivan and Otto Messmer's iconic Felix the Cat.

With the further work of the Disney studio, particularly in the decade between the first uses of its highly sophisticated multiplane camera in the late 1930s and the return to hybrid animation techniques in the postwar years, we can see a far more elaborate tracing out of this same conflict. Moving beyond the "stereoscopic" mouse that first brought Disney such great success, chapter 6 examines—and questions—the studio's later exploitation of various reality effects, as it drew together two spatial technologies: the multiplane camera, which would bring the studio an Academy Award for Technical Achievement with *The Old Mill* (1937), and hybrid animation, the process through which the studio had effectively come into existence with its Alice comedies of 1923–1927. In the course of developing the illusion-of-life aesthetic that would, for a time, become the hallmark of Disney animation, the studio would create the camera system that allowed films like *The Old Mill* and *Snow White and the Seven Dwarfs* (1937) to draw on a sense of three-dimensional space and to produce a naturalistic impression of parallax. The narratives that ensued become, as a result, not only intriguing and highly popular fables, but also practically dramas of space, of the relationship of their characters or creatures to the physical world, as the later work *Bambi* (1942), with its visual explorations of the forest world of its characters, especially demonstrates. As the studio tried to integrate this technology into its series of hybrid films in the postwar era, and even tried to recoup some of its earlier avant-garde reputation through various reflexive effects that can be observed in those films, however, it would move in a rather different, surprising, and, unfortunately, often forgotten direction. For when the reality effect of the multiplane camera met real characters in such films as *The Three Caballeros* (1945), *Song of the South* (1946), and *Fun and Fancy Free* (1947), the product actually proved to be a more fantastic dimension for its films—and a dimension that Disney critics have typically overlooked. These films are characterized by what can only be termed more a "liminal" than a traditionally realistic vision, one that suggests a desire to bridge the real and the fantastic worlds, to bind together the two promises of animation—albeit a promise that largely went unfulfilled. In effect, they begin to provide us with a glimpse of the lost dimension that Virilio describes and thus look toward the sort of postmodern spatiality that he forecasts for later films.

With their more "looney" thrust, Warner Bros.' Looney Tunes and Merrie Melodies cartoons almost invariably seem, as chapter 7 shows, to stake out very different territory from that of the Disney works. Untroubled by a single house aesthetic or a similar fascination with verisimilitude—thanks to the laissez-faire approach of the producer Leon Schlesinger and the development of multiple director-auteurs, often with somewhat different visions of the house characters[5]—the Warner Bros. cartoons play far more freely at the fringes of the real and explore many of the potentials of a form wherein, as Esther Leslie puts it, "everything in the drawn world is of the same stuff" (23). And yet here too we can find a curious fascination with the reality effect consistently rearing its head. In most of the Warner Bros. cartoons, but most pointedly in those created by the animation unit's most lauded director, Chuck Jones, we see a repeated concern with narratizing space, with shifting the terms of interrogation from animation's style to what we might term *style-in-action,* that is, to the ways in which the substance of animated reality becomes central to the story itself. The result is, of course, simply a different sort of reflexive thrust, as if it were not so much a figure coming "out of the inkwell," but the ground itself that was being constructed or inked before our eyes. Thus, a repeated fascination with the stage and its implications for our sense of onscreen and offscreen space, with the rabbit hole of Bugs Bunny, which allows for his easy appearances and disappearances, and with the vast highways and canyons through which the Roadrunner and Wile E. Coyote endlessly chase, increasingly becomes a signature of the Warner Bros. films as they work out a new, highly designed relationship between the space of animation and the animated figures that thrive within its characteristically chaotic, improbable, or unchartable spaces. Virilio argues that one of the hallmarks of the postmodern world is the way in which a traditional sense of space gives way to what he terms "speed-space" (*Lost* 102), that is, to relative movement within space, and it is a description that seems to correspond quite neatly to the world of the Roadrunner and Coyote, as well as the various other chase narratives (such as those involving Pepe LePew and Speedy Gonzales) that would become so central to the Warner Bros. canon in the late 1940s and 1950s.

Chapter 8 deals with animated films following what Norman Klein terms the death of the conventional seven-minute cartoon, as its cinematic incarnation gave way to television and its early emphasis on restricted animation.[6] In the wake of this tide of animation that would turn space into a static stage for dialogue by seldom-moving characters, I examine two feature films that self-consciously explore the dynamics of animation as they look both backward and forward in terms of animating space and the sort of characters who inhabit, and at times chafe at inhabiting, the cartoon world. The chapter's primary focus is on *Who Framed Roger Rabbit* (1988), a work that brings together both Disney's and Warner Bros.' approaches to animation—as well as their characters—in a retronarrative that is fundamentally about spatial change, about the buying up of "Toontown" and erasing it so that a new world of "speed-space" might be constructed: the world of the freeways that have come to crisscross contemporary America and allow people to move rapidly across its landscape like a nation of roadrunners and coyotes, while also discouraging them from ever really stopping to inhabit or appreciate a particular space. It is a narrative that, appropriately, is spatially arranged around the division between the real world and the animated one, the worlds of people and of "Toons." And it is the same spatial scheme that we find worked out in a near imitation of *Roger Rabbit*, Ralph Bakshi's equally evocative *Cool World* (1992). Bakshi's film is a similarly hybrid effort with a similarly nostalgic nod to a post–World War II America and its fondness for traditional cartoons. And it too explores the boundaries between the Cool World of "doodles," or cartoon characters, and the real world of "noids," or humanoids, while describing the possible consequences of a breakdown of those borders. Yet though *Roger Rabbit* offers a hopeful vision of the possibility of integrating its very different spaces, ending, in fact, with the destruction of a wall between the human and "Toon" realms, *Cool World* suggests that nearly apocalyptic consequences might follow if such mingling occurs, and in the process it points to a kind of fear of that lost dimension Virilio describes (which is partly bound up in the style of animation that Bakshi champions).

Chapter 9, which focuses on the work of the leading name in digital animation, Pixar Animation Studios (a subsidiary of the Walt Disney Company), looks into the new spatial world that has evoked the anxiety we find informing the two films treated in the previous chapter. Particularly, we shall look at how computer-generated imagery (CGI) technology has affected traditional cartoon work. Though cutting-edge digital technology has allowed a new breed of animators to work in a compelling three-dimensional realm, creating seemingly habitable spaces and living characters, it has also highlighted the problem of such reproduc-

The human rendered as a computer animation in Disney's *Tron* (1982).

tion, of how far one can go in fashioning a simulacrum of reality—of the potential limits on that reality effect Virilio notes. Pixar's singular record of success in digital animation comes with its development of a special software that has since become the animation industry standard, RenderMan. Originally designated by the acronym REYES, this software's name proclaims its vaulting ambitions: "*Render Everything You Ever Saw.*" Yet the Pixar works consistently pull back from that totalizing potential to explore the very problems of reproduction, including what we have termed "animating space," as we see in the studio's first feature, *Toy Story* (1995), and as perhaps its best film to date, *The Incredibles* (2005), further develops. In these films the space of animation essentially becomes the stuff of narrative, and the value of difference (live versus animated) is posed—both aesthetically and thematically —for the audience.

Finally, chapter 10 assesses the changes that contemporary cinema is seeing as the techniques and technology demonstrated in Pixar's animated films increasingly migrate to and affect the world of live-action cinema, as the lines between the two become increasingly blurred, and as the very term *animation* seems to be taking on new meaning. Specifically, it looks at works that suggest the range of animation hybridity today: works in which live action and actors mix with the digitally animated, as in *Pirates of the Caribbean: The Curse of the Black Pearl* (2003); works in which live actors are set down in a totally digitally animated realm, such as *Sky Captain and the World of Tomorrow* (2004); and works in which digital motion capture produces an animated narrative that completely replaces the live action of traditional cinema, as

Beowulf (2007) demonstrates. These works can help us measure the spatial effect of digital animation on live action, as, for example, in *Pirates of the Caribbean* when we see a real hand reach across the frame and gradually turn skeletal. In such instances, space once again—as in the modernist turn—seems to be freighted with anxiety, to become something rather uncanny, even though we know it is little more than, as Virilio would remind us, a reality effect. But now it has become a measure of our own immersion in that world of "effects," our own "cinematization"—an effect literalized through the "performance capture" technique used so successfully in *Beowulf*. In fact, it suggests a growing sense that our own space might not be so different from what we have termed animating space.

With the growth of CGI effects in feature films, the proliferation of digital animation production companies, the appearance of an international array of broadcast and cable-delivered animation programs, and the full flowering of the computer game industry, animation has obviously become both big business and an increasingly fashionable field for study. That status derives not only from the fact that it is more essential to the realms of visual entertainment, advertising, and instruction, but also because it suggests the very real possibility of a paradigm shift in visually based media, as it promises to replace or radically alter components of these realms that we have come to take for granted. It is a situation that has become particularly apparent in the film industry, where we find ever more experiments at merging live-action with animated characters, props, and settings, seen most spectacularly in the *Lord of the Rings* films, and even completely substituting rotoscoped and motion-captured worlds for the live, as works like *A Scanner Darkly* (2006), *300* (2006), and *Beowulf* demonstrate. As the experimental flavor increasingly dissipates from these experiments, as they seem simply to point to the new norm for a variety of screen-based entertainments, including video games, they also suggest that animation has entered a very new stage. Such significant developments argue for the necessity of a new assessment of the form that, particularly in the American context, is taking center stage in this drama of media development. It is an assessment that the following chapters can at least begin to undertake.

1

EARLY ANIMATION

Of Figures and Spaces

One of the abiding images of early animation is of a hand reaching into the film frame to sketch a variety of characters or things on a sheet of paper, a large easel-mounted pad, or a chalkboard. Whatever is sketched then usually undergoes a series of amazing or simply amusing transformations at the hand of "the hand." As most historians have noted, this signature scene, which we can find in the work of J. Stuart Blackton, Emile Cohl, Harry S. Palmer, Earl Hurd, the Fleischer brothers, Walt Disney, and others, emerged from the tradition of the "lightning sketch," a common act in vaudeville programs and music hall shows of the late nineteenth and early twentieth centuries. Described by Donald Crafton as "a hybrid of graphic and performing art" (48), these live presentations centered on an artist, alternately facing the drawing matter and then facing the audience, as he quickly illustrated a figure or scene and proceeded, with a few rapid changes of line or shading, to produce a surprising alteration in the image. This standard type of entertainment is certainly one of the key influences on early animation, not only because it provided the subject matter for many films in an era that Tom Gunning has evocatively labeled "the cinema of attractions" ("Cinema" 63), but also because of the way in which it forecast the early animated film's recurrent emphasis on amazing transformations. Yet in that reaching or sketching hand, I suggest, we might see more than just a lingering trace of influence, of the transition from one sort of entertainment to another.

Almost like a pointing finger, the sketching hand directs our attention to a boundary—or several boundaries—crucial to the emergence of the animated film, almost as if it were tracing the form's early history. Most obviously that hand calls our attention to a fundamental media border, that between the live lecture presentation from which these works emerged and the filmed entertainment that was already bidding to take the place of such vaudeville-style amusements. It also designates what we might term a generic border, one separating a live-action cinema that had first been unveiled to the public around 1895 and that had quickly developed a focus on narrative and a set of common practices for producing narrative, and a world of animated images that was still developing its own conventions and audience appeal, and for both of which it drew heavily on other media, such as the newspaper comic strip and magazine cartoon. Moreover, the sketching hand signals a fundamental aesthetic distinction, that between a three-dimensional world that was captured in the live-action portion of the presentation and a flat, two-dimensional one that often recalled those newspaper and magazine entries. It is in the crossing—or in some cases, the intentional blurring—of these different borders that our various standard histories of animation have essentially measured out the historical emergence of the form.

But all these boundaries or borders share a more fundamental importance for the films in this vein, since they also point up some key dynamics of the form. All these early animated efforts "draw" much of their capital from the nature of that liminal play they depict, that is, from their filmmakers' ability to violate or play at and with those borders. As an example we might consider a work that is still thoroughly informed by the lightning sketch model, is widely available, and is often cited today, J. Stuart Blackton's *The Enchanted Drawing* (1900).[1] This film produces its humorous effects through the depicted artist's ability to "enchant" drawn material so that it seemingly—and in lightninglike fashion—turns into real objects that can then be grasped and used by the artist who has materialized them (Blackton himself). Thus, a sketched bottle of wine and a glass, thanks to stop-motion effects, become a real bottle and glass in Blackton's hands, and the expression on the face of a man he has also drawn instantly changes to one of displeasure when the sketched material disappears from the paper world he occupies. Blackton then repeats the process with a hat and cigar, drawing both, liberating them from the canvas via stop-motion, demonstrating his use of these now three-dimensional objects, and then returning them to the sketchpad, again producing a changed expression on the face of his drawn man, who is now visibly pleased with what he has. It is a sense of pleasure, we might assume, that the film's viewers shared at Blackton's ability not only to *enter into* or affect that sketched world, but also to *draw out* from it practically anything he might desire, even a recognizably human response from a figure he has manifestly created. This bringing drawings to life that we find in *The Enchanted Drawing,* as well as such similar Blackton efforts as *Humorous Phases of Funny Faces* (1906) and *Lightning Sketches* (1907), is not, strictly speaking, true animation, but it does point to both a common impulse and a common satisfaction to be found in these proto-animation efforts—that found in the power of transformation and in the very plastic nature of the world these films envision.

With a nod to the prevalence of such scenes of drawing, inking, or demonstrating, Crafton in his landmark history of early animation argues that they also signal one of the central characteristics of the form throughout its first three decades. They are all signs, he says, of a common pattern, as I noted in the introduction, of "self-figuration, the tendency of the filmmaker to interject himself into his film," which seemed to give the animator a "special status"—as "a demigod, a purveyor of life itself" (11). And he ties the attraction of these initial efforts directly to this reflexive dimension, suggesting that audiences found a very real appeal not just in the rather primitive illusion of life that the animated film put on display, but also in their "vicarious participation in the ritual of incarnation" (12), in their own implied figuration. It is an appealing argument, especially insofar as it can help us better appreciate that still-formative relationship between viewers and filmmakers that was evolving in the early cinema. Moreover, it dovetails with Michael O'Pray's theory that one of the key pleasures we viewers derive from animation lies in its "objectification of our own desire for omnipotence" or control (200). We might remember, however, that Crafton's interpretation depends on a relatively few surviving films, those that, as he notes, managed to escape the prevailing attitude that animated films were "better suited for the dustbin than for any other repository" (4);

and, too, it is an explanation that ultimately calls for some amendment or expansion that can easily be found if only we follow those pointing hands of the lightning sketchers.

This recurrent image of figuration not only frames the artist in the context of his animation; it also underscores the relationship between the real and animated worlds. It points up all that is out there—or, to be more precise, all that is *in there,* in the world of animating space. On the one hand, it hints at a kind of *mise-en-abyme,* at the potential for an almost infinite movement within the frame, as frames themselves become fluid or movable (as we see in a work like Emile Cohl's *La retapeur de cervelles,* 1911), and as a single point or line can quite literally become the starting point for all sorts of new and surprising images (as happens in Cohl's *Fantasmagorie,* 1908). But on the other, it also points up the difficulty of that movement within, as these other planes of action simply do not resemble our world and seem bound by different rules—to be, as Cohl might have put it, phantasmagorical. If at the end of his famous *Gertie the Dinosaur* (1914) the artist and presenter Winsor McCay seems to enter the frame of his drawn world to ride off on his "pet" dinosaur's back, it is a feat he accomplishes, as we see on close inspection, only by fashioning a cartoon figure of himself, that is, by willing himself into this other space and becoming an image of the same nature as his creation Gertie. And yet that moment of entry is certainly one of the most effective parts of the film, an unexpected "topper" for all the other tricks Gertie has done and a hint of the attraction that inheres in the deep—and still unexplored—space of the frame.

This ability to move within represents a very fundamental appeal of animation, yet it is also of another sort than just the figurative. It speaks to a new sense of space—and of the individual's experience of space, even of trying to control space—that, as I noted in the introduction, was characteristic of the modern world and that was finding representation across the arts in this period, although most notably in architecture, the graphic arts, and especially film, where the camera was readily demonstrating how easily we might construct—or reconstruct—reality, and where those constructions seemed to point to a correlative possibility for reshaping or controlling our own world. On the one hand, that movement within signals an increasing effort in early animation at imitating live-action cinema, at following the path that André Bazin has famously staked out as the movies' own, that of a "complete illusion of life" (22). But on the other, it also suggests a rather uncanny sense of space that, as Anthony Vidler has argued, was emerging in late modernist culture and that would find a new means of expression in the novel realms of animation. For that uncanny effect, Vidler notes, "destabilizes traditional notions of center and periphery" (*Architectural* 10), causing us to reassess our normal sense of boundaries, much as do those drawing, gesturing, pointing hands of the lightning sketchers.

It is to the various strategies at revisioning space—a space that could be used to stage and mobilize the sort of possibilities Vidler describes, as well as to further that Bazinian myth—that I turn here to set the stage for our more detailed case studies of the relationship between those figural and spatial forces, or what we might more simply term the figural-spatial dynamics of the form. The early history of animation demonstrates a great many different approaches to animating space, as practitioners set about exploring both the broad parameters of their art and a dominant direction that it would take. Though the drawn mode rather quickly assumed a primary position in the world of animation, its own approach to spatial matters had to be worked out over time, particularly as animators sorted out the relationship of their essentially two-dimensional art to the still developing patterns and conventions of live-action cinema, and as their own methods, such as the use of multiple cels, became standardized. At the same time, other techniques—some further emphasizing that two-dimensional character and others moving in quite the opposite direction, grounding themselves in a pointedly three-dimensional world—appeared. Thus, early cinematic animation encompassed not only the hybrid efforts that recall the lightning sketch, but also conventionally drawn films, silhouette films, doll and puppet films, Claymation, and the like. All could stake a claim as a type of animation thanks to their common concern with giving life to things, that is, with *animating* space, but all are equally interesting for their different strategies at constructing or appropriating an animating space, for fashioning a world that, as those sketching hands suggest, invites us in. And more fundamentally, all include the two most basic factors that Charles Solomon has described as fundamental to "a workable definition of animation: (1)

the imagery is recorded frame-by-frame and (2) the illusion of motion is created, rather than recorded" (10).

One approach to opening the door into the animated world is very similar to the tactic of live-action cinema, that is, the creation of a mise-en-scène that furthers the illusion of depth. Among the most effective visual tactics that had become commonplace even in early live-action film were such effects as layering, directed motion, emphasis on a vanishing point, lighting and shadow effects, and the use of oblique lines to direct the eye into the scene. Some early cartoons, in part because they were based on comic strips or magazine cartoons that employed elaborate visual styles, naturally drew on these established techniques. As Norman Klein observes, they were often viewed as "an expansion of the illustrated or printed page" (5), as we see with Winsor McCay's efforts that recall his work as a comic-strip artist for the *New York Evening Telegram* and *Herald*. Because of the immense labor that was involved, though, McCay, who did almost all the drawing himself, was able to produce relatively few animated films in his career. Given the work involved in doing shading, detailed backgrounds, and complex line schemes, most others only sketchily employed these techniques, opting instead for a more streamlined graphic style that could be adapted to a quickly evolving assembly-line approach to cartooning.[2] In the various Phables cartoons (1916) that he illustrated, for example, another former cartoonist and key pioneer of the form, Raoul Barré, seldom provides backgrounds for the action, and a lack of perspective lines makes the action seem to be happening in an almost abstract space.

Like several other companies, William Randolph Hearst's International Film Service produced and distributed a number of series that capitalized on the various comic strips that his newspapers were already syndicating, including Tom E. Powers's *Phat Phables* series (on which Barré worked), George Herriman's *Krazy Kat*, and Frederick Opper's *Happy Hooligan*. That sort of dual development of the same property was quite natural since, as Crafton notes, "the films would publicize the comics, and vice versa, and that was good business" (178). Though the comics' creators were seldom involved with the film adaptations of their work and the various animators who were employed—and these included some of the most noteworthy illustrators of the day, such as Leon Searl,

Gregory La Cava, and Frank Moser—pointedly tried to imitate their styles, it was always within the constraints imposed by the rapidly evolving "industrialization of the cartoon" (Crafton 162) and thus, in effect, by certain "house" practices. The result was, in the period 1916–1918, a cartoon style that both recalled those comic-strip antecedents *and* stood as testimony to the new fascination with, and need for, speed and efficiency in both production and content. Graphic complexity was generally deemphasized, and the line became the governing principle in what Norman Klein has termed "the typographical cartoon" (5) of this era.

As an especially noteworthy example of that adapted style—one that emphasized the figural while offering a context that still suggested the world of the comics—we might briefly consider one of the many newspaper cartoonists who turned his attention to film animation in these early days of cinema. Earl Hurd, who had drawn the comic strips *Trials of Elder Mouse* (1911–1915) and *Brick Bodkin's Pa* (1912), created a series of Bobby Bumps cartoons, first for Universal and then for Bray Productions, the dominant American animation studio from 1914 to 1920. In moving into the animation field, Hurd developed several new techniques that eventually became standard practices for cartoons, while also providing new means for promoting their sense of depth. He used a single background sketched on paper that was then overlaid with characters drawn on a transparent medium—celluloid, or cels, as they came to be known. This technique not only increased efficiency, since only the image produced on each cel would have to be redrawn for every element of a character's motion, but also produced an effective visual separation of characters and backgrounds. And those effects would only be enhanced by adding other cels, which made it possible to do multiple layers of animation, thereby suggesting a more complex, indeed more natural, world. The effect of that approach shows up repeatedly in the composition of many of his Bobby Bumps efforts. For not only are his scenes highly detailed and marked by a sense of perspective that leads the eye into the frame, but they also typically make effective use of off-screen and layered spaces—in effect, of a newly conventionalized three-dimensionality that was further empowered by those technical developments he had brought to the industry-leading Bray studio.[3]

To illustrate these techniques, we might consider a relatively early entry in this series, *Bobby Bumps Starts a Lodge* (1916). In this film young Bobby enters pulling a rope attached to something offscreen, a stubborn goat, we learn, when it suddenly appears and butts Bobby into an adjoining yard, into another offscreen space, but this one hidden by a foreground fence. Though this play of offscreen and onscreen space is basically horizontal, Hurd resorts to a diagonal plan for the subsequent scene in which Bobby tries to share his pain by getting the goat to similarly butt a black friend: Bobby places the goat in the frame's background, arranges his intended victim in the foreground at an angle, and then sets the goat running on a diagonal, only to have his friend foil the trick by turning at the last moment. When Bobby then chases his friend, the action again shifts to conventional horizontal movement, but Hurd adds a layering effect by arranging various pieces of foreground scenery—shrubs and rocks—in the space between the camera and the running boys, and the entire chase is done with a "tracking" camera to further suggest movement within real space. An added spatial effect occurs when the black boy finds himself up a tree and trapped there by a bear. Again, most of this scene is played out in a conventionally horizontal manner (Bobby on the left and his friend, the tree, and the bear on the right side of the frame), but Hurd inserts an inventive high-angle shot as Bobby bargains to help the other boy. Not simply a closer shot, it is one in which the point of view shifts to a diagonal on the previous action while also looking down, as if we have actually moved—tracked in and right while craning up over the treed boy's shoulder—within the previous scene. That vantage allows Hurd to maintain the visual relationship between the two boys as they bargain, while also dramatically linking the viewers to the precariously positioned boy in the tree and thus aligning not only our point of view but also our sympathies with the little black boy. In this short film, then, Hurd manages to deploy an impressive array of visual techniques. Though some of these techniques could be found as well in both comic strips and the live-action cinema, they also point to a desire to capitalize on the spatial possibilities of film animation by exploring some of its own properties. The result, in this case, is that space becomes a fundamental part of the narrative, the defining element of its comic suspense.

That desire would, in relatively short order, find some fulfillment as animators became more ambitious, as certain processes (such as the use of cels) became more widespread, and as sound asserted its own influ-

Staging action on the diagonal in *Bobby Bumps Starts a Lodge* (1916).

ence. The Pat Sullivan–Otto Messmer Felix the Cat cartoons, for example, not only present their central character as fully inhabiting a physical world, but also constantly show him able to manipulate parts of that world, to transform them into props that aid him in his adventures, to bring that world, however sketchily realized, into the work of narrative. And even before Disney would fully syncopate cartoon action in the Silly Symphony series, we would find buildings dancing in *Felix the Cat Woos Whoopee* (1928), backgrounds becoming a shade that could be lifted to reveal *another background* in the Fleischers' *KoKo the Cop* (1927), and trolleys, along with their tracks, coming alive in Disney's *Trolley Troubles* (1927). Sound, moreover, would necessitate further dimensional thinking for the drawn world, particularly in terms of perspective and the relationship between onscreen and offscreen spaces. Thus, even a primitive sound effort like Disney's *Steamboat Willie* (1928) has the faint sounds of a steamboat anticipate its appearance around a river bend in the background, and a parrot that Mickey Mouse knocks out of a porthole on the steamboat produces an audible splash from offscreen. Certainly, some of these effects can just be passed off as anthropomorphizing, a source of humor long before there were cartoons, or be seen as proof that animation actively sought to imitate live-action film. But Paul Wells offers a keener appreciation of these tendencies in the world of pre- and early sound-era cartoons when he observes how they "invested the taken-for-granted aspects of the material environment with their own kinetic aesthetic and found in them the 'essence' of autonomy" (30). Implicit in that notion of the "taken-for-granted" is a key line of development that the cartoon would follow: a tapping into the modernist vision that saw an effective, even uncanny power in the spaces of everyday life, and in animation's simultaneous ability to reproduce and to undermine the appearances of conventional reality.

Another approach to negotiating the spatial potential of animation that was advanced in the form's early years was to deploy a qualitatively different *style* of animation. One of these different styles was the shadow play or silhouette, which was rooted in much older entertainment types, such as the ancient Chinese shadow play and Javanese wayang theater, and the relatively more recent Italian *ombri cinesi* and French *ombres chinoises* of the eighteenth century. Though Crafton describes the silhouette film as "among the more archaic forms" (265) of early animation precisely because of its links to these antecedents, it did allow for a very different spatial experience through its novel style of relief between background and foreground. It typically achieved that effect by employing a light source in back of the image, while the black cutouts of movable figures—the real focus of the animation—occupied the foreground. It is a technique that had a relatively limited, if at times ambitious, role in animation's early development, being used in several series, such as the Bray-Gilbert Silhouette Fantasies of 1915–1916 and Tony Sarg's Almanac cartoons from 1921 to 1924, as well as in a number of German films, most notably Lotte Reiniger's feature-length *Adventures of Prince Achmed* (1926). Yet because of its built-in limitations on depicting action and developing characters, the silhouette film had only a negligible effect on animation's spatial explorations, although its influence can still be seen in more recent efforts at what is termed backlit animation, prominently featured in the Disney science fiction film *Tron* (1982).

We can observe both the basic principles of the silhouette film and some of those limitations that the style entailed by considering one of the early efforts in Tony Sarg's series, *The First Circus* (1921). Even by the standards of this period, the animation is limited, even awkward, the film's primary appeal apparently resting in its extended comic comparison to a contemporary circus and its unconventional depth illusion. After a title card refers to P. T. Barnum's first circus of 1871, the film introduces a "Stonehenge Circus" of thousands of years before, includ-

Silhouette animation in Tony Sarg's *The First Circus* (1921).

ing a stone-age entrepreneur who evokes Winsor McCay's *Gertie* as he introduces his own trained dinosaur to an assembled crowd—three silhouetted figures occupying the left side of the screen. Against a hazy background of Stonehenge-like rock structures, the trainer then pokes and prods his silhouetted beast to make it leave the spectators alone and concentrate on its tricks. He jumps about on the creature's back, head, and tail and introduces a cavewoman—incongruously carrying a parasol—who also balances atop the dinosaur, while a snake forms a tightrope between the creature's head and tail, which the woman then walks. Eventually the dinosaur loses interest in performing, sending those on its back tumbling, and grabs a member of the audience, thus ending the show.

Because of the very nature of the silhouettes—here roughly cut from black cardboard, the figures having few moving joints—all the characters, including the dinosaur, are only crudely realized and capable of little action. What action does transpire is staged horizontally on the foreground plane, as the dinosaur faces and interacts with the small audience on the left of the frame. In fact, the only shift from horizontal movement in *The First Circus* is provided by the vertical leaps and bounces of the trainer and tightrope walker. In the dinosaur's grabbing—and, we presume, eating—of a spectator, however, the film manages a dramatic closure for its limited action that also profits from the nature of the form. As simple black silhouettes, the onscreen spectators are neither detailed nor personified, so a potentially horrifying conclusion becomes instead one more comic demonstration of the dinosaur's failed training. The vaguely sketched but lighter backgrounds help create a visual relief, then, but the severely limited animation does little to capitalize on that effect, leaving us essentially with a flat, horizontally constructed screen world.

In Lotte Reiniger's ambitious *Silhouettenfilm The Adventures of Prince Achmed*, we find a far more complex effort at exploring the potential of this ancient and alternative style of animation.[4] Done only a few years after Sarg's efforts, Reiniger's feature offered audiences delicately conceived, carefully cut-out, and multijointed characters who actually do more than function in, as Esther Leslie describes the film, "a curious side-on world" (50). Often—and strikingly—they actually turn to face the audience, as we see when the African wizard first appears or when he is captured by the Caliph's guards. In such scenes these figures, cut out of black cardboard or thin sheets of lead, their limbs joined to their bodies by fine wire hinges, seem to manifest a kind of hidden dimensionality, an effect only furthered by Reiniger's simultaneous development of an early multiplane camera setup, which she termed her "trick table" (Reiniger 86). That device, consisting of a glass-topped table with diffused lighting underneath, frames to hold multiple images, and a camera situated above and able to move both horizontally and vertically (E. White 10), draws far more effective capital from the usual relief effect of the silhouette by adding multiple ornate background layers and camera movements to many scenes. The film repeatedly seems far more interested in demonstrating the sort of elaborate surface patterns that might be formed, however, as Reiniger frequently arranges multiple characters in the frame in ways that produce what can only be described as ornate images that seem more fundamentally linked to the stylings of Art Nouveau (or the German Jugendstil) than to anything modernist. In fact, Leslie suggests that Reiniger's work essentially failed because its only connection "with modernism's logic" was through its "oscillation between a stark flatness and the exploration of depth through its fakery" (50)—that is, insofar as it made audiences aware of its limited efforts at constructing space. And indeed, these silhouette films, consonant with their theatrical origins, seem to carry a far greater weight of obvious artifice than other forms of animation, and thus a greater sense of the boundaries or limitations within which they worked.

But Reiniger's ability to draw an unusual and even unexpected depth out of this sort of material, and even to explore how the world might, from a different perspective, produce its own curious and appealing patterns, also suggests its kinship to the expressionist cinema of the period and its potential for offering its own commentary on a modernist sense of space.

Yet another approach to developing the figural-spatial relationship that we might briefly consider involves radically changing the nature of the game, that is, employing the concept of animation in its root sense by giving life or spirit to otherwise lifeless objects, such as dolls, manikins, models, or clay figures. Certainly, a great variety of such efforts flourished during the early days of animation, some quite striking in their choice of materials for animation, such as the insect films of Ladislaw Starewicz. This branch of animation, generally known as stop-motion and encompassing such practices as object animation, puppet animation, Claymation, and so on, staked out its own long line of development, one that includes, among others, the figure animation of the former conventional cartoonist Charles Bowers in the 1930s, George Pal's Puppetoon shorts of the 1930s and 1940s, Art Clokey's Claymation Gumby shorts, Aardman Animations' Wallace and Gromit films, Tim Burton's stop-motion features, such as *The Nightmare before Christmas* (1993) and *Corpse Bride* (2005), the experimental work of the Brothers Quay, the puppet films of the Czech animator Jiří Trnka, as well as the stop-motion/live-action combinations created by the two masters of this form, Willis O'Brien and Ray Harryhausen. In fact, this broad field of stop-motion animation has developed such an identity of its own and so broad a following that Tim Burton pointedly tried to imitate its look (to evoke its heyday in the 1950s) when he employed a stylized computer animation for his film *Mars Attacks!* (1996).

In animation's early era, we can find a wide range of efforts using not only commonplace figures, such as posed puppets and toys, but also highly unusual subjects, like preserved insects and stuffed animals. This unusual category shows most prominently in the work of the Russian filmmaker Starewicz, as we see in such early films as *The Ant and the Grasshopper* (1911), *The Cameraman's Revenge* (1912), *The Insects' Christmas* (1913), *The Frogs Who Wanted a King* (1922), and *Voice of the Nightingale* (1923). Perhaps the most famous of his works, *The*

Cameraman's Revenge is certainly remarkable for what Crafton, rather understating the case, terms its "total lack of 'cuteness'" (242). The film tells a story of infidelity and retribution in the insect world by using dead insects—beetles, grasshoppers, a dragonfly—whose limbs have been detached and then reconnected with wax so that they can be sequentially posed. Though the roughly animated insects are themselves fascinating and evidence of Starewicz's keen interest in natural history, the creation of a fully three-dimensional world for them is just as striking and revealing of his larger strategy.

Before taking up filmmaking, Starewicz was, we should note, head of a museum of natural history in Kaunas, Lithuania, and that background seems to have inspired not only his choice of materials but also his methods: of carefully detailed presentation and of consistent parallels between the various creatures that make up that natural world. In keeping with that approach, *The Cameraman's Revenge* uses a number of highly detailed sets, all realized in depth—a depth that, moreover, consistently proves central to the narrative's key dramatic moments. For example, the Hotel d'Amour, where Mr. Beetle takes his dragonfly girlfriend, has double doors that occupy the center of the frame, and beyond them is a flight of stairs that we see the couple climb to their room, and to which they are followed by a jealous grasshopper, the eponymous cameraman. A cut to the landing outside their door reveals the grasshopper looking through the room's keyhole and then positioning his camera to shoot through it, as an insert shot of the couple embracing, framed by a keyhole mask, shows. A parallel tryst between Mrs. Beetle and her artist-lover occurs in a parlor containing an elaborate fireplace in the far-right corner—which proves a convenient escape route for the lover when Mr. Beetle unexpectedly returns and enters from the other side of the frame. The outside of their house is elaborately landscaped; there are trees in the foreground and another tree in the middle of the frame, and the double-doored house is in the background. When Mr. Beetle comes through the doors and sees the lover, a chase ensues around that mid-frame tree, which the lover uses to help his getaway. Finally, the narrative's revenge is staged at a cinema, where a "forgiving" Mr. Beetle has taken his wife—and where the cameraman grasshopper works. Seated in the foreground in front of a large screen on which his own infidelities are surprisingly played for all to see, Mr. Beetle finds that the only escape from his wife's wrath is to jump through the movie screen, into the background. Of course, that sort of movement in depth, into the full reaches of the frame, only parallels Starewicz's larger strategy, which is to take his audience into a normally unseen or hidden realm, thereby revealing not only its depths but also its similarities to our own world and, ultimately, the normally unseen—or purposely hidden—dimensions of that world.

Of course, Starewicz's ability to exploit the film frame's spatial possibilities in part speaks to the very nature of stop-motion animation, particularly its ability when properly scaled and detailed to create an uncanny illusion of life or to suggest another world parallel to our own. But his skills also remind us of the difficulties involved in taking this sort of painstaking path to animation. Though creating and animating a subject using stop-motion is every bit as time-consuming as the production of conventional cel animation, producing the *animating space* introduces far more complexity into the animation process, as we can see in some works of Starewicz's competitors. Far more conventional, yet also more crudely animated, are efforts like the Motoy Comedies produced by Toyland Films. *Mary and Gretel* (1917)—a mélange of various fantasy elements, including *Alice in Wonderland, Rip Van Winkle, Hansel and Gretel,* and *Pinocchio*—is a case in point. The animated dolls employed for this film move awkwardly, and their limbs have little articulation. More to the point, though, is that they have little to do, and the action takes place entirely in a poorly realized forest and

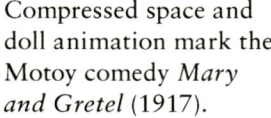

Compressed space and doll animation mark the Motoy comedy *Mary and Gretel* (1917).

cave. The title characters, brought to life by a fairy, simply wander through the forest, where they watch three dwarfs bowl and drink ale, see a white rabbit also indulge and become drunk, and pluck flowers, whereupon the fairy reappears and deanimates them. The forest is composed of a few out-of-scale bushes and twigs that merely provide a shallow background for the dolls' movements and remind us that one of the most difficult tasks involved in this sort of animation is the construction of the miniature sets within which the action unfolds. Because of that difficulty, the only scene composed in depth is that of the dwarfs bowling, and even here the space is truncated to fit everything into the frame; movement into the frame is eliminated because of that necessarily compressed space. The emphasis is on the largely side-to-side movements of the three-dimensional figures, the fantasy context serving as license for the sketchily rendered world of the film.

Rather more ambitious were the early efforts of one of the most important figures in the development of stop-motion animation, Willis O'Brien, who created a series of eight comic shorts for the Edison company, all on a prehistoric theme, including *The Dinosaur and the Missing Link, The Birth of a Flivver,* and *R.F.D. 10,000 B.C.* (all 1917). As the title of a work like *The Birth of a Flivver* suggests, these films all play on the same appeal that would later drive *The Flintstones* cartoons: incongruously viewing stone-age people and creatures through the filter of contemporary culture. Though there were some efforts at animating dinosaurs and other prehistoric creatures, it was usually done briefly and in the context of the larger comic focus of the films, as we see when a "mail truck" arrives in *R.F.D. 10,000 B.C.* It is a cart drawn by a small dinosaur and carrying a prehistoric mailman, his position signified by his "RFD" cap; a title card adds a pun by identifying the pair as "Harry Saurus and his miss Dinah." The animation itself is far from smooth, but the modeled cavemen, dinosaurs, and the "Missing Link" of a film like *The Dinosaur and the Missing Link* are themselves well detailed, and the mise-en-scène is conceived with a mindfulness of live-action cinematic space. In this film (the first in the series), for example, the milquetoast protagonist, Theophilus, enters from the foreground and discovers that Wild Willy, the "Missing Link" who has been terrorizing the people, has been knocked senseless by a dinosaur. After assuring himself that Willy is either dead or unconscious and sensing the

The stop-motion animation pioneer Willis O'Brien developed his technique in films such as *The Dinosaur and the Missing Link* (1917).

approach of others from the rear, he picks up a club and adopts a triumphant pose over the fallen Willy, as if he were the cause of Willy's drubbing. When his girlfriend and her father emerge from the background, they simply assume that he has performed the heroic feat and congratulate him for his courage. The scene suggests not only Theophilus's own awareness of space and the possibilities of staging for effect, but also O'Brien's ability to build gags around such spatial relationships, here between background and foreground action. And that ability forecasts an element of the fame that O'Brien would later earn as he ambitiously sought not only to animate a variety of fantastic figures, such as dinosaurs and giant apes, but also to visualize entire fantasy worlds, as *The Lost World* (1925) and the Skull Island scenes of *King Kong* (1933) most famously attest.

But as Paul Wells rightly notes, the work of O'Brien and others operating in the broad vein of stop-motion animation has often been "absorbed within the Effects tradition rather than receiving recognition in its own right" as animation (52). That is, its very ability to give life to figures within a real space, even to stage that space as one would in a live-action film, has often seemed to argue for a different kinship, as if the real value of this approach lay in its ability to add another dimension to conventional cinema, to open up a fantastic dimension that live action might not otherwise achieve. And certainly figures such as O'Brien and the key inheritor of his position, Ray Harryhausen, helped reinforce that thinking by pursuing projects that consistently showcased their three-dimensional animations by "starring" them in live-action productions where they were seemingly surrounded by real actors and full-sized sets or placed in real locations. It is perhaps for this reason that the various historical accounts of animation, such as those of Barrier, Maltin, Kanfer, and Klein, omit O'Brien from their discussions and give very little or no mention to the likes of George Pal's Puppetoons, Clokey's Gumby, or the Wallace and Gromit films.[5] The very three-dimensionality of these and the earlier works discussed above clearly forecast the eventual trajectory followed by much of the field of animation, however, particularly as it has developed in recent years through CGI and performance-capture technology. In fact, the creation of strikingly "real" figures and their ability to inhabit seemingly three-dimensional worlds —albeit typically stylized or exaggerated worlds—has become almost a commonplace of contemporary digital animation.

Another approach to animating space that bears mention—and that has also converged with recent developments in computer-assisted animation—is the purely technological solution found in optical 3-D processes. Though 3-D did not really become popular until the 1950s, and even then was used primarily for live-action films, a few films appeared earlier that clearly bear the mantle of animation. Among the more prominent of these was *In Tune with Tomorrow,* a film created for the Chrysler Motors Pavilion at the 1939 New York World's Fair. In it a polarized 3-D system was combined with stop-motion animation to create the illusion of a car assembling itself "right in the midst of the audience," as the World's Fair program described it.[6] Attesting to its popularity is the fact that the film would later be reshot in color and released for theatrical play under the titles *New Dimensions* and *Motor Rhythm.* Also for the fair, the former cartoonist Charles Bowers combined the same 3-D process with puppet animation to produce another publicity film, *Pete-Roleum and His Cousins,* a celebration of the contributions of petroleum products to modern life. Though its central characters, animated petroleum droplets, hold little appeal, the film effectively exploits the spatial potential of its 3-D process with surrealistically exaggerated landscapes and canted buildings that loom into the foreground, and it too would eventually make its way to theaters as a short subject, one that remains widely available today. Later, and spurred by the live-action vogue for the form, a number of conventionally drawn cartoons would also be produced in 3-D, among them Warner Bros.' Bugs Bunny film *Lumber Jack-Rabbit* (1954), the Casper the Friendly Ghost effort *Boo Moon* (1954), the Popeye *Ace of Space* (1953), the Woody Woodpecker *Hypnotic Hick* (1953), and two Disney efforts, *Melody* and the Chip 'n Dale cartoon *Working for Peanuts* (both 1953). But the quick collapse of both audience and industry interest in 3-D films in 1954 effectively cut short this line of development.

Much of both the appeal and the problem with these 3-D efforts resides precisely in their treatment of space. John Belton nicely diagnoses the issue in his commentary on the advertising for many 3-D films; as he explains, "Instead of audiences' entering into the world depicted on the screen, the space on screen was represented . . . as invading that of the audience" (189–90)—which is precisely the point emphasized in the guidebook description of *In Tune with Tomorrow*. Indeed, in their use of 3-D, these films typically never so much open up the space of the cinematic image as they do our own space, while also suggesting that this space, including as it does our spectator position, might prove to be in some way unstable or vulnerable to intrusion. In short, the uncanny space of the modernist text becomes *our* space. Yet that sense of what Belton terms "the copresence of image and audience" (190) has retained a fascination, perhaps partly in response to that nagging postmodern impression of what Virilio terms a lost dimension, of something we would do well to get back in touch with, and it has in recent years found renewed application in film generally and in animation more particularly. Though the 3-D modeling programs of computer graphics have provided some element of that dimensionality for all of today's digital animation, we are also increasingly seeing the limited release of specially processed 3-D animated features, such as Disney's *Chicken Little* (2005), *Meet the Robinsons* (2007), and *Bolt* (2008), as well as the Disney-Pixar *Up* (2009), all done in the new Real-D format. These films, designed from the outset to make effective use of that "copresence" effect, suggest that there might be new possibilities for mining what we could term the superspatial effects of true 3-D animation.

This brief survey suggests that the spatial project of animation is an enormously rich field for study, but the following chapters have a rather more limited scope. To allow for detailed examination of some of the key texts in animation history in the context of our shifting cultural sense of space and, more specifically, of the relationship between figure and space, I want to focus primarily on the most common form animation has taken, what I have labeled drawn animation. This is, after all, what most commonly springs to mind when any discussion of animation history or techniques begins, and it is the form that has probably had the most influence on our theorizing about animation. Moreover, that limited focus lets us easily observe the larger trajectory that animation has followed from drawn paper and cels, to computer-assisted drawing, to digitally realized images—a trajectory that ultimately reminds us, as the animator Philip Kelly Denslow has recently suggested, that "with the future digitalization of all media, all forms of production will perhaps be as much animation as anything else" (4). Given this perspective, we might suggest that the trajectory traced here effectively encompasses that of most animation.

Though that future Denslow describes remains open to debate, it is a possibility that I hope to connect with by pursuing certain spatial concerns and developments in the history of animation. As I noted in the introduction, "animating space" involves both the bringing to life of a figure and the creation of a space to support life, meaning, and spirit. And those dual impulses—what we might term the vital and the ecological—that have consistently been at the heart of animation's historical development also provide us with a needed perspective on the increasing fusion between animated and live-action cinema. It is a linkage that Winsor McCay certainly anticipated when he figured himself into the fantastic space of his drawings and rode off atop his dinosaur creation in *Gertie the Dinosaur*. And it is a line of development that all those various pointing, gesturing, drawing hands of the many early lightning sketch–like films essentially invited us to inspect. Look inside, even step inside, this world, they offered, and subsequent animators and audiences have accepted the offer, finding in that animating space not only the pleasures of what Crafton terms figuration, but also the fascination of a surprisingly new and complex world, even a possible cognate of our own. And so let us too step inside some of those worlds.

2

WINSOR McCAY'S WARPED SPACES

An oft-repeated anecdote of early film history recounts how audience members at the Lumière brothers' first screening of their *Arrival of a Train at La Ciotat* (1895) recoiled in fear as the train moved from deep background toward the foreground and eventually off the frame, as if expecting the mechanism to emerge from the screen and enter into their world. It is a story that, though perhaps spurious,[1] has been so frequently recounted precisely because it suggests the sort of phenomenal power of those first projected images, while also hinting at the new cinematic mechanism's ability to suture—somewhat disturbingly—two different sorts of space, the reproduced world of cinematic space and the real world of human experience. I recall this anecdote because of its curious parallel in animation history, as Winsor McCay reversed this fear-inducing effect with his famed vaudeville piece *Gertie the Dinosaur* (1914).[2] Accompanying his cartoon, McCay presents himself as the trainer of his animated dinosaur and, at the act's conclusion, appears to walk into the cartoon's space, there to be taken up by Gertie and move off into the deep background, perched atop her head. Of course, that movement from offscreen space into the depth of the filmed world, into animating space, was apparently meant for a different effect, one of amusement and awe rather than fear, thanks to the manner in which it pointedly toys with reality, emphasizing the skills of the showman-animator and the constructed nature of the filmic space. And yet it is an effect that, I suggest, still carries its own weight of anxiety because of the modernist attitude toward space that it demonstrates—an attitude that, as the previous chapters have suggested, represents an important legacy for the animated cartoon.

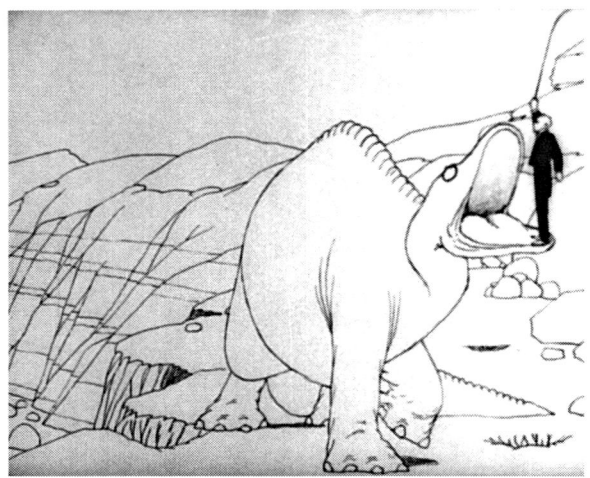

Winsor McCay "enters" the animated world of Gertie in *Gertie the Dinosaur* (1914).

Much of the critical discussion surrounding the early history of animation has recently come to focus on its shifting relationship to the avant-garde; there has been a particular emphasis on how the early cartoon especially, with its essentially flat, fluid, and even reflexive characteristics, was often perceived as effecting the same sort of challenge to the status quo as did much of modernist art. Esther Leslie typifies this approach as she compares early developments in animation to an avant-garde movement that typically "takes fragmentation and disintegration into its law of form, making clear how constructed not only it is but also the social world—ripe for transformation" (122). And following this same focus on animation's ideological implications, Paul Wells reminds us of how the "positioning of animated films" and, by implication, of animation itself as "merely populist texts" has "proved to be inhibiting in properly acknowledging its omnipresent significance as a potentially radical art form" (1). That emphasis on formal parallels between animation and avant-garde art in terms of both technique and political intention, though, has tended to gloss over the nature of some of those connections, particularly the manner in which early animation addresses one of its most fundamental properties, the space that the animator or cartoonist must fill up or leave empty,[3] the animating space that through his or her own creative efforts the animator must, as McCay seemingly does in *Gertie the Dinosaur,* almost literally enter. I suggest that when we look more closely at how McCay's films engage with space, we can see another dimension of that modernist spirit at work, for we find that his work implicates an assault not simply on the social status quo, but also on what we might term the phenomenological status quo, that is, on both the organization of and the audience's experience of space itself.

As we have previously observed, Anthony Vidler, in his study of space, culture, and architecture in the early modern era, provides us with an important lead in this direction. He notes that the turn of the century introduced, along with its insights into psychology and culture, a new sense of space that he terms "warped space," and he suggests that this development was so crucial that we might well think of it as the key leit-motiv of modernity (*Warped* 5). Drawing on the work of Freud, Walter Benjamin, and Georg Simmel, he describes how the new urban world—that which was populated by the audience for that equally new phenome-non of film—had become invested not only with a fresh awareness of what we might term *internal spaces* or psychological space, but also, and corre-sponding to these internal spaces, with a variety of space-oriented neuro-ses and phobias resulting from processes of "psychological projection or introjection" (*Warped* 8).[4] As part of this investment, space was no longer simply perceived to be a "stable container" or neatly measurable realm, but was increasingly seen "as a product of subjective projection," an incon-stant and shifting world that might best be described by the emerging vocabularies of "displacement and fracture, torquing and twisting, pres-sure and release, void and block," and one that popularly measured out, particularly among the new urban populations, a rising sense of alienation that even produced a symptomatic agoraphobia (*Warped* 1).

One result is that artists and architects of the modernist era—like the cartoonists and animators whose task was to give shape to or fill up a spatial void—also had to address or account for this "architectural uncanny," as Vidler terms it (*Architectural* 11). As traditional notions of center and periphery were effectively disappearing, and as perspective became unanchored, they would increasingly find it necessary to break the boundaries of convention in order to depict space in these new ways, seeking to "produce effects of techniques of movement and space-time interpenetration" (*Warped* 100), perhaps most famously demonstrated in Duchamp's *Nude Descending a Staircase* (1912), wherein space is multiply fragmented to present movement in time.

McCay is especially well positioned in animation history to help us gauge this new world of warped or uncanny space and its effect on the early development of this mode of cinema. His work, as Donald Crafton has shown, clearly straddles different eras and approaches to the drawn world. His early manner of presentation drew on the model of the vaudeville performance and capitalized on the common practice of the lightning sketch—originally a Victorian parlor entertainment before migrating into vaudeville, and already popularized in the cinema through the work of Georges Méliès, Emile Cohl, and J. Stuart Blackton. That approach tends to frame him less as a cartoonist—that is, as someone who has created a drawn product for the audience's entertainment or amusement—than as an entertainer himself, someone who, like Cohl or Blackton, primarily aims to amaze viewers with this technique for producing rapid transformations in the image (Crafton 48).[5] And in combining his animated efforts with live-action scenes of himself as animator, in demonstrating to audiences how the show of animation works in films like *Little Nemo* (1911) and *Gertie the Dinosaur*, McCay only underscored that performative dimension of his work.

To that approach, which pointedly emphasizes the element of self-figuration that Crafton has identified as central to early animation, McCay added an emphatic spatial sense. For he generally drew in what Michael Barrier describes as "an elaborate illustration style" (33), one that had been honed in his artist-reporter background at the *Cincinnati Commercial Tribune* and his early print cartoons for the *New York Herald*. That style clearly ill suited the pace and procedures of an industrial animated cartoon production—which helps explain his relatively short career as a film animator—and at first glance it seems far removed from the world of the avant-garde, Yet as Leonard Maltin notes, McCay's films also seem to offer "a continuous parade of movement, metamorphosis, and exaggeration" (*Of Mice* 3), precisely the sort of features that would quickly become synonymous with the new animated cartoon and its potentially subversive nature. In fact, one of the most striking characteristics of all of his films is their almost self-conscious devotion to motion and change—elements that also align them with what Esther Leslie describes as the modernist "universe of transformation, overturning, and provisionality" (vi).

And yet, in her account of early animation's links to modernist art

Leslie almost dismisses McCay's efforts, simply noting that they "were detailed, beautiful, and took many months to produce" (12). That hint of disregard seems to result from the sort of mixed nature of his work that I have described above, as it perhaps, following his own lead, too easily assigned him to the rank of entertainer—admittedly of an innovative sort—while paying too little attention to the nature or style of his entertainments, and particularly to the aesthetic of "movement . . . and exaggeration" that his films were gradually developing and that would become one of his key legacies to the world of animation. In his discussion of modernist art in the early twentieth century, Paul Virilio describes how its development brought with it "a crisis of representation," owing not only to the disappearance of a stable sense of space, as conventional space increasingly seemed to become a "lost dimension" of everyday life, but also to the way in which it was being replaced by the often disorienting experiences of speed and motion (*Lost* 112). And in McCay's films, I would suggest, we can already begin to glimpse important elements of this development, elements that, despite Leslie's near dismissal of his work, give reason to Michael Barrier's description of him as "the first American animator of consequence" (10).

We need not look that far ahead, though, to see how McCay's films repeatedly invest space with a kind of anxiety that results in a version of that warped or phobic space Vidler has described. As a most obvious instance we might briefly consider a film that viewers tend to see as his most realistic effort, *The Sinking of the Lusitania* (1918). It is a work that achieves its propagandistic shock effect by interweaving two very different spatial conceptions: a literal concern with actual space and a stylized treatment of space. On the one hand, as part of what a title card describes as the "historical record," the film dramatically details the headline-making event of its title, showing how danger hides in the impenetrable depths of the sea; a German submarine's periscope is glimpsed above the water and then torpedoes suddenly strike the British liner, causing it to explode and sink—all rendered in what Crafton accurately describes as a "realistic graphic style" reinforced by an editing technique that imitates newsreels of the day, such as the *Universal Weekly* (116). But, on the other hand, it uses the stylistic possibilities implicit in that real space of anxiety to add a further unsettling dimension, as if the submarine lurking in those depths were metaphoric of

A submarine's periscope produces a threatening space in *The Sinking of the Lusitania* (1918).

some other sort of anxiety or threat that was more difficult to articulate or visualize. More specifically, we see the almost abstractly rendered blank surface of the sea—essentially a sea of white space that is as well the nearly undifferentiated space of the film frame—swallow up the carefully drawn and detailed victims of the attack, fashioning in its collision of styles an effective visual anxiety and suggesting a dangerous void. What McCay managed to tap into with this spatial combination was a new fear of space that, as Vidler has chronicled, had been "forged in the early modernist period itself with the introduction of . . . psychological projection or introjection" (*Warped* 8).

Responding primarily to its ideological thrust, Paul Wells has fittingly described this film as "a seminal moment in the development of the animated film" (33), largely because of the way it effectively combined near-documentary elements with a pointedly propagandistic impulse. In that very combination he sees the film tracing "the contradictions of the modern age," and especially of "animation as a Modernist practice" (31, 30). Yet beyond its obvious ideological implications, as I suggested above, this film points to a kind of stylistic difficulty—or perhaps a contradiction—that we can see being negotiated successfully here and that also surfaces in various ways in McCay's other films. Particularly—and as an amplification of Wells's assessment of the "contradictions" at work in *Lusitania*—I suggest that we view McCay's animated work as an effort at balancing what we might term created space with the film frame's negative space. The former takes shape from both a dominant realist aesthetic of the period and McCay's own grounding in what Wells terms "a journalistic mode of representational realism" (31), both of which invited efforts at naturalistic reproduction. And the latter denotes that nagging emptiness of the frame that was the fundamental condition and starting point for both animated and live-action film. That negative space was always laden with anxiety—or hints of the uncanny—because it automatically evoked both that element of "psychological projection or introjection," that is, the world of repressed forces and unseen depths whose power Freud had just begun to explore and articulate in this period, and the basic difficulty of creation itself, of filling up the void with images drawn from within the self. The drama to which *The Sinking of the Lusitania* attests and purports to record, then, is not just the one involved in the real and momentous historical event, or even in the specific challenge to the animator as he tries to give shape to this tragic event, but also that implicit in the pregnant spaces of every frame and every image. In the way he exploited the tension between these spaces, McCay effectively underscores an important if generally overlooked link between animation and the avant-garde: a reminder not simply of animation's subversive possibilities and ideological positioning, but also of its ability to tap into the evocative, even disturbing power of space itself.

As examples of the sort of tension or negotiation I am describing, I turn to two of McCay's films that correspond to two key dimensions of his career: his vaudeville experience and his newspaper cartoon background, particularly as modeled in his most famous comic strips, *Dreams of a Rarebit Fiend* (1904–1913) and *Little Nemo in Slumberland* (1905–1914). For the former example I consider *Bug Vaudeville* (1921), a film that, while not employing the sort of stage interaction between the animated world and the real world that we see so prominently displayed in films like *Little Nemo* and *Gertie the Dinosaur*, presents its material as if it were part of a vaudeville-style show. In effect, it deploys that vaudeville dynamic, the supposed live performance, as a crucial support for its narrative. For the latter I look at *The Flying House* (1921), a cartoon in the vein of McCay's various other Dreams of a Rarebit Fiend film efforts, all of which drew on his previous newspaper work by depicting wildly exaggerated adventures resulting from a spicy dish eaten before retiring. Of course, both are actually set up as dream narratives and thus ultimately suggest a level on which McCay's films almost invariably proceed from an oneiric impulse, one that, as does all dreaming, always seems to be negotiating between our sense of real space and imaginary space, and thus always speaking to the sort of spatial negotiation that, as I have suggested, seems so fundamental to much early animation.

Like many other McCay films, *Bug Vaudeville* begins with a realistic rationale for its ensuing fantastic imagery, as a tramp emerges from behind a stand of elaborately drawn trees, announces in a title card that he is sleepy, and anticipates the narrative to follow by observing that "cheese cakes are bad. They make me have such queer dreams." That verbal context punctuates some of the best examples of McCay's "painstakingly realistic" animation, as Michael Barrier describes it (17): highly detailed images of trees, bushes, plants, and of the tramp himself, yet all framing a curiously empty white central background that hints of a dream space that is about to open up to him and to the audience. That mise-en-scène of elaborately drawn foreground and negative space in the rear of the frame then reverses ground, as a curtain appears and a title card announces "The Program": a series of sketchily realized bugs doing dancing, juggling, bicycling, tumbling, and boxing acts in mid-frame, all of them set against highly detailed vaudeville-style stage backdrops. This reversal of ground is noteworthy because it underscores the fakery inherent in the false perspectives that decorate these elaborately conceived backdrops, establishing space here as itself a kind of performance, the work of the artist—or dreamer—much as McCay himself established it in his vaudeville stint with *Gertie the Dinosaur*.

At the same time, the various elements of the "show"—backdrop, stage area, performing bugs, proscenium arch—point toward a new negative space, an unaccounted for one in the foreground that only slowly calls attention to itself when, at the conclusion of each act, the hands of a single figure, the back of its head seen in silhouette, rise up and applaud the performance, making us aware of what had seemed to be just an empty area of the foreground. That glimpsed figure effectively stands in for both the film audience and the tramp from whose "queer dreams" we suppose all these strange performances have emanated. Reduced to a shadowy presence, this singular audience not only responds appreciatively, but effectively frames the unusual action, putting the apparently giant-sized bugs in a traditional space demarcated by the backdrops and proscenium arch and organized by the vanishing point implicit in his gaze. This familiar situation of performance and appreciation seems to render the nightmare, despite all its strangeness, harmless and conventional, even amusing. And the movement of the performers only underscores this impression, as the dancing daddy longlegs, bicycling cockroach, and tumbling bugs consistently move in left-to-right and right-to-left fashion, and a butterfly and beetle fly about in circular patterns, thereby reassuring us that this is a regular, if also carefully constructed, space, all arranged for that viewer's perspective and, more important, that these uncanny effects are safely contained within its theatrical conventionality.

In a surprising conclusion to the film, however, this space—not to mention the performers—also reveals another dimension. A spider emerges from above this artificial realm, reaches across the proscenium arch, grabs that silhouetted audience figure from the foreground, and swallows him. It is a most unsettling end, not just because of that surprising and horrific attack—precisely the stuff, after all, that audiences probably should have expected from such "rare" dreams—but also because of the way it assaults (or torpedoes) that conventional sense of space, pulling in the audience, as if it were enacting another version of that move noted at the conclusion of *Gertie the Dinosaur*. This unset-

An animated spider of *Bug Vaudeville* (1921) violates the space of the audience.

tling finale reminds us of what *real* space, in contrast to the neatly arranged arena of stage and performance, is actually like. It is warped or phobic, filled with our darkest anxieties, and open to the unexpected, whereas our conventional sense of space is rather that which we carefully construct—with frames, vanishing points, and an artfully controlled perspective—as a kind of distraction, even protection, from the reality of life.

If the conclusion to *Bug Vaudeville* seems a bit like a nasty joke—one in keeping with the "queer dreams" motif established at the film's start—it is one that follows a pattern in McCay's work, of spaces that become laden with surprise, even menace. Of course, the "empty" sea of *The Sinking of the Lusitania* offers the most obvious example. We see the same pattern at work in the case of the outsized mosquito that slowly makes its way across a transom to attack a sleeping man in McCay's early effort *How a Mosquito Operates* (1912). And at the start of *Gertie the Dinosaur* we watch the "playful" Gertie saunter from background to foreground to greet the audience, but almost immediately grab for the only substantial object in the foreground—and nearest the audience—a tree, which she then easily plucks and swallows. When another character, Jumbo the elephant, appears from offscreen and threatens to upstage her, Gertie soon picks him up and flings him into the deep background, demonstrating her power over this cartoon space. There is at least a hint in both these scenes that this primitive force could easily reach farther into the foreground, even offscreen, like the spider of *Bug Vaudeville,* to violate our space and undermine our carefully constructed world, were it not controlled by the ultimate master of these spaces, the animator McCay.

A slightly later effort, *The Flying House,* further develops this assault on conventional space, while more pointedly linking that effort to the sort of questioning of the cultural and social status quo that we usually associate with the avant-garde. Its ground is not the artifice of the vaudeville stage, but rather the artifice of an increasingly urbanized and suburbanized American society of the 1910s and 1920s. As Howard P. Segal has described this development, the late nineteenth and early twentieth centuries saw the appearance of a great number of highly designed communities, some industrialized utopian villages, connected to large factory complexes, as in Gary, Indiana, and other greenbelt suburbs, closely linked to larger urban-industrial centers, as was the case with Forest Hills Gardens in New York. All were "well planned and modernized—the machine making possible the modernized garden" (20); the communities were typically arranged on a grid, the straight-line streets regularly dividing the grid's sections, and similar houses on similar-sized lots further regularizing the living space. It is this highly conventionalized space—its artifice normally obscured from the vantage of its inhabitants—that is revealed and explored when one house in such a modern grid suddenly takes flight.

That larger social vision is once again framed by the dream mechanism to which McCay often resorted, as a woman notes to her husband that she is afraid the rarebit she had for dinner might produce a nightmare, and a subsequent title card announcing "The Dream" quickly supports that fear. Yet the images that immediately follow prove quite conventional and demonstrate some of the clean yet finely detailed drawing for which McCay was so well known—realistically rendered domestic images of their bedroom, a staircase, and the attic. Save for their strange emptiness, these domestic spaces hardly seem the stuff of nightmares. In the attic, however, the film begins to open onto a seemingly surrealist dimension, one that initiates the work's assault on both the everyday world and its conventionalized spaces. For there we see the woman's husband tending a massive engine that fills the room and to which we later see him hoisting up a huge propeller that he attaches to a shaft that extends outside, apparently making their house ready for flight. These strange preparations, as we learn, are his reaction to a letter from their unseen landlord, George A. Profiteer, who has announced he is going to dispossess (or torpedo) them for a lack of payment. Rather than lose their home and their place in this carefully constructed society, the husband announces his unconventional response, that they will simply "steal the house," as a title card offers. That theft begins with a long shot of the propeller-equipped house; we see the house slowly breaking free from its foundations, the house flying toward the camera and then up and out of the frame—after the fashion of the Lumières' train and of McCay astride his pet Gertie.

As it violates the spatial constraints of the frame—as well as the laws of gravity and probability—the flying house leaves behind an almost completely empty space, a regular spot on the neighborhood grid, on

The nightmarish implication of *The Flying House* (1922)—the threat of placelessness.

which the camera then focuses. There is, of course, a multiply subversive effect within that now empty space. It represents, foremost, a strike at the very core of property rights and the capitalist system, denoting both the theft from Mr. Profiteer and the empty promise of the highly planned community. Additionally, that emptiness suggests the fears of loss and dispossession, the anxieties that drive this seemingly most conventional couple to this extreme act, while also hinting at a repressed revolutionary spirit lurking even within the traditional domestic world. Finally, there is a phenomenological insistence here, as that vacated space underscores how easily this world might become warped, its spaces transformed, its solidity revealed as just another illusion maintained by the conventions of everyday life.

In detailing the couple's subsequent adventures in their flying house, the rest of the film swerves into another sort of nightmare, one whose power draws less from the ideological than from the phenomenological implications of that emptiness. For the narrative then becomes a terrifying story of placelessness—and an interesting interpretation of the Freudian *unheimlich*—as the couple determine to "fly around till we find a place where" their landlord "will *never* find us" or their stolen house. But in sharp contrast to their former home site, the places to which they resort are all rough and unplanned, off the grid and clearly inhospitable: a swamp, a factory smokestack, the ocean, even the moon, where they are quickly chased away by a giant Man in the Moon wielding a flyswatter. And to underline that contrast, McCay depicts them looking wistfully at the conventional spaces below, neat squares and rectangular plots of land, like the neat lot they had abandoned, criss-crossed by roads and rivers—the constructed space that seems most appropriate to the domestic world they have left behind. One implica-tion, of course, is that there might not be anywhere in the modern world free of landlords, no space outside of that which has been culturally constructed and apportioned. Yet the wife's fearful recognition that they might become simply "lost in the sky" voices a darker corollary, a fear that once we open onto that emptiness we might not be able to regain a secure place in this "planned" world. Her anxiety is precisely that bound up in Vidler's sense of "phobic space" and even in Virilio's later notion of a lost dimension. The fact that the house eventually runs out of gas and is then struck by a rocket fired from an experimental army gun, however, brings a more practical end to this dream—or nightmare—of flight and escape. As they fall from the sky and land—or awaken—in their bed, the starting point of the narrative, and the wife realizes, "I was dreaming," *The Flying House* resolves these multiple anxieties for us. Relieved and returned to their realistically drawn domestic space, back in their spot on the community grid, the couple reminds us of how we remain bound to this world and to its cultural constructions, even if we become aware—or dream—of other possibili-ties, an open space of motion and change that, under life's pressures, powerfully beckons. It is a note comically struck earlier in the flight when the husband accidentally knocks over a water tank with the flying house and his wife observes, "They will make you pay for that"—a quip he tries to ignore.

Yet that open space wherein the couple can, for a brief time, escape any payment suggests a further dimension of the narrative, particularly in the way it signals a stylistic shift here. For it also represents the ani-mator's own free space, the realm in which an artist like McCay can imaginatively play, can "warp" space as he sees fit, much as his comic strip character Little Nemo would do in his dreams, or the title charac-ter of his *Little Sammy Sneeze* would do in the final panel of each comic with his powerful sneezes that were, at times, even able to burst the gridlike boundaries of the comic strip frame.[6] It is a point that *The Fly-ing House* underscores particularly when, during the house's flight into space beyond the earth, a title card strikes a surprisingly self-conscious note, advising us to admire the "remarkable piece of animation which follows." Though we are assured that these images of the Earth, Moon, and "the beautiful constellation Orion" have all been "drawn true to astronomical calculations," the rapid changes in perspective and the sudden appearance of an unlikely-looking Man in the Moon, as well as the outlandish shift in scale that this giant figure introduces, quickly blast away that notion of scientific concern and accuracy. In its place, and in an example of what Crafton has described as McCay's "remarkable reflexiveness" (129), the film asserts the animator's freedom to explore and develop a sense of space for both comic effect and social satire. The extra, malleable space of the cartoon, the space that reminds us of what can and cannot be bound within the conventionally constructed world—or the typical film frame, or as McCay's newspaper entries suggest, even the comic strip frame—is that which the very act of animation, the movement via pen or pencil from outside the frame to within, most fundamentally reveals and attests to.

In trying to gauge the sort of allusive use of space that marks McCay's films, I have followed Paul Wells's lead in his discussion of the cultural power of early animation. He suggests that in the early modern era the animated film "was *the* language of presence and absence" (43). Yet that description, as accurate as it is, needs to be extended and read in the context of more than just the ideological, for it also points us in the direction of both the raw material of animation, space itself, and the role of the animator, as himself a figure of "presence and absence." In McCay's films *constructed space,* the space of culture, the space of presence, even the space of conventional community, is continually foregrounded and interrogated to reveal not just the constructions of the social world, but also its own corollary, the *warped space* of experience, the subversive space of the imagination, the space of absence. If the latter typically emerges or discloses itself in the space of a dream—or the nightmare of war, as we see most vividly in *The Sinking of the Lusitania*—it intimates the difficulty of negotiating between these two sorts of space, and even the degree to which the latter was seen as repressed by the power of the former—a point that would repeatedly be made by the avant-garde art of McCay's time.

Key to this spatial negotiation is the animator himself, in this instance

Winsor McCay, whose presence, as I have suggested, can be felt even when he does not, as showman, pointedly step into the frame, as he does at the end of *Gertie*. His presence is repeatedly measured out in the negative or warped spaces of his films, in every instance when he injects a note of surprise that suddenly apprises the audience of the animator's hand, precisely because of the way in which the images undermine a conventionally constructed space and, in the best modernist tradition, hint of an alternative. In this context we might briefly consider McCay's film *The Pet* (1921), with its narrative about a couple's adoption of a strange creature that they soon discover has a prodigious appetite, one that prompts it to eat practically everything it encounters—a bowl of milk, but also the pet cat, the couple's breakfast, including their place settings and coffee urn, the coal pile, various house furnishings, a barrel of rat poison, trees, a car, a trolley, various buildings, planes, and even a dirigible—all the while growing ever larger and becoming an even bigger menace. This unknown, unidentified, and vaguely drawn species simply gouges ever greater holes in the detailed and conventional landscape McCay has drawn, and in a highly ironic way, I suggest, points toward the work of the artist, as the figure who both creates and erases, always suggesting other possibilities, always dueling with that empty space. It is also clearly a figure (both "pet" and artist) freighted with anxiety because of its very capacity for opening up these holes, for threatening our conventional sense of space, ultimately for challenging our worldview. We might even think of it as the very specter of modernism, stalking through the animated world, reminding us of how pliable cinematic space is and how similarly malleable, despite all our efforts at planning and construction, the real world might also prove to be. Creating that vision seems to have been McCay's own "pet" project after all, and perhaps his key legacy to the world of animation.

3

THE STEREOSCOPIC MICKEY

If most film histories have conveniently located animation's origins in the work of McCay and the appearance of his dinosaur Gertie, they have also tended to link its emergence as a mature form and a fundamental component of the American film industry to the work of the Fleischer brothers and Walt Disney, especially with the introduction of the latter's iconic character, Mickey Mouse. Chapter 4 will examine some of the Fleischers' key contributions, but here I focus on Disney's signal creation, the mouse that he would subsequently credit with being the foundation of his entire entertainment empire, and on the style that attaches to that mouse, at least in his early creation. For although the Fleischers would precede the Disney brothers in the industry and, thanks to their KoKo the Clown, would quickly establish a reputation for both inventive cartoons and technological innovation, the mouse soon after his introduction in 1928's *Steamboat Willie* would become the most famous of all cartoon figures and would even be trumpeted in a *Film Daily* ad of 1930 as "The Most Popular Character in Screendom."[1] In introducing the first episode of his landmark *Disneyland* television show in 1954, Walt Disney would himself point to this significant appearance, reminding audiences, as he referred to the entertainment empire that he was even then expanding, that "we mustn't forget that it all started with a mouse."[2] The historian Gregory Waller underscores the extent of this influence as he chronicles how, in the wake of the mouse's appearance, "for almost all critics and journalists and reviewers of the 1930s and early 1940s, the animated cartoon was quite literally Disney's land" (57). Disney's point, then, is one that we might justifiably stretch a bit to take in much of animation's history, for it was "with a mouse," more than with a Fleischer clown, that animation made some of its largest early gains, particularly in its exploration of that new modernist sense of space.

Yet we should note from the start that many readings of the early Mickey Mouse cartoons—and to some extent of all the Disney Studio's early animation efforts—have been partially obscured by their very accomplishment. For with what was actually the third Mickey cartoon, the fully synchronized *Steamboat Willie,* they have been inextricably linked to the coming of sound and largely discussed in the context of their successful application of that technology. In fact, the earliest Mickey efforts—*Plane Crazy* and *The Gallopin' Gaucho* (both 1928), along with *Steamboat Willie*—have been both praised and attacked from this vantage. Michael Barrier in his history of the Hollywood cartoon, for example, emphasizes their singular achievement, how "from the first, Disney grasped sound's potential for involving his audience in what was happening on the screen" (57), whereas Esther Leslie in her discussion of modernism and animation argues that, in their use of sound, these films demonstrate almost from the start "Disney's accomplished sell-out of the quintessence of cartoons, their modernistic dissolution of conventional reality" (149).[3] Certainly there is some accuracy in both assessments; however, what they and other historical accounts typically omit is an appreciation of their visual styles, particularly of how these films confronted the problems of space and constructed a character—Mickey Mouse—who would have to seem at home in that space. This omission is particularly significant, since it tends to cast Disney's later development of a "realistic" style in a simplistic light,[4] while it also interferes with our understanding of the studio's problematic relation to modernism.

In this vein, we might note that Leonard Maltin's history of the American cartoon claims that "there was nothing special or different" about the first Mickey Mouse cartoons, that essentially they were similar to Disney's silent Oswald the Lucky Rabbit efforts, the design of which had also been determined largely by Walt's friend and early partner Ub Iwerks (*Of Mice* 34). The first two Mickeys, *Plane Crazy* and *The Gallopin' Gaucho,* center on a mischievous and highly inventive character, the gags mix physical slapstick with an element of what Barrier terms "psychological" humor (47), and the new mouse hero is a

familiar type—"a formulaic mouse of a kind that had long been plentiful in competitors' cartoons" (Barrier 49), or as Neal Gabler suggests
more simply, "essentially Oswald with shorter ears" (113). Yet for the
most part, that similarity was all to the good, since by this point the
cartoons produced by the Disney studio had a reputation for their work-
manship and were already being studied by other animators.[5] That
sense of imitation or sameness, however, has often been used to prop up
the conclusion that sound—when introduced in *Steamboat Willie* and
later added to these first efforts—was essentially all that distinguished
this new creation and was the real source of Mickey's popularity. Yet
there is something else different about the first Mickeys, for these cartoons, especially *Plane Crazy* and *The Gallopin' Gaucho,* which were
both designed for a silent world, also use space differently and link their
new central character to this world in a way that even many of the later
Mickey cartoons—those burdened by what the contemporary critic Gilbert Seldes describes as a felt need to "give him too much to say" (170),
to *use* sound as a narrative underpinning—would not.

Sound is, of course, what first interested distributors in Disney's new
product, largely because it had suddenly become the cinematic fashion
in the wake of Warners' *The Jazz Singer* (1927). And the success of Disney's first sound release, *Steamboat Willie,* quickly prompted the studio
to revisit its first efforts with the mouse and add sound to both *Plane
Crazy* and *The Gallopin' Gaucho.* But as Maltin's comment reflects, the
prevailing wisdom is that those first efforts were very primitive and
largely, as Gabler assesses, "the product of desperation and calcula-
tion," done "as quickly as possible so that Walt could find a distributor
and keep his company afloat" after losing the rights to his Oswald character to Universal (114–15). Gabler also notes, however, that two repre-
sentatives of MGM, Howard Dietz and Felix Feist, liked the silent *Plane
Crazy* enough to recommend it to Nicholas Schenck, president of the
parent company Loew's, and to arrange a special showing. Why Schenck
decided not to contract for a series of Mickey Mouse films is unknown
but may simply reflect his primary focus on the company's business
operations, in which capacity he had primarily overseen its theatrical
holdings. There clearly was something very attractive about these first
efforts, although something that would be qualified as sound increasingly came into play.

To better understand the significance of the first Mickey Mouse cartoons, and eventually to better gauge Disney's emergence with sound's introduction as a premier animation studio, we also need to see these efforts in another context, one closer to their position within an evolving animation aesthetic. We should specifically consider their relationship to that modernist fascination with space that I described in the introduction. For there was, I would argue, something more three-dimensional about the mouse, something that we might—to use the phrasing of one contemporary commentator—even term *stereoscopic*. As Leslie chronicles, animation was early on linked to the modernist spirit and seen to reflect many of the same concerns as early twentieth-century avant-garde art. She describes how modernist artists and critics tended to see cartoons as operating within a universe of impermanence, constant transformation, and shifting expectation (vi). More particularly, Leslie suggests that their superficial emphasis of such characteristics was generally viewed as "a virtue, a motive and a motif," since their "dissolution of form" pointed to something more significant: "a chance to return to the drawing board of social formation" (vii). It is a point made by the noted director Sergei Eisenstein, who early on championed animation and especially Mickey Mouse, finding in the work of Disney "an upheaval, a unique protest against the metaphysical immobility of the once-and-forever given" (*Eisenstein* 33). For some, then, the cartoon, including the early Disney efforts that were praised by Eisenstein, as well as by such figures of the aesthetic and social avant-garde as Salvador Dalí and Walter Benjamin, embodied the modernist spirit of change, while also marking an interesting meeting ground between high and low art, and the worlds of politics and entertainment.

Yet Leslie's interpretation of that modernist affinity bears further consideration, for she bases her linkage to the avant-garde spirit on what she describes as the essential "flatness" of early cartoons, the two-dimensionality that highlights their constructed nature and seems to many so primitive today. Thus, she argues that the "flatland" they depicted and of which their characters were a part was important precisely because it subverted a realist sensibility, particularly that associated with Hollywood narrative, while promising to reveal how, in the grip of modern capitalist society, audiences were "just as lifeless as the figures on the screen" (181). Yet in discussing that same modernist spirit from the perspective of architecture and graphic arts, Vidler offers a very different take on how space, form, and dimensionality were read in this period. As we have already noted, he believes that a new sense of space was the central leitmotiv of modernity (*Warped* 5), particularly as space came to take on psychological and social dimensions and, in so doing, to hint, also subversively, at the incommensurateness of many of our other normal categories—such as those of class, gender, and nationality. Nowhere was that modernist art of space more in evidence, he suggests, than in film; for there, especially in those forms that most explored the possibilities of graphic design—expressionist, constructivist, and animated film—a new sense of space most clearly seemed "to transform reality itself. . . . The surroundings no longer surrounded, but entered the experience as presence" ("Explosion" 14–15), not flattening space out so much as revealing its further dimensions. In effect, whereas Leslie, drawing on a Marxist perspective, sees a subversive power in the marked absence of dimension in much early animation, and thus in its tendency to flatten out and abstract our sense of the real, Vidler, with his phenomenological vantage and following the lead of Walter Benjamin,[6] locates that same power in a kind of expansive and revelatory power of filmic space, its ability to explore unseen dimensions, to play with form and dimension, to make space visible and give it a voice—a point similarly made by Stephen Kern as he describes space in this period as constituting a new "form of understanding" (134). As a German art critic of the period, Herman Scheffauer, would describe this effect, it represented the cinema's capacity for "the vivifying of space," for projecting an image not so much of the real world, but of a new "stereoscopic universe" (79).

Against the backdrop of these different approaches and their dissimilar appreciations of spatial significance, we might begin to better gauge the appearance—and early popularity—of Disney's mouse, who was clearly a native of that stereoscopic realm. The mouse was from the start more than just a new character, and, I would argue, more too than a one-off version of Disney's previous "star," Oswald. As we have noted, Mickey evokes something of Oswald's appeal, which Russell Merritt and J. B. Kaufman ascribe to his "ebullient energy and high spirits" (86). But Mickey is also a figure who is placed in a more complex world than the one Oswald or a more daunting competitor such as Felix the

Cat occupies; and he is a figure who is more focused on finding ways of coping with this stereoscopic world and participating in what Eisenstein describes as "the liberation of forms" (*Eisenstein* 21), the transformative and ultimately subversive power of film images. In fact, this encounter is key to his own modernist dimension, as he must address the challenge of modernism's "flux of form" (Vidler, "Explosion" 22), operate in an often satiric landscape, and live in a world that is every bit as alive and dimensional as he is—as the apparently "conscious" steamboat whistles that nudge each other in *Steamboat Willie,* the church steeple that "dodges" Mickey's plane in *Plane Crazy,* or even an outhouse that avoids bullets and bombs in *The Barnyard Battle* (1929) demonstrate.

Rising to this challenge, confronting space at a time when, as Vidler notes, it was becoming freighted with the weight of "psychological projection or introjection" (*Warped* 8), is a key marker of the first Mickey cartoons, if also a characteristic they later deemphasized as Mickey did indeed become bound (in the later 1930s and 1940s) to a conventional world. It is certainly *part* of their kinship to the era's Felix cartoons, which found their own "special attraction," as Donald Crafton terms it, in their character's emphasis on the "polymorphous plasticism" (329) of both his body and his environment. But even as the Messmer-Sullivan cartoons emphasized Felix's ingenious use of that plasticism—as we see in his ability to turn his tail or a graphic flourish like an exclamation point into a useful, narrative-furthering prop, thus all the more flattening out the world, making "everything in the drawn world . . . of the same stuff," as Leslie suggests (23)—the early Mickeys seem far more intent on making space function within the narrative so that it might thereby reveal itself.

Of course, *Plane Crazy* rather quickly demonstrates its—and its new central character's—fascination with such spatial matters through its very subject: building a plane to transcend the limited world of the farmyard, inhabited by Mickey and a variety of other animals and depicted in great detail as the film opens. As Vidler might suggest, the narrative almost immediately attaches a psychological dimension to this effort to fly, as it introduces Mickey with an iris-in (that is, a circular darkening of the frame) on him reading a book, *How to Fly.* But more than simply forecasting the mouse's intention, this opening speaks of a kind of popular desire at work, one underscored when he turns a page, sees a picture of "Lucky Lindy," smiles, and, with the help of a mirror, immediately starts to transform himself into the pictured aviator—tousling his fur and crinkling his eyes to achieve the same casual look as his idol. It is an effort at transformation that runs throughout the film, as a dachshund becomes a twisted rubber band to turn the plane's propeller or a turkey's tail feathers become its rudder. From the start, though, with the book, plane, and Lindbergh "look," Mickey is positioned within what we might term the spirit of the age, as part of a technological effort to move beyond our limitations, as both plane and sky become freighted with a popular desire.[7]

This context already suggests that the cartoon merits more consideration than Robert Sklar's dismissal of it as a simple romantic escapade allows. In his commentary he mistakenly superimposes on the film a conventional romantic plot, describing it as a narrative about Mickey's effort to build a plane "to impress his girl friend, Minnie, and get her up in the air where she won't be able to run away from his advances" ("Making of Cultural Myths" 62). The film shows Mickey fashioning two planes, however, the first of which has only one seat, cannot accommodate a passenger, and quickly crashes into a tree. The second, cobbled together from an old flivver and various other found parts—including the turkey "rudder"—has a backseat that Mickey offers to Minnie in thanks only after she approaches him with a good-luck horseshoe. Any libidinous interest, such as his attempt to kiss Minnie once they are airborne, is more of an afterthought, or a hint of the rather delirious effect that flight has on him. More important, the focus on constructing and reconstructing planes underscores the ambition at the core of the film— to move, to soar, to break free of the barnyard world where everything occurs. And that imitative note—wherein Mickey attempts to ape Lindbergh and the other famous fliers of the era—only helps satirize that driving spirit here, along with its embodiment in a mouse.[8]

Yet just as important as this thematic embrace of the modernist spirit is the style in which it is presented. *Plane Crazy* effectively visualizes that attitude, placing Mickey and his sky adventures in what I have termed a stereoscopic context by the way it *spatializes* his actions: depicting them neither in a flatland nor within a conventionally realistic space, but rather using them to "warp" space, as Vidler puts it. Of course, the home-built plane itself helps accomplish this feat, because in quickly going out of control or, as the title suggests, "crazy"—as it seems to come alive, bucks Mickey off, and leaves Minnie a frightened passenger on a runaway mount—it shifts from the common horizontal movement of most cartoon conveyances of the day to various unpredictable loops and twists that allow the animator Ub Iwerks to explore every element of the frame, to let the plane itself become rubbery, almost fluid in form, and to build a series of gags around the unusually unstable perspective—anathema to conventional cinema—that results. Thus, as the "crazy" plane bears down on and then hits a frightened cow running into the frame's background, the cow flies up into the air and then into the camera, its white udders and black hide momentarily—and startlingly—blotting out the image. As the plane then veers toward the roadside and a telephone pole, the pole too briefly blacks out the image, as if there had been a violent collision. And when the plane turns back toward the road, heading into the depth of the frame, it comes upon a car moving into the foreground and seems to head directly into the vehicle, whose black radiator once again blacks out the frame. In repeating these same thrill scenes and implied impacts—with cow, pole, and car—and in emphasizing the impression of a subjective shot from within the plane, the film exploits our illusory occupation of an unpredictable space. Of course, such blacked-

Developing a spatial dynamic in Disney's *Plane Crazy* (1928).

68

out frames appear in some other cartoons of the era, but *Plane Crazy* pointedly uses those sudden shots to *spatially* convey the comic fear and anxiety of the possible collisions, effectively giving space a psychological and symbolic force.

With such shots the film also reaches for another improbable spatial effect, for in each case the implied camera does not simply veer improbably away from a collision; it seems to go *through* that space—as if the narrative had cut away to a slightly displaced position a moment later. In fact, each of these effects is a variation on a similar displacement shot that introduces the apparent collisions, as Minnie screams helplessly in close-up and the camera seemingly moves in on her face and into her mouth, which also serves to black out the image. This too is not a novel effect for animation of the period—it occurs in several of the Oswald shorts and later shows up in the Bosco cartoons of the ex-Disney animators Hugh Harmon and Rudolf Ising—but here it works to prepare us for the rapid spatial displacements that are, at the same time, experiments with creating three-dimensional effects and efforts at exploiting the affective possibilities of spatial disorientation, producing a very unrealistic or warped sense of space. It thus points to what we might describe as a spatial or stereoscopic consciousness at work here—one that would result in an obviously spatial gag that concludes the film. As Minnie pulls up her outrageously expanded bloomers that have para-

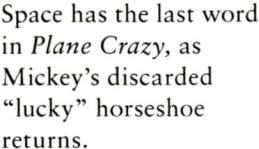

Space has the last word in *Plane Crazy,* as Mickey's discarded "lucky" horseshoe returns.

chuted her safely to earth and turns her back on the now crashed plane and its would-be Lindbergh, Mickey looks with disdain at the apparently unlucky horseshoe she had earlier given him and flings it into the deep background of the frame, from which it emerges, after describing a long arc, as if it were a boomerang, to ring him around the neck. Space here, it seems, incorporates our fears, admits of no easy mastery, and certainly has the last word, as it—three-dimensionally—mocks Mickey's efforts to emulate a "real" hero (and by extension, the cartoon's aspirations for a level of realism like that of live-action feature narratives).

The second silent Mickey, also quickly converted into a "talkie" after *Steamboat Willie*'s success, was *The Gallopin' Gaucho,* a work that, on the face of it, seems a bit more derivative and perhaps more nearly linked to the world of earlier silent film than *Plane Crazy,* but which similarly suggests something of that developing stereoscopic consciousness, drawing the film both toward and away from a realist register. Because of its obvious connection to popular Hollywood narrative, particularly to Douglas Fairbanks's hit *The Gaucho* (1927), Leslie dismisses it as a "Fairbanks pastiche" (26) and offers no commentary. Yet Mickey's character here equally recalls Felix the Cat, as he continually resorts to the sort of practice that had become identified with Felix, using his tail for comic effect, treating it like a surreal, infinitely manipulatable prop rather than a natural part of his body, and thus the source for a great variety of gags. When Mickey arrives at the Cantino Argentino, rather than entering through the door he turns his tail into a hook and jauntily uses it to swing into a window. Once he is seated on the windowsill, his tail again forms a hook to steal a mug of beer from a waiter's tray. As he watches Minnie dance, he snakes his tail around her, uses it to wind her up like a top, and then pulls it to spin her around. Later, in an effort to save her from Pete the Cat, he pulls his tail out from his body as if it were an endless rope, ties a noose, and uses it to lasso a post and hoist himself into the building where she is being held. Finally, as Mickey and Minnie ride off on his ostrich mount, both turn their tails into coil springs to cushion their ride and allow them to comfortably celebrate the rescue with a kiss. As is the case with Felix, such antics have a visual appeal, point up the clever nature of the character, and demonstrate his—and her—ability, despite all appearances, to triumph over various obstacles, in fact, over reality itself. Such gags, however, are much the stuff of silent cinema, of silent animation, and, indeed, of a flat world.

And yet two stylistic signatures mark off *The Gallopin' Gaucho* from much that had gone before, and certainly from the Felix cartoons. One is simply movement itself, the manifest liveliness—or alive-ness—of the central character, the same spirit that provides the impulse for the two plane constructions in *Plane Crazy*. The Mickey who enlivens these narratives is pointedly a rascal and almost constantly in motion here, seeming seldom to stop, as Felix so often does, to contemplate a problem before acting.[9] Rather, he quickly intuits the appropriate response to each situation, in part because a central tenet of his "character animation" (another phrase frequently applied to Disney cartoons) is that Mickey is a figure of movement—a constantly "gallopin'" gaucho—a point again established from the opening to the final scene. The cartoon begins with Mickey charging across the Argentine landscape, incongruously astride an ostrich, and it ends with his ostrich carrying him and Minnie off as they kiss—in love but also still in motion. In between—and indeed in usual Fairbanks fashion—Mickey vaults into windows, dances a tango with Minnie, fights with Pete, chases him across the landscape and over various physical obstacles, and then duels with him. Mickey is, in effect, constantly moving, suggesting the sort of figure that was especially suited to Machine Age culture, to a time and place when, as Cecelia Tichi has observed, "speed and the belief in cultural acceleration were proclaimed from every quarter to be . . . *the* defining characteristics" (101) of the age, yet also effectively satirizing that figure and the conventional film narratives that featured such characters.

And as we see in *Plane Crazy,* the other defining feature here is a stylistic fascination with space, with creating a more complex, or stereoscopic, world in which to place this new figure and one with which he might interact. As Michael Barrier notes, the Felix cartoons, like most efforts of this period, were usually marked by "dull, uniform staging"; the central figure is typically placed against spare, uninspired, and pointedly flat backgrounds (32)—a symptom of Leslie's flatland. In contrast, *The Gallopin' Gaucho,* like *Plane Crazy,* is pointedly a space-conscious effort, as is demonstrated by the use of background decor, an accent on complex structures and landscapes, and even a compositional emphasis on dimension. The interior scenes, for example, show detailed pictures and posters on the walls, cracks, and exposed brick. In fact, several shots let us glimpse in the deep background a reward poster for "El Gaucho," apparently a reference to Mickey's rascally character in this film and an unusual use of such depth to build characterization—in this instance, to explain the cautious attitude of many of the Cantino's folk when this diminutive figure enters. And when Pete kidnaps Minnie, we see in the rear of the Cantino another, and unexpected, use of that deep background that further reveals the film's dimensional design: behind this obviously very rough and dangerous place is a sign incongruously marked "Family Entrance"—out of which Mickey's drunk ostrich then staggers. And when the ostrich subsequently collapses while Mickey is chasing Pete, the deep background again provides the seed of a gag, as it shows laundry hanging on a line and a bucket of starch nearby, which Mickey runs to retrieve and uses to dip his ostrich, to stiffen his legs—and resolve—so they can resume the chase. Of course, such drawing together of background and foreground to construct gags is consistent with the film's narrative use of structures, such as the Cantino and the multistory building from which Mickey must later rescue Minnie. Nicely detailed and typically presented at angles to the frame line to increase the depth illusion, these structures frame Mickey's actions—dancing, fighting, dueling—within a three-dimensional world. Yet conditioned as we are by a later mode of criticism to see compositional depth simply as a signpost of realism, we lose some appreciation of what is being accomplished here. Certainly, this attention to dimension suggests a different sort of texture for the narrative world, moving it away from the almost abstract landscape of the Felix cartoons, but also toward a realm that is designed not so much for realism as to afford unexpected possibilities—surprise and even a surreal humor.

In any case, a more emphatic sense of dimension is not the only or even the primary result of that spatial sensibility here. As in *Plane Crazy,* we see a consistent effort to mine the space for a number of other effects, to give it a "voice" in the narrative. For example, in a move that *was* unusual for this period, offscreen space repeatedly becomes implicated in the narrative, as we see when Mickey and Minnie dance a tango. As this comic-romantic scene plays out, suddenly a hugely out-of-scale hairy paw with extended claws—truly a surreal intrusion—reaches into the frame from a previously unseen space on the right to grab Minnie

Gallopin' Gaucho
(1928) builds a gag
around foreground and
background space.

and pull her offscreen. This sudden warping in the narrative space breaks the happy mood, reestablishes the possibility for danger that had earlier been vaguely linked to "El Gaucho" himself, and embodies the fear that Minnie feels when Pete the Cat—owner of the paw—unexpectedly makes off with her. And later, when the two antagonists duel, all seems lost when Mickey stumbles, loses his sword, and tumbles offscreen, but it is into a previously unseen room where he reaches under a bed and discovers a chamber pot, which he flings, into the next shot, to miraculously finish off Pete and save Minnie. That use of offscreen or previously unseen space does more than simply build a spatial logic for the narrative; it suggests that the very depth and extensiveness of this world—of this pointedly *un*flatland—holds, as we have previously seen, possibility, surprise, or, in the instances noted here, both danger and hope.

Obviously the most heralded of the early Mickey Mouse cartoons and the first pointedly designed for sound, *Steamboat Willie* is in some ways less inventive visually than either of these predecessors. While offering little that might pass for dialogue, much less what Seldes describes as "verbal wit," the film does point to an almost "forced" desire for sound, often at the expense of Vidler's notion of "space conception." Though critics responded to it very favorably—the *Variety* reviewer described it as "a peach of a synchronization job" (qtd. in Barrier 55)—the film seems to aim for little beyond that signal accomplishment, offering no sound perspective, traveling sound, or fading sound, such as we have come to expect as hallmarks of an aural realism. Rather, sound is simply *there,* as narrative gives way to performance and space constricts around the performer. In fact, Barrier offers a dismissive summary of the film: "Mickey, his girlfriend Minnie, a cat captain, and a boatload of domestic animals make a tremendous variety of musical and nonmusical noises—but not much else" (55). Yet the nature of that enthronement of sound was distinctive enough, for here, as Neal Gabler in his recent biography of Walt Disney reminds us, was the first work "imagined . . . fully as a sound cartoon in which the music and effects were inextricable from the action" (127), helping to build a more complex world.

The action, perhaps because of a felt need to lay things out very simply, to make the link between sound and image both visible to the audience and easy for the animators to coordinate, is certainly less complex than in the previous Mickey cartoons. Though *Steamboat Willie* emphasizes the same spirit of change or transformation that marks many other cartoons of the period and is often seen as sharing their modernist character, it yokes the various demonstrations of that transformative spirit to the performance of sound, while rendering space somewhat secondary. Thus, when a goat on board the steamboat eats Minnie's sheet music and instrument, Mickey opens its mouth, as if he would somehow enter the suddenly outsized cavity to retrieve the musical materials, but then decides to turn the goat's mouth into a phonograph. As Minnie cranks its tail, the song "Turkey in the Straw" emerges from its mouth, as if from the funnel-shaped speaker of an old Victrola. Following that transformation, each animal on board, in turn, becomes an equally effective musical instrument in Mickey's hands. It is as if the goat's eating of the music—literally *internalizing* the potential for sound—inspires Mickey to *externalize* it, to recognize and then release the potential for music everywhere he sees it, in a kind of aural version of Vidler's notion of "projection." So to accompany this new phonograph, Mickey also pulls a cat's tail to punctuate the music and then swings the animal by its tail to produce a continuous sirenlike sound. A goose soon becomes a bagpipe, a pig proves another sort of wind instrument as he plays on its teats, and a cow's teeth stand in for a xylophone. In fact, the various animals Mickey uses—and abuses in the common fashion of early cartoons—easily mesh with other found instruments he plays—a washboard, pots, pans, a wooden tub—to suggest a world of unexpected aural potential that Mickey does not simply *produce* but *discovers* and *discloses,* to the delight of both Minnie and the audience, as this process of musical discovery, of turning sound into physical correlatives, essentially becomes the narrative. The ability to draw sound out of every object, to locate in a previously silent world an unexpected dimension—a capacity for speech, voice, and rhythms—is *Steamboat Willie's* version of *Plane Crazy's* and *The Gallopin' Gaucho's* efforts to disclose the unconventional possibilities of space and, through those possibilities, to transcend this world's limits.

Beyond this difficult equivalency, though, we find another dimension that is developed to accompany the film's aural emphasis, attesting to an effort at determining how sound might be used to enhance the narrative's spatial component. For *Steamboat Willie* not only synchronizes sound to action; it also uses sounds to real-ize space—that is, to bring it into being, to suggest its substance, and to suture spatial elements together. Much of the action is laid out in a conventional horizontal fashion, and there is little movement across the screen. But when Mickey's steamboat approaches Podunk Landing, we hear its whistle before it comes around a bend in the background, as sound heralds what

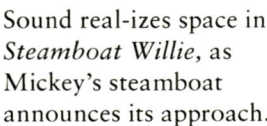

Sound real-izes space in *Steamboat Willie,* as Mickey's steamboat announces its approach.

screen space hides. And once Mickey starts up the goat-phonograph, its music similarly serves to build spatial reality by suturing offscreen and onscreen space. So when Mickey moves from the steamboat's deck to the ship's interior, we continue to hear "Turkey in the Straw," as if through a window, and when at the end of the film Mickey throws a potato at a mocking parrot and knocks it out a porthole, an audible splash and squawking indicate that the parrot has fallen in the river. Moreover, those sounds motivate Mickey's impish smile of satisfaction on which the film concludes. These and similar sound effects thus serve to help construct a more complex spatial environment by announcing an unseen presence, suggesting contiguous space, and even motivating character reaction to what happens offscreen. And that complexity, as sound comes to the narrative fore, serves less to create surprise or humor than it does to build our sense of this world.

In that substitution—or amplification—of an unexpected aural richness for a surprisingly evocative space, *Steamboat Willie* thus suggests something of both the strength and weakness of the early Mickey Mouse cartoons. That process of discovery, the revelation that sound too might hold an unexpected potential, attractively links all these cartoons, helps establish the new mouse's identity as a revealer or discoverer of different sorts of depth (both aural and visual), and ties them, both narratively and stylistically, to the modernist impulse earlier described. That turn also forecasts a move away from the modernist spirit, however, not simply because of the shift in emphasis from the visual to the aural register, but because of a manifest concern with using sound to help construct a more realistic cartoon world—suturing onscreen and offscreen space, constructing narrative-temporal continuity, even building character motivation. And in gaining a voice—Walt Disney's own voice, we should note—Mickey himself would, as Seldes observes, become increasingly bound to that reality, tamed because he has been "forced" into a "verbal" world (170).

And yet, a somewhat later Mickey cartoon, and one that also heralded a new technology that some would see as another step in a realistic direction, reminds us of the need for a more complex view of these early Mickeys. For with *The Band Concert* (1935), Mickey's first foray into Technicolor,[10] Disney crafted a film that pointedly revolves around these issues of space, sound, and the mouse. By this point, as numerous

commentators have noted, Mickey had become a much more domesticated mouse, less the trickster, explorer, and daredevil, since Donald
Duck was being groomed for such roles. *The Band Concert* underscores
this change, depicting Mickey in a proper and traditional role, as the
conductor of a rural orchestra, but outfitted in an oversized uniform,
one that takes up more space than he does. And because of its size, the
uniform repeatedly trips him up and mocks his efforts at conducting—
that is, at keeping other unruly, rambunctious types in order, especially
a constantly intrusive Donald, who repeatedly tries to subvert the band's
classical performance with a penny flute version of "Turkey in the
Straw," ironically the very number that signals Mickey's similarly subversive high spirits in *Steamboat Willie*.

Just when Mickey seems to have achieved some sort of harmony, to
have brought his ragged group of musicians in line, even to have silenced
the duck and his repeated subversive sounds, the deep background forecasts another possibility. It undergoes a visual transformation, as the
pastel-colored pastoral scene suddenly darkens to announce the surprise
appearance of a cyclone that gradually devastates the countryside and
then wreaks havoc with the concert. While Mickey and his fellow musicians find themselves suddenly sucked up into its funnel and whirled
about, they comically try to continue their actions—conducting, reading the music, playing their instruments—in empty, almost abstract
space. In the chaotic, even absurdist scene that results, one in which
dimension, direction, and orientation are shown as completely unstable,
as the aural tries to maintain its sway in the midst of visual chaos, we
might see a kind of revenge of modernist space, at least a reminder of
how much remains outside and unaccounted for in our conventional
conceptions of space as well as sound. And with Donald having the last
say—or sound—as he emerges from the devastation to toot "Turkey in
the Straw" one last time, the film also reminds us of the sort of character who was so appealingly native to that earlier world.

We might, in fact, see *The Band Concert* as a reflexive meditation on
the earlier Mickey Mouse cartoons and on that central character's
appeal, even as it couches that reflection within the conventional illusion-of-life style that was coming to mark much of Disney animation by
the mid-1930s. And it was a moment that would recur in several other
Mickeys of the later 1930s, most notably in *Mickey's Trailer* (1938),

which begins with a trailer set against a pleasant pastoral sunrise backdrop. Quickly, though, discordant mechanical sounds intrude, sounds that seem completely disjointed from the image, and then the deep background literally begins to deconstruct. In fact, the scenery folds up like a fan, showing that it was an accessory part of the trailer, revealing that the trailer is actually parked in a dirty junkyard, and reminding us, in the process, of the constructed nature of space in all such narratives. Here space is not only implicated in the narrative right from the start, but it takes center stage, pointing up the characters' dreams of a different reality. Such instances of narratizing space suggest many of the tensions that lingered in Disney animation, particularly as the studio moved to create characters and worlds that were indeed more aligned with the evolving potential of sound and with conventional film narrative. For they clearly recall the complex, surprising, even subversive spirit that marks the very first Mickey Mouse films, while also underscoring how, after being given a voice and placed in a complex aural environment, Mickey and his world are slowly being pressed—or in this case, folded—into conformity.

Yet the fact that films like *The Band Concert* and *Mickey's Trailer* could so effectively mock that development and even narratize the tensions between the original mouse and his later incarnations precisely in terms of a struggle between space and sound suggests that, at least in this period, something of that spirit lingered at Disney, even as the studio pushed toward additional moves in a realistic direction—as the initial steps toward producing a feature film (*Snow White and the Seven Dwarfs,* 1937) and developing its signature spatial technology, the multiplane camera, got under way. The stereoscopic mouse still reared his head, letting us glimpse something of his character and his world, indeed, of a visual style that had originally so appealed to audiences and attested to Disney's own links to a modernist spirit.

4

THE DOUBLE SPACE OF
THE FLEISCHER FILMS

It is as naïve to doubt that the stereoscopic film is the tomorrow of
the cinema as it is to doubt that tomorrow will come.
—Sergei Eisenstein, *Notes of a Film Director,* 129

As we noted at the start of chapter 3, the Fleischer brothers, Max and
Dave, are certainly among the most significant figures in the history of
animation. Between the late 1910s and the early 1940s, they created a
number of enduring cartoon characters, such as KoKo the Clown and
Betty Boop, pioneered the use of sound with their Talkertoons, and
helped introduce into animated films what Norman Klein describes as
"the New Humor" of ethnic vaudeville skits (20). At the same time,
they developed several key animation technologies that advanced both
the efficiency of animation production and the reality illusion that
would, for a time, become a primary focus of the form's development.
Moreover, though the image of KoKo emerging "out of the inkwell" of
Max Fleischer in films of 1919–1929 both illustrates that basic pattern of "figuration" Crafton describes and embodies the form's animating potential, the Fleischer brothers' work also helps us see how
important the notion of animating *space* was becoming for a developing animation aesthetic.

Most discussion of the Fleischer films has proceeded from either of
two directions. In attempting to frame Max and Dave's efforts in the
context of an early, sometimes anarchic era of animation, Paul Wells
has suggested that we see their films as working "in the service of ani-

mation as a radical form aesthetically *and* socially," and as all part of what he terms a "radical Modernity intrinsic to the form" (38, 40). Yet in light of the Fleischers' development of the rotoscope and rotograph, devices that were designed to produce more naturalistic motion and to seamlessly combine animated motion with live action, they have just as often been credited as pioneers of a realistic strain of animation.[1] Thus, Crafton argues that the great attraction of their first cartoons "was not so much the elaboration of the 'out of the inkwell' formula [of their KoKo the Clown films] as the magical sense of realistic movement made possible by the rotoscope" (174). And somewhat paradoxically, each of these arguments has been deployed to frame their work in relation to the Disney Studio's, either as anticipating the realistic aesthetic that has most often been associated with Disney, or as confirming their resistance to and divergence from that studio's illusion-of-life approach. As we might expect, there is a level on which both vantages have validity, on which realist and radical interpretations merge and, in the process, point to both the potential and the problems inherent in what we might loosely term the Fleischer style.

As earlier comments have suggested, the key links between what is often referred to as golden age animation, particularly that of the period 1910–1940, and the world of modernist art are typically seen as residing in early animation's radical approach to space or dimensionality and its protean treatment of the material with which it populated or organized that space. Thus, Esther Leslie argues that cartoonists of this era were typically conscious of space as "not geographical but graphic" in nature and thus were, for the most part, "not tempted to imitate theatre, to produce an illusion in three dimensions," but rather felt free to experiment or play in a world of flatness (19). Within that flatland they typically demonstrated a kind of "ideographic playfulness" (23) that readily translated into a vision of ready and rapid transformation, or as Michael Barrier describes it, "metamorphosis—a device integral to animation since the earliest animated films" (26–27). The ultimate effect of such a vision, intentionally or not, was to implicate the real world as a candidate for and similarly open to reconception, even radical change, much as did the era's avant-garde art. Certainly, between the mid-1920s, when the Fleischers' was one of the top animation studios in America, and 1941, when Paramount effectively took control of—and ultimately altered—it, the Fleischer brothers never created as iconic a figure of change as Felix the Cat or quite as surreal a context as that of the Pat Sullivan–Otto Messmer films. They did in their early efforts, however, offer a KoKo the Clown, emerging from his inkwell to encounter a world that was always new and surprising, and later Betty Boop, "hip-swaying her way through impossible encounters in space," and narratives that, Leslie suggests, "unfold things gag by gag" (174), rather than in the fashion of classical narrative's predictable, conventionalized trajectories. The overall effect was to suggest a world that, while recalling the everyday, did indeed seem to suggest alternatives by operating according to its own, often unpredictable laws.

And yet for all of their "eccentric" character (Barrier 27) the Fleischer cartoons gradually became populated with more conventional characters, such as a domesticated version of Betty Boop, Popeye the Sailor, and even Superman, and they also increasingly demonstrated a more conventional sensibility, including a more straightforwardly "geographical" sense of space, although it is a sensibility that, I would argue, was always implicit in the development of the Fleischers' landmark technology, the rotoscope. Leslie and others have tended to attribute that conventionalizing or taming of the Fleischer cartoons more to the influence of the Hays Office (174–75) and its efforts at censorship, particularly after 1934, as the motion picture industry sought to rein in the sometimes outrageous images and implications of Hollywood films—including the sexual innuendo and suggestive imagery that certainly distinguished many of the early Betty Boop efforts from their competition at Disney and elsewhere. And in another attempt to account for this conventionalized turn, Barrier notes how the Fleischer films become marked by a "continual friction between a rigorously mechanical approach to filmmaking, on the one hand, and an utterly whimsical, not to say careless, attitude toward stories and animation, on the other" (28). That yoking of the "mechanical" and the "whimsical" presents us with a difficult interpretation of the Fleischer films, one that conventionally hints at a source in the often at-odds personalities of Max and Dave Fleischer and that obscures their films' links to the larger trajectory of animation in this period, particularly to a more general movement away from what Leslie somewhat hyperbolically describes as "the surrealistic and analytical cinematic dynamite of the optical unconscious" and toward what

Theodor Adorno and Walter Benjamin would derisively term a "naïve realism" (attributed to both in Leslie 121).

What also tends to be obscured, even in ideological analyses such as those by Leslie and Paul Wells, is the attitude toward the most fundamental problem facing the animator, that of addressing—or filling up—space itself. But it is the approach to space, the manner in which one might turn negative space into animated product or expression, that is, as I have already suggested, a key subject of experimentation in this era, probably the most important link between the avant-garde and the general world of animation, and even the true ground for many of the ideological interpretations of early animation. And in the case of the Fleischer films, that approach to space, and more specifically to the representation of depth, would continue to occupy the brothers, leading them to develop their "Stereoptical Apparatus," or turntable camera, and to produce with it some of the studio's most elaborate and distinctive cartoons of the 1930s and early 1940s.

As background to a discussion of these films, we might first recall the world of avant-garde art and animation against which commentators have often framed them. In this context we need to include, for example, the contemporaneous abstract efforts of Hans Richter, such as his *Rhythmus* films (1921, 1923, and 1925), with their collages of variously shaded squares, rectangles, and bars, constantly rearranging patterns in screen space; Walther Ruttmann's *Opus No. 1* (1921), with its combinations of geometric cutouts and painterly brushstrokes; or the work of Viking Eggeling, such as *Diagonal Symphony* (1925), which, as Leslie suggests, sought to "set the line in motion . . . lines twisting and turning, forming spirals" that "hold the centre of the screen" so that "the film frame seems like the space of a concert hall" (54). While generally freed from a concern with narrative, with character, or with the demands of a correspondence to the real such as we find in most cartoons of the era, including most of those described in earlier chapters, such films ultimately implicate a very similar "story." That is, they describe the exploration and tenuous occupation of space itself, as they set about investigating what Anthony Vidler terms "the conditions for thinking [through] fundamental problems in vision and spatiality [that] were forged in the early modernist period" (*Warped* 8). In this period space was beginning to be seen quite differently, "as a central category for modeling social relations," as representative of the "crowded disorder" (*Warped* 67) of modern life, as part of the scientific investigation of the "distinctive spatial orientations" of various life forms (Kern 137), but most important as something that was no longer objective, firm, and easily measurable, but phantom, constantly mutating, and, as we have repeatedly termed it, warped.

Practically from the start, the Fleischer brothers' cartoons betrayed a curious, almost paradoxical attitude toward the issue of space, an attitude that, for all their conventional narrative thrust, offers some hint of the "social" function Vidler notes, but perhaps more tellingly shows traces of that warped sense of space he describes. On the one hand, their Out of the Inkwell cartoons took their central principle from the pointedly reflexive efforts of KoKo the Clown to move offscreen, to emerge not only from the inkwell that was essentially the fount of his lifeblood, but also from the conventional space of animation in order to enter the real world, in effect to escape from conventional screen space and, by implication, from his established social role. The result was an often surreal and certainly entertaining combination of live action and animation, as Koko interacts with Max Fleischer and moves about in the human world, when, for example, he walks through the streets of New York, searching for Max in *Bedtime* (1923), and in one instance even becomes the artist himself, reversing field and function by seemingly "drawing" Max and the real world in *KoKo Gets Egg-Cited* (1927). Yet on the other, Max Fleischer's development of the rotoscoping and rotographing processes ensured that such hybrid situations were never quite as jarring as those we often find, for example, in Disney's primary effort in this same period, the Alice comedies of 1923–1927, which place a real girl within a cartoon world. These processes not only naturalized the motion of the animated figures (the rotoscope), but also helped suture the cartoon figures into the filmic space (the rotograph) by ensuring that the various Fleischer creations would fit almost seamlessly within the real world the films depict and thus that an element of their anarchic potential—their transformative power—would be more easily tamed.

A key result is what we might describe as a double sense of space, one that is consistent with another primary characteristic of the early Fleischer efforts, namely their persistently reflexive dimension. Following Donald Crafton's leading comments on the "figural" nature of early animation, Leslie and others have noted how, for the Fleischers, "consciousness of the medium" quite frequently seemed to be "part of the entertainment" (14). And though that element is especially prominent in the Out of the Inkwell series, it would also prove a continuing legacy in their Betty Boop and Popeye cartoons. Richard Koszarski goes a bit further, noting the highly "self-reflexive quality" of this series, but at the same time reminding us that this characteristic runs "through . . . almost the whole of silent animation" (342). As a result, he sees the Fleischer films' comic confrontations with the form's fundamental artifice—and thus the meeting point of two different sorts of space—as typical of early animation, of a film type that, unlike live-action cinema, both was mindful of its nature and often tried to capitalize on it. Yet even after the emergence of sound, we sometimes encounter this same spirit, or what Stefan Kanfer, in light of the increasingly realistic turn of other animation of the era, translates as a "perverse" character (97). In the Popeye film *What, No Spinach?* (1936), for example, Popeye, in the midst of one of his customary fights with his adversary, Bluto, actually addresses the audience, asking, "Is there any spinach in the house?"—a request followed by a long shot of a live-action boy in a theater, watching this film in which Popeye "stars." We then see the child pull a can out of his grocery bag and toss it into the screen world, magically penetrating its sudden depths, to help out his hero. Here and elsewhere, this sort of "knocking down the proscenium," as Kanfer terms it, serves more than to just remind viewers "that they are watching a world of make-believe" (97). Rather, it suggests that the Fleischers were well aware of the self-evidently artificial nature of the form in which they were working and understood that they could always mine that characteristic for additional jokes or for narrative effect, particularly by exploiting the different categories of space that were implied: the artificial space of the narrative and a contiguous, even—somehow—continuous space surrounding it. Ultimately, the Fleischers felt they could effectively exploit the space of artifice only by grounding it in a more stable context, by, in effect, *accepting* the proscenium rather than simply "knocking" it "down."

I would suggest, then, that many of the more striking effects found in the Fleischer films essentially spring from the characteristically double sense of space that emerges, and that not only links their work to the earliest film animation, but also helps explain its seemingly simultaneous kinship to both the avant-garde and realist traditions. It is an approach that allowed them, by turns, to accept the boundaries of a conventional cinematic space or to open up—often quite suddenly and unexpectedly, as in *What, No Spinach?*—another, extradiegetic space that reveals the artifice or showcases the show itself for comic effect. Thus, throughout the early Betty Boop cartoons we find an effort both to create a plausible animated world and to undermine its consistency, typified by the embedding of Betty in a recognizable narrative and her frequent emergence from it to address or perform for an extradiegetic audience. Michael Barrier effectively describes this loose narrative sense as evidence of "an aesthetic credo directly opposed to the one emerging in the Disney cartoons" of the early and mid-1930s—an aesthetic in which the real attraction was never the "purposeful" trajectory of narrative, but rather "everything" that "happens around the edges," such as in the Fleischer version of *Snow-White* (1933), a film in which, he says, the "narrative thread is . . . of no interest" (182). This explanation suggests that, even as they were becoming more narrative-oriented and character-driven, the Fleischer films also "remained fundamentally dependent on happy accidents" (183), that is, on the various jokes that the animators could cleverly and consistently sprinkle "around the edges" during the production process, as well as on an aesthetic approach that readily accommodated that "sprinkling."

Yet, even as their films frequently renewed the connection with the spirit of those persistently reflexive Out of the Inkwell cartoons and earlier works, and even as they seem ruled by a loose structure that Gerald Mast, in describing comedy of the silent and early sound eras, has described simply as comic "riffing" or "goofing" (7), the Fleischers were also constantly pursuing initiatives in more conventional directions, in fact toward the sort of realistic representation that was becoming linked to the Disney project and to a more naturalistic presentation of character. Thus, Mark Langer has chronicled how, from the 1920s through the early 1940s, the Fleischers and Disney seemed to be continually trying to top each other in terms of technological and artistic developments, as each in turn began working with sound, color, multiplane devices, and feature production, and as each sought "to find some advantage over its competitor" (351) by leveraging the latest—and often most costly—innovation, which was, in turn, featured in ever more ambitious productions.

Certainly their early development of the rotoscope and rotograph devices, in addition to speeding up the animation process, had already signaled a move in a realist direction, primarily by allowing animators to capture—by tracing—real human motion. But late in 1933 Max Fleischer introduced a new device that promised a spatial complement to that figural emphasis built into the use of the rotoscope.[2] This system, described as a "setback" in the studio, or a turntable camera, and dubbed the "Stereoptical Process and Apparatus" on their film credits,[3] paralleled similar work being done at the same time by Ub Iwerks on a multiplane camera, and it anticipated Disney's slightly later—and more heralded—development of a far more complex multiplane device. Like these other developments, the Fleischer setup was aimed mainly at producing a more natural illusion of depth—long considered one of the primary hallmarks of a cinematic realism and, as no less a revolutionary than Sergei Eisenstein would at one time proclaim, "the tomorrow of the cinema" (*Eisenstein* 129). While Fleischer's patent application of November 2, 1933, made twenty-three claims for his creation, those claims focused principally on three concerns, all serving the stated purpose of making the cartoon "appear more natural and realistic": enhancing the "illusion of distance"; allowing for a more natural "change in perspective"; and creating "proper relative illumination" of the cartoon scene (M. Fleischer).

To achieve these ends, Max Fleischer, working with his assistant Johnny Burkes, produced a design for a relatively simple and cheap mechanism. This initial design was essentially a long table with a camera placed at one end and a pie-wedge platform attached to the other, with a pivot at the point of the wedge and at the opposite end from the camera, allowing the platform to move panoramically in relation to the camera. The animation cels for each shot, containing the central character or image in the scene, could be mounted vertically between glass plates, fixed before the camera and adjacent to the wide end of the pie wedge. On the wedge—or "oscillatable bed," as the patent description terms it—were placed miniature sets or additional drawings (or both) mounted on separate supports and arranged "in different vertical planes" (up to four) to produce real spatial separation. Furthering that impression were additional miniature objects or cutout drawings that could be mounted on an extension of the pie-wedge that jutted into the foreground between the camera and the cel holder, and the set itself could be turned on its pivot to produce a panning effect, thereby also altering perspective, since set elements would appear to diminish in size or get larger as the wedge pivoted toward or away from the camera's position. Furthermore, lighting could be arranged separately for each plane to produce realistic shadowing and highlight effects. As Barrier describes the result, "The idea was that the animated characters on the cels would seem to be performing on a three-dimensional stage" (185).

Though producing an often striking sense of depth, this "setback" system had its drawbacks, most directly connected to that "stage" paradigm. Unlike rotoscoping, this process actually proved more difficult, expensive, and time-consuming than conventional animation. A primary reason was that this Stereoscopic Apparatus grew to be a more complex and unwieldy mechanism. As Max's son, the noted director Richard Fleischer, describes it, the device evolved into "a huge turntable that weighed two and a half tons and needed a real Rube Goldberg conglomeration of gears, wheels, pipes, and cranks to operate it" (84). Moreover, furnishing this miniature theater with complete sets—or, more often, stagelike "flats"—also done in miniature required additional skilled personnel, materials, and an uncharacteristic (for the Fleischer Studio) expenditure of time. Ultimately, the painstaking creation and photographing of these sets proved the point that Leonard Maltin has made about the Fleischer Studio, that frequently "economic feasibility took a back seat to mechanical innovation" (*Of Mice* 110). Eventually the bottom line would win out, as Max found that these effects, as his son Richard notes, simply "cost too much money" (85). Moreover, since the apparatus itself emphasized movement along the horizontal plane, those effects were constantly yoked to an outmoded, conventionally theatrical style of presentation. Together, these various circumstances would dictate that the Fleischers use the process for fewer and fewer films, although it still shows up in their last effort at competing with Disney in the feature market with *Mr. Bug Goes to Town* (1941). But perhaps more tellingly, it would be employed only in a very limited way in most of the studio's films.

We will now examine how the Stereoptical Process was applied in a range of Fleischer cartoons in order to better gauge how successfully the Fleischer Studio, like a number of other studios in the same period, addressed this issue of depth (and the developing sense of realism in animation), and to further sketch what I have termed their double sense of space. Maltin has suggested that the flaw here—if there is a flaw—lay in the person of Max Fleischer, since, "like so many other inventors, once he developed the machines he didn't know how best to implement and exploit them" (*Of Mice* 110). Yet by looking at a range of the Fleischer cartoons, we can also see a level on which the mechanism followed from and played into that sense of a combinatory avant-garde and realist aesthetic, and thus of the double sense of space we have noted. That vantage might also, in turn, better explain how the Fleischer device helped set the stage for Disney's more successful application of a similar apparatus only a short time later, and thus further trace the extent of the Fleischer influence on Disney.[4]

Fleischer first employed the Stereoptical Process in *Poor Cinderella* (1934), a two-reel cartoon "starring" the studio's key creation of the era, Betty Boop, and done in color.[5] It would subsequently be used for individual scenes in a variety of Betty Boop and Popeye one-reel black-and-white efforts, such as *For Better or Worser* (1935), *Betty Boop and Grampy* (1935), *Betty Boop and the Little King* (1936), *Grampy's Indoor Outing* (1936), and *House Cleaning Blues* (1937), although it shows to greatest effect in two of the Fleischers' most successful efforts, the color Popeye "specials" of the late 1930s, *Popeye the Sailor Meets Sindbad the Sailor* (1936) and *Popeye the Sailor Meets Ali Baba's Forty Thieves* (1937). In fact, as a measure of the effort that went into these longer and more expensive Popeye films, we might note that the first of these was not only the first color Popeye—using the more costly three-strip Technicolor process by this time—but also the first of any Fleischer cartoons to be nominated for an Academy Award, a distinction that certainly owes something to its more elaborate efforts at exploring that new sense of depth.

Because of its uncharacteristic use of color, *Poor Cinderella* immediately announces its own rather "special" status among the Betty Boop series of films (which, including her appearances in the Fleischers' Talkertoons, dated back to 1930). Lacking the surrealistic effects or what Maltin more generally terms the "compelling strain of silliness" that had marked most of the earlier Betty Boop cartoons (*Of Mice* 101), *Poor Cinderella* offers a conventional story line, one that yokes its various visual transformations and narrative improbabilities to the presence of a Disney-like fairy godmother and her magic powers, and thus one that excuses its subversive potential as the work of fantasy. An opening proscenium and curtain on which we view the credits frame the following action as a kind of artifice, although the first shot of the narrative proper, done as a "setback," quickly qualifies that frame, providing us with a three-dimensional scene as two heralds march right to left against a multiplane backdrop of trees, hills, and a dimly glimpsed castle. The scene suggests movement for the sake of movement, as if the film were simply showing off the depth effect here, since in a conventionally flat shot, the next image has the heralds facing the camera and unfurling a banner—a kind of return to the proscenium and curtain—that announces a "Public Ball To-Night" and adds, on a democratic note, that all are invited. But the subsequent introduction of Cinderella (Betty Boop), also done conventionally, gives some point to the differing visual styles, as we see Cinderella alone in a dingy room, dressed in rags and singing to a mirror that she is "just a poor Cinderella," as if her relegation to this flat world were a correlative to her inability to escape her class and her servitude or to attend the ball.

There are actually few Stereoptical scenes in the rest of the narrative, but they all similarly support this stylistic-thematic link. For the dimensional scenes are those depicting her magical coach's trip to the ball, the Prince's entrance and dancing with Cinderella, and eventually the royal carriage's whisking her away with the Prince to his castle—all steps in her gradual transformation from "a poor Cinderella" to a Princess, as if the film's development of its Stereoptical potential were commensurate with her own achievement, her freedom from servitude. Apart from this link, though, the dimensional effect is not impressive, since it is used only in scenes involving simple horizontal motion, typically in the foreground and set against flat elements arrayed in different background planes. Even the ball, probably the most complex scene in the film, arranges a series of flat, static character images in the background to set off the animated movement of Cinderella and the Prince. The resulting contrast between moving and static images, between the conventionally animated pair and the motionless crowd placed in several background planes, between what

Betty Boop as Cinderella dances in a multiplane scene from the Fleischer Color Classic *Poor Cinderella* (1934).

is conventionally referred to as positive space and negative space, leaves us not so much with the sense of a three-dimensional world as with the illusion of two worlds, of two contiguous spaces that the filmic event inhabits.[6] And it is an illusion from which the film eventually retreats, as it closes with a conventional shot of the Prince's carriage moving into the background, taking Cinderella to her new home in his castle.

In several ways a more interesting effort is *Betty Boop and the Little King* (1936), an effort to bring Otto Soglow's cartoon strip figure the Little King, previously the "star" of ten Van Beuren Studio cartoons, into the Fleischer character stable. It would seem an unlikely choice for a Stereoptical film, since the Little King is a pointedly uncinematic sort of character—flat, highly stylized, and visually right at home in the flat and exaggerated world of the comic strips. Helping in that adaptation, though, *Betty Boop and the Little King* naturalizes an element of artifice by playing to the reflexive character of the earlier Fleischer cartoons, here casting Betty, naturally, as a performer—a singer, dancer, and horse trainer—who is appearing in a vaudeville-type theater. The narrative sets her low art in parallel to a "Special Performance in Honor of His Majesty the King," as a banner announces, at the nearby Imperial Opera House—a performance by a conventionally oversized diva, set against a flat and empty background, that is clearly not to the King's liking, as his efforts to escape this "honor" demonstrate. In fact, his exit utilizes the Stereoptical Process most effectively to suggest an almost revolutionary break with that world, as he emerges from the Opera House, set in the background, into a three-dimensional realm and moves from background to foreground, past two flanking lines of guards leading from the theater lobby to the street. Done as aloof-looking setback figures—cutouts receding in size as they lead into the frame—the guards nicely measure out the King's desire to escape from the artifice of the opera, from the imprisoning nature of his official role, and into the real world. The subsequent extended tracking shot from right to left, as the King moves out into the world of his subjects and encounters the nearby vaudeville house, underscores the impression of his having entered a different and more complex realm, yet one clearly continuous with the artifice of the opera house.[7] Though his entrance into the vaudeville theater returns us to a conventionally animated context, the performance the King encounters there is pointedly staged with an eye to three-dimensional arrangements (and thus the three-dimensional world through which he has just passed): the image emphasizes the proscenium as a dividing line between performer and audience; within the proscenium Betty sings as she moves all around the stage and addresses the offstage onlookers; and she introduces her trained horse, which then performs within a riding circle that links the front of the stage to the rear and allows for movement in all directions. The King's subsequent participation in her act, as he crosses the proscenium, enters the riding circle, and, with her permission and direction, even mounts the horse, answers his desire for entry and participation in a complex,

Betty Boop and the Little King (1936) combines flat character styling with in-depth composition.

91

three-dimensional world, although it is also only a momentary satisfaction, since duty calls and he must eventually make his way back to the Opera House, to his disapproving Queen, and to those same guards who have been sent to find the missing King.

The Stereoptical Process is employed only in those transitional scenes—in the movement out of the Opera House, down the street, into the vaudeville theater, and then back again—but it effectively visualizes the key point of the film, the Little King's yearning to escape from his confining situation and become part of the real or common world. In that world, as we see when he purchases a peanut vendor's stock and then enjoys himself by flinging packs of peanuts to the vaudeville audience, he can democratically mingle with the other patrons and respond demonstratively to Betty's performance, things he simply could not do in the Opera House under the watchful eye of his Queen and the assembled nobility. That three-dimensional space, consequently, configures a kind of call for change that is built into this narrative. And yet it is also a very limited figuration, precisely because of the way that the film's three-dimensional effects are bracketed into a transitional space, cordoned off from the space of narrative action. The effect is to produce a kind of *dream* of change or difference—hence the movement back to the Opera House and the Queen, the *finding* of the missing King, the return to two-dimensionality, even if the King does manage, surreptitiously, to invite Betty into his carriage in the concluding shot.

The more ambitious Popeye efforts that would follow, the two-reelers *Popeye the Sailor Meets Sindbad the Sailor* and *Popeye the Sailor Meets Ali Baba's Forty Thieves,* deploy the Stereoptical Process far more extensively, although in the process they also point up the limitations that generally mark its use. Vidler has described how, in architectural drawing from the late nineteenth century onward, three-dimensional styling was typically employed "in order to bring the private into the public realm, to reveal the complex inner life of private space to the outsider" (156). And that is, after a fashion, the effect we find in these films. In the former the Stereoptical technique is used to characterize the world of Sindbad: as he is introduced and walks along his island, singing about what a "most remarkable, extraordinary fellow" he is; as he sends his pet Rokh, a monstrous bird of prey, to attack Popeye's ship and kidnap Olive Oyl; as Popeye enters the cave on his island; and as

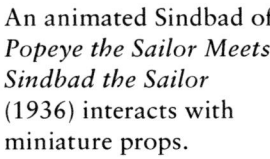

An animated Sindbad of *Popeye the Sailor Meets Sindbad the Sailor* (1936) interacts with miniature props.

Popeye and Sindbad have their final confrontation. In contrast to the simple, almost naturally two-dimensional world of the open sea that Popeye inhabits—an openness and simplicity that match up with his frequent refrain, "I yam what I yam"—it is pointedly a complex, exotic realm, with trees, rocks, chains, and structures in foreground and background as Sindbad moves about the island, with jagged rock formations and ominous skulls and bones as Popeye makes his way through the cave, and with rocks and various monstrous figures crowding all around the scene as Sindbad and Popeye square off.

And yet an exotic effect is practically all that this technique offers here. Unlike Ub Iwerks's multiplane camera developed at the same time, the Fleischer apparatus did, at least in its original patent form, allow for the tracking in and out of its otherwise fixed camera.[8] In these films, however, we find no such movement, but rather a horizontal emphasis and a kind of foreshortening of perspective that together qualify its Stereoptical impression. Thus, in each of the scenes described above, the action consistently occurs along the horizontal frame line, and it is composed in the center of the frame, against a flat backdrop and with shadowy projections in the foreground. The effect is to create a kind of central tunnel for action, a three-dimensional space set against two-dimensional space, often with two-dimensional cutouts helping produce the usual layering pattern of a three-dimensional world. The imaginary space of film, consequently, here becomes highly stylized, or as I earlier described it, a kind of double sense of space, a *cartoonish* version of real space wrapped within (or, to take Vidler's terminology, *warped around*) the traditional two-dimensionality of animation and geared not so much to imitating reality but to producing a striking, if rather bizarre stage— a new sort of proscenium—for its heightened actions.

Framing these elaborate effects are more conventional treatments of space that seem designed to lead up to and to build on the Stereoptical scenes. The film opens, for example, with an elaborate tracking motion to introduce Sindbad's island and to take us up a winding path, past various monsters, to the gate of his castle. And subsequently the film deploys particular events to signify the play of depth and distance here, as when Sindbad spies Popeye's ship through his telescope and when Popeye, through his own telescope, views Sindbad menacing Olive. These actions are worked out conventionally, with an iris frame effect to physically mark the space of the action and the distance of the observer. And though a number of actions are actually played out three-dimensionally, such as when the Rokh flies Olive into the deep background to Sindbad's island, when it similarly takes Popeye into the background to a nearby volcano, when Popeye returns bearing a roasted Rokh, or when Sindbad's various monsters and minions gather in the background, as if in a natural amphitheater, to watch Popeye and Sindbad battle in the foreground, the Fleischers never exploit those dimensional possibilities with their apparatus. Rather, such scenes are all done as a series of conventional long shots to contain the action, which is, finally, just another variation on the by-now-familiar escalating confrontations between Popeye and his oversized nemesis.

In the latter film, *Popeye the Sailor Meets Ali Baba's Forty Thieves*, these patterns are largely repeated, although there are more Stereoptical scenes and a greater variety in their use. What is perhaps more important, those scenes are set in contrast to a highly conventionalized sense of space, what we might think of as the typical "representative" space of most animated film. For example, the credits appear against a crude image of a cave, not only suggesting the cave of Abu Hassan (rather than the titular Ali Baba), which will figure prominently in the narrative, but also evoking a traditional proscenium arch, the stage on which this curious mixture of the Arabian Nights and contemporary action will be played out. To bring these mythic and contemporary worlds together, the film employs a familiar convention, a drawn and pointedly unscaled image of a turning globe, as Popeye, Olive, and Wimpy literally fly around the world in response to an urgent alert about the criminal Abu Hassan. And to depict the influence of Abu Hassan's approach on a town, the film resorts to the sort of exaggerated spatial tricks that mark much early animation: a frightened, full-sized man dives into a small jar, clearly too small to hold him; the numbers and hands on a clock hide from fear; a figure in a painting runs away from the frame. All are effective visual gags, but they are also the familiar stuff of animation of the era, solidly lodged in two-dimensional cartooning and its self-conscious joking about its own spatial limitations.

In contrast, the film uses its more numerous Stereoptical scenes to open up that tunnel spatial effect, particularly by emphasizing the foreground space that was barely glimpsed in the earlier Fleischer films. Though much of the film is built around the expected horizontal movement of characters, the opening scene, for example, unconventionally shifts that movement—of Abu Hassan and the forty thieves—into the deep background, while the foreground presents a three-dimensional desert landscape of miniature sand dunes, littered with rocks, skulls, bones, and an occasional desert plant—all scaled miniatures. Later in the narrative, the appearance of Popeye, Olive, and Wimpy in the desert repeats the same shot composition—a brightly lit set of sand dunes, rocks, and bones again occupying the foreground, effectively showcasing the Stereoptical Process by having us look *through* those three-dimensional objects to see the background action. In the middle of the narrative the film returns to the tunnel effect that dominates *Popeye the Sailor Meets Sindbad the Sailor,* although each of the Stereoptical scenes seems more richly done, with greater attention to set detailing. Thus, Popeye's ride through an Arab city shows off a variety of three-dimensional structures in the background and foreground as he moves through the center of the frame, and when Popeye enters Abu Hassan's cave, he passes an assortment of miniature treasures—chests of jewels, piles of gold—as he searches for Olive. The film concludes, though, with the action staged in the foreground, amid a variety of three-dimensional props. In this instance, we see Popeye, Olive, and Wimpy perched victoriously atop a wagon loaded with jewels, being pulled by Abu Hassan and the other thieves through a Stereoptical landscape. The pattern is perhaps obvi-

Popeye walks through a three-dimensional version of Ali Baba's cave in *Popeye the Sailor Meets Ali Baba's Forty Thieves* (1937).

ous but nonetheless appropriate, as the narrative has gradually brought the action from the background into a three-dimensional foreground, as if it were progressively shifting into the "real" world. This dramatic appeal to space, its increasing prominence in the narrative, nicely balances those conventional depictions cited earlier, while also using that juxtaposition of two-dimensional and three-dimensional spaces to underscore Popeye's victory over those forces of a legendary and repressive past—almost as if the film were metaphorically enacting its own triumph over a more traditional visual style.

The narrative of *Popeye the Sailor Meets Ali Baba's Forty Thieves* ultimately differs little from that of *Popeye the Sailor Meets Sindbad the Sailor*—thanks, of course, to the dominant figure of Popeye and the story that typically attaches to this figure—but it does at least suggest that the Fleischers were reaching for a more ambitious and an even more intriguing use of space, certainly something more than just a decorative enhancement of its story. Popeye's commonplace victory over his thuggish opponents is here coded, somewhat after the fashion seen in *Betty Boop and the Little King*, as a triumph for the modern (over the mythic), for the common (over the exotic), and for a new (Western) order (over a tyrannical Eastern status quo), and all set in parallel to that gradually foregrounded Stereoptical effect. The result is a narrative that, like those of a number of other Fleischer films of the later 1930s, retains at least a spirit of the challenge identified with the avant-garde, even as it explores

An animated Popeye, Olive, and Wimpy ride off on a live-action miniature wagon at the end of *Popeye the Sailor Meets Ali Baba's Forty Thieves.*

how its technology might ultimately affect or enhance the animated film's reality illusion.

Of course, it might be argued, as Mark Langer does, that the Fleischers were only trying to better compete with their chief competitor, Disney, and particularly with the emerging illusion-of-life aesthetic that had come to characterize the latter's cartoons and to draw increasing critical praise. The new sense of depth produced by their Stereoptical technique certainly represented another, less conventional solution to the depth illusion that the Disney animators were, at that time, still addressing with more traditional animation techniques—with layering, shading, perspective, movement, color gradation, and so on—and thus it effectively threw down a gauntlet that Disney and the Ub Iwerks studio, thanks to their similar technological interests, would attempt—similarly—to address. Yet it would also, as we have noted, seem to pose a challenge to the modernist impulses at work in the earlier Fleischer films and perhaps help account for what Paul Wells has termed "the tension in the aesthetic styling" that we often find there (56). Combined with their rotoscoping and rotographing techniques, the Fleischers' Stereoptics would, on the one hand, underscore efforts at a realistic animation and suggest what Eisenstein, not unproblematically and perhaps a bit too enthusiastically, would term "the tomorrow of the cinema." But on the other hand, that approach would never quite satisfy, would prove to be a costly and time-consuming practice, and would ultimately inject its own interrogation of the real—an interrogation deriving from the strangely doubled or warped space that it produced.

What we see in the various efforts described here, and especially in the "special" Popeye cartoons, is what might well be described as a kind of decorative use of the Stereoptical Process. It often serves little narrative purpose and functions mainly to confirm that we have indeed entered unusual, fantastic worlds—such as a fairy-tale kingdom, Sindbad's mysterious island, or Abu Hassan's treasure cave. It holds out—almost as if, like so much later 3-D cinema, it were inviting us to touch it—a seemingly solid reality, while also deferring that contact, setting off that reality in a wholly other space. And in this respect at least, with its sense of a frustratingly elusive other world, the Fleischers' Stereoptical vision still suggests some of that interrogative thrust that marked their earlier animation. The double sense of space that it produced allowed, if a bit unsatisfactorily and too expensively, their work to look to both their past and the Disney future. Both realist and radical accounts of the Fleischers' work might benefit from this perspective, for each, taken alone, tends to obscure a kind of compromise aesthetic that was emerging at this point—an aesthetic that a competitor such as Ub Iwerks would never quite manage to negotiate, that the Disney studio would almost intrinsically understand and exploit, and that the Fleischers would, at least until their studio's takeover by Paramount and refashioning as Famous Studios, continue to explore.

That compromise aesthetic underwent further and in some ways more interesting development during the final years of the Fleischer studio. As part of their ongoing competition with Disney, Max and Dave Fleischer produced two feature films, *Gulliver's Travels* (1939) and *Mr. Bug Goes to Town* (1941), both of which draw to varying degrees on the studio's key figural and spatial technologies, the rotoscope and the Stereoptical Apparatus. The former film sets a rotoscoped Gulliver amid a world of animated characters who, as Michael Barrier notes, "lack the sharp individuality" common to other animated figures of the era. The resulting combination is one that he judges to be, simply, "odd" (29). The latter uses limited rotoscoping, mainly for the human figures seen early in the film, but it deploys an elaborate three-dimensional New York cityscape to begin the narrative. This detailed model, along with the

Rotoscoped characters establish the human world at the start of the Fleischer feature *Mr. Bug Goes to Town* (1941).

first sequence in the town of Bugville, is part of the Fleischer setback technique, used to lead us gradually from the human world deeper into the insect realm, as if reminding us that different species have different spatial experiences. Neither film would provide a major challenge to the Disney hegemony, however, perhaps because of their conditions of production—the first film required far more trained animators than the Fleischers could readily muster, and the second was rushed through production while the Fleischers bargained for control of the studio with their distributor, Paramount.[9] Though these ambitious efforts show the Fleischers further exploring their animation technologies, weighing their potential against their inherent limits, the most revealing use of those technologies may show to best effect in their Superman cartoons of 1941–1943, which were also the final efforts of their own studio.[10]

Citing a kind of "technological determinism" (38), Paul Wells has suggested that the Fleischers' use of the rotoscope and multiplane technique fostered a style that imitated the conventional realism of Hollywood cinema, while moving away from the "fundamental questioning and interrogation of the representational apparatus" that is implicit in all cartoons (12). Both their Betty Boop and Popeye shorts occasionally employ these technologies, but the Fleischers' abiding aesthetic in the 1930s could never really be described as realist, although the label of "perverse surreality" that Wells applies to some of those efforts (55) does not fully bring to bear, either. Certainly the Fleischers' style had fundamentally changed since their earliest Out of the Inkwell cartoons, some examples of which, because of the rotoscoping, earned Barrier's criticism that it "was not really animation at all" (22). We have noted how in the 1930s their cartoons showed evidence of a kind of compromise vision, as they played out the appeals of figure and space linked to their key technologies. Their cartoons thus emphasized caricatured human figures like Betty, Popeye, and even the Little King—figures generally bound to realistic laws of probability and propriety—while situating them within pointedly unusual contexts, as in the case of Betty Boop's *Snow-White* and *The Old Man of the Mountain* (both 1933). Yet Barrier suggests that, from the mid-1930s, there was "no sign . . . of any real interest in the characters" (185) per se, and that much of the attraction in these character-driven cartoons lay in what "happens around the edges" (182), in the increasingly elaborate space surrounding the central figures. A bit more exaggeratedly, Stefan Kanfer describes the Fleischer product in this period as "a cascade of visual and musical astonishments" (71). The seventeen Superman cartoons produced in 1941–1943 also offer many such "visual . . . astonishments," but they seem to make a much stronger claim on the real, thanks to their real-world settings, character styles, and frequent grounding in current events, all of which would seem consistent with a more elaborate application of the Fleischer technologies. Yet that claim ultimately proved rather illusory and instead might help us make out the kind of double vision at work in these films as the Fleischer Studio—and later Famous Studios—grappled with the difficulties of doing what we might term realistic fantasy.

This sense of a double vision might also help explain the general disagreement about the achievement of the Superman cartoons. In assessing his father's contributions to animation, Richard Fleischer boasts that these last studio efforts are "among the best cartoons ever put on screen" (105). Tempering that praise, Leonard Maltin, focusing on the Superman films' technical accomplishments, terms them "the most cinematically sophisticated the studio ever produced" (*Of Mice* 117). Barrier's history of American animation, which tends to prize realistic styling, gives reason to that qualification, noting that despite the cartoons' expense, whatever "pains taken" with the animation "did not extend to striving for realistic movement" and that character was generally subordinated "to extraordinarily plentiful explosions and robots" (304). Meanwhile, Wells's study of American animation, like Kanfer's history, simply omits them from the discussion. Part of the problem may lie in their problematic authorship, since nine of the films were done under the auspices of the Fleischer brothers—Dave was directing— whereas the remaining eight were produced after Paramount took over the studio in 1942, renamed it Famous Studios, and split the cartoons' supervision between Max Fleischer's son-in-law Seymour Kneitel and several remaining Fleischer animators. Thus, the Superman films do not easily fit the sort of studio vision on which animation studies have often focused. But the greater difficulty, as Barrier's comment hints at, proba- bly goes back to the perception that they were working in a manner dif- ferent from that used in most other cartoons, as the "more or less realistic" characters (Barrier 304) received little development, while a fantastic spatial design—one that indeed owes much to the comic-book source—became a central attraction.

Actually, most accounts of the Superman shorts suggest that the main challenge the Fleischers faced in this series was financial, since if the cartoons emulated the detailed style of the popular comic books on which they were based, they would be too expensive to produce under the studio's normal procedures, wherein, as the animator Gordon Shee- han suggests, "quantity was the big item" (qtd. in Barrier 187). Para- mount, as distributor, however, readily agreed to underwrite those increased costs.[11] A more substantial challenge came from what was implicit in the cost estimates. In agreeing to adapt the Jerry Siegel and Joe Schuster comic-book character, the Fleischers found that the real- world settings, characters, and contemporary events anchored the films in a very different and in some ways more constrained context than the Popeye or Betty Boop cartoons that had been the studio's stock-in-trade, practically forcing them to take a more elaborate—and in some ways more realistic—approach that was similar to the comics. As Richard Fleischer notes, they recognized that the comics "had a distinctive style. The characters were very realistically drawn human beings, and the compositions in each panel were well designed and dramatically com- posed" (104). As a result, Barrier suggests, these cartoons were initially "produced with care like that given to the Fleischer features" (304), that is, to the more ambitious and costly *Gulliver's Travels* and *Mr. Bug*

Goes to Town, which had to compete with Disney's elaborate features. Another was that the studio deployed the full variety of its technological effects to help meet that realistic challenge. So besides being shot in Technicolor, the entire series of Superman cartoons would use to some extent both the Fleischer multiplane process and rotoscoping, as well as actors who would "act the stuff out" while the animators sketched them (Barrier 304)—elements that could well have pushed the cartoons even closer to the conventionalized realism of classical Hollywood narrative than to the rough but highly imaginative style of their usual shorts.

That effort would thus become a site of what Neil Postman has termed technological "negotiation," a process that, he says, "is inescapable" and usually involves us in "a bargain . . . in which technology giveth and technology taketh away" (5). In the case of the Superman cartoons, that negotiation would center on the difficult relationship between the films' realistic styling and concerns and their source in a comic-book fantasy. Though in their previous films the Fleischers had felt free to use one of those technological embellishments as part of a menu of various "astonishments," here they had to find ways of striking a balance between the imperatives of an animated realism and a cartoon fantasy. One element of that negotiation can immediately be seen in the cartoons' technologically enhanced mise-en-scène. Every Superman title includes a credit for the Fleischers' patented Stereoptical Process and Apparatus, a note that again underscores the competition with Disney, since the latter's much-heralded multiplane camera had by that point become a highlight of its feature films. As we have noted, it was first employed in the Betty Boop cartoon *Poor Cinderella* (1934) to emphasize the spatial spectacle of the Prince's castle and to underscore character movement therein, as if in a real world. But because in these instances it mainly combined three-dimensional miniatures with two-dimensional drawings, the result was not so much realistic as a strangely compromised sense of the real. As Mark Langer states, here and in other Betty Boop efforts, the unusual spatial effect produced "a rupture of the films' visual continuity" (357), rendering such scenes systemically self-conscious and, ultimately, astonishingly *unreal.* And since this process was both time consuming and costly, it was used sparingly, further calling attention to the few scenes in which it is employed.

Trying to avoid that sense of "rupture," the Superman cartoons typically use the process in conventional ways, such as in establishing shots, for example at the beginning of *The Bulleteers* (1942) and *Electronic Earthquake* (1942). Both films open with extreme long shots of the city, seen through animated foreground clouds. In the former film, a tracking shot takes us into the city in the background and ends with a shot of police headquarters, which is soon attacked by the flying bullet car on which the narrative focuses. In the latter a similar contextual shot eventually leads into the *Daily Planet* building, where a dissolve shows an American Indian scientist threatening destruction if Manhattan is not returned to his people. Having established this three-dimensional context, though, both narratives then largely abandon it, resorting to heavy shading and varying color saturation—made possible by the use of Technicolor stock—to suggest their worlds' dimensionality. In fact, they similarly shift from the almost conventional sense of three-dimensionality produced by the Stereoptical and tracking shots to highly stylized renderings of the city, presented with a noirish low-key lighting scheme and in a great many canted or "Dutch-angle" images (wherein the camera is tilted to create tension), offered in a quick-cut montage fashion that projects a nightmarish sense of instability or disorder—a spatial emphasis that contributes to the fantasy aspect of the narratives. Of course, that visual style well suits the subjects, particularly when the *Bulleteer* gangsters launch their various assaults on the city and its institutions or the American Indian scientist unleashes his electronic earthquake machine that sends structures toppling. Both provide a threat to normalcy—or as the introductory narration idealistically styles it, "to truth and justice"—that Superman then has to vanquish. Moreover, that style approaches the dynamism and almost expressionistic style of the comic books' panels. It markedly contrasts with the sort of visual realism initially produced by the Stereoptical scenes, however, and hints at a desire to provide more than just a simple depth illusion for these films.

To that end, we find the Stereoptical Process used in a number of the cartoons, such as the early *Mechanical Monsters* (1941) and one of the last efforts, *The Underground World* (1943), not simply to foster a dimensional realism for the mise-en-scène, but also to contribute spatially to that larger atmospheric styling, even to help measure the menacing and subversive powers at work in the "normal" world of these

Superman "trapped" in a deep-space composition, courtesy of the Fleischers' Stereoptical Apparatus, in *The Mechanical Monsters* (1941).

films. In *The Mechanical Monsters,* for example, while chasing one of the film's robotic monsters, Superman is thrown into high voltage wires. We then see him in a process shot, framed by intertwined trees and craggy rocks in the foreground plane that effectively replicate the tangle of electrical cables with which he struggles in mid-frame, while providing visual continuity with the forest in the scene's deep background and suggesting how the natural and unnatural elements of this world seem to conspire against Superman. And the following scene introduces the underground lair of the robots' inventor with an elaborate tracking shot along a cavern path that lets us glimpse, through intermittent openings in the rocky foreground, a dungeonlike background containing machinery for constructing his robots, vats of molten metal for forging their bodies, and a torture device with which he intends to pry information from a captured Lois Lane. These ever more fantastic images, along with the dark foreground and only partial glimpses of his activities, help build the sense of mystery and menace, while also recalling the manner in which Superman, like Lois in this scene, seems to have been swallowed up by this world and by the dangers constructed by this unnamed villain. Similarly, *The Underground World* offers a series of tracking shots as first Lois and Professor Henderson and later Clark make their way down an underground river, their movements all framed and partially obscured by dark stalagmites and stalactites that crowd in from the foreground. Those ominous images, darkening the foreground

The Stereoptical Apparatus is used to create an ominous atmosphere in one of the last Superman cartoons, *Underground World* (1943).

while seeming physically to close in around the characters, forecast impending danger, as Lois and Henderson are effectively enveloped by this world—trapped and captured by its fantastic denizens.[12] Both cartoons, like other Superman films, ultimately cue us to see their Stereoptical effects *not* as coded signs of the real, as demonstrations of this world's three-dimensionality, but rather as atmospheric and even thematic tropes, even as another voice through which the narrative might speak of the dark and subversive forces at work in this world. It is an effective compromise on the studio's customary use of that process and one that suggests how these cartoons had begun to prompt a more imaginative application of that technology—translating the conventional signs of realism into other terms.

Another dimension of negotiation can be seen in the fact that the studio approached the drawing of the Superman character differently from the way it had addressed its previous major figures. Whereas some accounts suggest that Joe Shuster actually supplied model sheets to the Fleischers as they prepared the series,[13] Leslie Cabarga credits Dave Fleischer with recognizing that Superman, because he was such a thoroughly modern and realistic character, would pose a "drawing problem," one that he claimed to have solved "by substituting blocks and wedges for the usual circles and ovals that all comical cartoon characters were composed of" (136) and that had been used for the studio's other "human" stars, Betty Boop and Popeye. In fact, a surviving model sheet for Superman contains notations, presumably by Dave Fleischer, who signed it, emphasizing how the use of blocks for "roughing out [the] figure" should be employed to "help keep proportions and perspective" (Cabarga 137–38), in effect, to maintain a realistic sense of character, proportion, and scene design, even if such hard geometrics would make it more difficult to incorporate some of the naturalistic methods Disney had pioneered, such as squash-and-stretch or follow-through, or even to mesh with some of the more expressionist spatial features we have noted.[14]

That strategy was certainly partially successful, since the more angular, hard-edged stylistic approach clearly distanced the Fleischers' version of the superhero from the more rounded and pliable cartoon characters of the era, while approximating the comics' dynamic and hard-edged aesthetic. As Scott Bukatman nicely describes him, the comics' "man of steel" was from the start drawn as a figure of steellike stability and visual authority, that is, a character whose deliberate styling emphasized the fact that he stood for the forces of "transparency, control, and knowledge" (*Matters* 198) often associated with the real world. Carrying that characterization beyond dynamic poses and into motion, however, would prove more difficult precisely because that stylization got in the way of any efforts at employing Disney-like illusion-of-life techniques. Thus, the intermittent motions of the crudely drawn evil scientist of the first cartoon *Superman* (1941), the awkward action of Clark Kent as he exits a phone booth in *The Mechanical Monsters,* or the jerky motions of the Japanese spy in the opening of *Japoteurs* (1942) all support Barrier's simple observation about a lack of "realistic movement" in the cartoons. And the frequent loss of scale in films like *Terror on the Midway* (1942), *The Arctic Giant* (1942), and *Japoteurs*—all of which place Superman in the context of various outsized figures or "astonishments" (a giant ape, a reanimated Tyrannosaurus, the "World's Largest Bomber")— demonstrate another way in which realism sometimes posed a stylistic problem here, particularly when Superman was combined in the same shots with figures like the giant ape or dinosaur, which were not drawn in the same angular, hard-edged style. The result is a world that seems strangely conceived, pointedly a fantasy realm.

Some of those difficulties were disguised by two simple stylistic moves, both of which suggest the influence of the comics. One was to emphasize human detail; the opening scene of *Japoteurs,* for example, cuts from a medium shot of the awkwardly moving spy boss to a close-up of his hand holding a cigarette, which, in a slight move, touches the photograph of a new bomber on the *Daily Planet*'s front page, thereby shifting focus from the figural to the spatial, to a key but static image and prompting a scene change. Such dramatic detail and static shots abound in the Superman films: a hand holding a threatening letter in *Superman;* hands throwing levers and fingers pushing buttons in *The Mechanical Monsters, The Magnetic Telescope* (1943), and, indeed, in most of the films; a fist pounding a desk, a hand holding a poster, Lois Lane's legs poised against a wall in *Eleventh Hour* (1942); native hands pounding drums, fingers turning a radio dial in *Jungle Drums* (1943). This emphasis on close-up or detail shots effectively transforms the figural into a spatial feature, while also resulting in another sort of compromise, in this case an unusual editing pattern for cartoons. As the animator Myron Waldman notes, "There were many more scene cuts" than in any other Fleischer cartoons (qtd. in Maltin, *Of Mice* 117). The result, however, was a faster pace overall, and one that better accommodated the comics' emphasis on individual panels of action.

A second strategy was to use tableaux to minimize the need for realistic movement. Thus, as a robot in *The Mechanical Monsters* attacks the city, we see a line of police officers all in the same pose, firing machine guns. *Terror on the Midway* simply offers crowds of people, standing still, watching the circus sideshows. When the Bulleteers attack in the film of that title, long shots show panic-stricken crowds in the streets, as is also the case when *The Arctic Giant*'s revived Tyrannosaurus goes on a rampage. Though hardly unusual, such shots point to the sort of restricted animation style that would become popular a decade later, as the animation industry shifted into television production and sought to lessen the time and cost of production. Here they effectively submerge the figure into the group, movement into mass spectacle, the figural into the spatial, thereby minimizing or rendering motion unnecessary, while also balancing the quick-cut montages noted above.

But of equal importance was the studio's pointedly technological solution for dealing with realistic movement, one that goes back to the Fleischers' first animation efforts. By photographing his brother Dave in a clown suit and tracing the results, Max Fleischer found that he could relatively quickly and with minimal resources produce highly lifelike character movement or, as he describes the result, accurately "get the perspective and related motions of reality" (qtd. in Crafton 167). Thus, with the patent on the rotoscope that was issued in 1917, the Fleischers' first major cartoon character, KoKo the Clown, had been born. And though the realistic movements of that character and his frequent combination with actual photographed backgrounds in the early Out of the Inkwell cartoons moved the Fleischers' films in a different direction from the amazing transformative world that marked popular cartoons like Felix the Cat, they soon managed to combine the two impulses. As a result, the Inkwell films ultimately present audiences with a world in which, as Barrier allows, "appearances are simultaneously true and false" (27), in which realistic (or photographic) effects and fantastic astonishments become complementary—an accomplishment that forecast the sort of negotiation that the Superman films seemingly aim for.

For these reasons it is often supposed that the Fleischers freely employed the rotoscope to cope with the Superman project's realistic thrust, including the different stylistic approach needed for the character. Yet curiously, there is no consensus about how much or in what way the rotoscope was actually used. Philip Skerry and Chris Lambert, for example, suggest that most of the series' animation was produced by rotoscoping and even stress its importance for animation history, as they credit the Fleischers' use of the technique with successfully "integrating the human body with cartoon adventures" (65) at a time when Hollywood was preoccupied with cute cartoon animals. Leonard Maltin qualifies this judgment. Drawing on firsthand accounts, he notes that "rotoscoping was used to a degree, but the animators had to rely on their own sense of proportion and perspective to make these human characters work" (Of Mice 117); Seymour Kneitel's daughter, Ginny Mahoney, has told me that "there was some minor rotoscoping done," but she suggests that it was often done "to study things like the motion of the figure."[15] In contrast, Michael Barrier cites the former Fleischer animator Bob Bemiller's recollection that "there was no rotoscoping, just animating from sketches" of live actors (304). Cabarga's otherwise highly detailed history of the Fleischer operation is curiously silent on the matter. Close observation shows that in some instances the human characters seem fully hand-drawn, notably in the case of the crudely conceived evil scientist of the first entry, *Superman;* he is a figure who seems clearly in the mold of the caricatured humans that the Fleischers usually employed. In other instances, jerky movement and inconsistent proportions—often the case with Lois Lane—would seem to support Bemiller's reminiscence. There are also numerous scenes, however, that differ so markedly from these examples that they seem the likely result of rotoscope technology and point to a kind of technical and narrative negotiation at work, as the animators sought to fit a more naturally conceived figure into spaces that were at times realistically conceived and at others quite fanciful.

Such scenes hardly need cataloguing, but we might note the main types of scenes in which the process seems to occur. Practically every one of the films offers mundane scenes, bringing together Clark Kent, Lois Lane, and their editor, Perry White. When gathered around a desk, observing something offscreen, or in simple conversation, as, for example, at the start of *The Underground World* when Perry hands out an assignment, the figures often seem fully rotoscoped, perhaps simply because the scenes were so routine that they posed no challenge for—or evoked little interest from—the animators, yet they also involve highly detailed arm, hand, and head motions. Other seemingly obvious instances of rotoscoping involve Lois Lane—for example, in *Japoteurs* as she sneaks into the giant bomber's cockpit, and in *The Mechanical Monsters* when she hides inside a robot monster. These scenes involve very complex and carefully coordinated human movements, as is also the case when we see Lois, Clark, and Dr. Henderson loading their expedition boats in *The Underground World.* Then, too, they involve a character, Lois, who seems to have posed some animation problems, as shifts in the general look of her figure throughout the series might suggest. Yet another sort of scene is that which involves highly dramatic or exaggerated human actions. Here a prime example is the scientist-inventor of *The Magnetic Telescope,* particularly as he defies the police and, with a series of elaborate gestures, warns against any interference with his machinery. By rotoscoping such dramatic actions, of course, the animators could keep them within a normal human register, even when more exaggerated events—Barrier's "plentiful explosions and robots"—are occurring all around the central characters.

Yet such possible uses of rotoscoping, like that of the Stereoptical

Process, ultimately serve not so much to produce a realistic-seeming world as to fashion a compromise vision, one in which the real and the fantastic can be interwoven, much as the comic books themselves seek to do. Ultimately, it seems that the studio (both Fleischer and Famous) used rotoscoping fairly sparingly, particularly since, as Barrier notes, there was an apparent lack of "interest" in character (185). Rotoscoping thus became just one aid in producing some of the realistic styling that the comics seemed to call for, and such treatments were readily mixed with restricted animation and more stylized renderings, such as that of the cartoonishly comic office boy or the fake Superman figure in *Showdown* (1942). In fact, that film pointedly mines this stylistic difference as a key support for the narrative, which is about public confusion between the true Superman, who is rendered in a highly realistic style here, and a criminal masquerading as Superman who is drawn as a slack-jawed grotesque. The studio's approach, in any case, represents a major shift from its earliest use of the technology and seems to echo the experience of Disney's animators with rotoscoping, as Frank Thomas and Ollie Johnston recall. They note how, "whenever we stayed too close to the Photostats [produced by the rotoscope], or directly copied even a tiny piece of human action, the results looked very strange. The moves appeared real enough, but the figure lost the illusion of life. . . . The actor's movements had to be reinterpreted in the world of our designs and shapes and forms" (323). In effect, a compromise to full rotoscoping seems to have been necessary, as both how the technique should be used and just what its effect was continued to be debated.

Though the Superman series' relatively short lifespan—seventeen cartoons in all—certainly owed something to the cost and difficulty involved in applying such technologies, then, it also seems to speak to some of the aesthetic difficulties that this mix produced, as the Fleischers sought to work out a stylistic balance between figural and spatial thrusts. The issue of realism is prominent in most mentions of these cartoons, but we should be cautious about simply tying it to a "technological determinism." Perhaps we might recall John Ellis's caveat about the very slipperiness of the "realism" label, how it typically refers to "a whole series of principles of artistic construction and of audience expectation alike" (6) that do not always coincide—a series of "realisms" (8), including one that dictates a particular approach to the issue of space.

In this case, the Fleischer Studio was trying to meld the techniques and technologies it had developed for an earlier sort of animation to a very different type of material, while also trying to meet the expectations of both a cartoon and a comics audience. And as we have noted, some of those effects tend to call attention to themselves, resulting in sequences that evoke not just the world of a conventionally realist cinema, but also ones that threaten to puncture its conventional vision, that seem to shift valence between the realistic and the astonishing—that always seem to be part of a negotiation between different "realisms."

Yet we should not forget the key role the Superman figure himself plays here. The figure is the very reason for these cartoons' being, yet he is one whose fundamental story is about trying to disappear as hero, to hide his identity, to find an inconspicuous place for himself. In that regard he embodies the very aesthetic "problem" that these cartoons trace for us—of a dynamic, constantly shifting relationship between figure and space, in this case, of the figure that can come to center stage only when the world—the background, as it were—requires him. Always forced to negotiate a precarious identity, to disguise the points of juncture between the astonishments of his superhuman powers and the limits of his conventional identity, he is ultimately forced by narrative circumstance into taking action, "starring" in the narrative, but even then only by disappearing into nondescript spaces like phone booths, supply closets, and dark alleys, into the empty areas of the frame. And the character who eventually emerges is hardly the sort that would typically drive classical narrative; rather, once in action he is seen as a fantastic figure, embodying what Rosemary Jackson describes as one of the fundamental effects of the fantastic text, its "assault upon the 'sign' of unified character" (87). The *Superman* cartoons typically conclude on this note, drawing their narrative closure out of an ironic assertion, usually from Lois Lane, about the "real" difference between her milquetoast colleague Clark Kent and the fantastic hero Superman by whom she has often just been rescued.[16]

Of course, the truth is otherwise—that the real and the fantastic exist in the same figure and in the same spaces. And that narrative point dovetails with the stylistic problem on which we have focused here, not only because Superman constantly finds himself battling with or attempting to tame a threatening technology—much as did the Fleischers themselves—but also because of the way this fantasy figure who moves through a world that is supposed to be as real, as fully dimensional (or "stereoptical") as our own, has to be both the real Superman and a kind of tracing (or what we might think of as a *rotoscope*) of that reality, Clark Kent, as he has to take center stage as the figural focus of the narrative and as he has to blend into the narrative space. For just as Superman's essential story remains one of constant and difficult negotiation between the dictates of his adopted human identity and the powerful, machinelike nature that is part of his Krypton heritage, the cartoons featuring him also had to find ways of bargaining between the astonishments and transformations of animation and the conventions of realist cinema, between a fantasy figure conceived in realistic terms and the realistic technologies being used to convey a fantastic vision. Friedrich Kittler reminds us of how early filmmakers and theorists, in their own sort of negotiation, frequently "turned the handicaps of contemporary technology into aesthetics" (172), drawing out of the new medium's emerging technologies new discursive practices. In the Superman series we might well see traces of the Fleischers working in this vein, trying to flesh out a still developing, even conflicted animation aesthetic in which "astonishments" and the real could have equal play. It is, I would suggest, one of their key legacies to animation history. That the place of this series in our histories remains unsettled and in many cases even ignored only attests to the difficulties involved in such negotiations, and indeed in many of our ongoing efforts to sort out animation's relationship to a realistic or live-action cinema.

5

UB IWERKS'S (MULTI)PLAIN CINEMA

This had always been the objective of modernism: to flatten out,
to bring to the surface in order to make the base show itself for
what it is.

—Esther Leslie, *Hollywood Flatlands*, 297

In his history of the American cartoon, Leonard Maltin assesses as
mediocre the contributions of Ub Iwerks, a figure who has become
almost legendary in the field. He describes Iwerks as "a second-
echelon cartoon producer" and the products of his own studio, the various Flip the Frog, Willie Whopper, and ComiColor fairy-tale films, as
"basically unmemorable cartoons" (*Of Mice* 185, 192). Similarly, Michael
Barrier describes Iwerks as an animator of "narrow technical skills"
whose cartoons lacked "a distinct comic or narrative shape" (168, 166).
Though both assessments certainly have much truth to them, they also
suggest a kind of corrective response to a legend that has grown up
around Iwerks in light of his early fame among fellow cartoonists, his
signal contributions to the creation of Disney's iconic Mickey Mouse,
his near single-handed animation of the first Mickey cartoons, and his
involvement in the spectacularly successful Silly Symphony cartoons,
with their early and innovative use of synchronized sound. Because of
these connections it was often suggested that Iwerks was really the
genius behind the mouse, or as Russell Merritt and J. B. Kaufman put
it, "the strong foundation on which the [Disney] studio depended" in its
early years (64). Of course, these views are not necessarily contradic-
tory, but the relative neglect of Iwerks's independent efforts has raised
the questions of where his own cartoons went wrong, and of how some-

one of near-legendary status could, in many cases, simply be relegated to the footnotes of animation history.

Because of his reputation for his drawing speed and seemingly innate understanding of the basic principles of the animated cartoon (squash and stretch, recoil, follow-through, etc.), Iwerks has been described as essentially a master technician—a view only reinforced by his professed interest in various mechanisms that would support the animation process, and his development, after returning to Disney in 1940, of such devices as the Xerographic Fusing Apparatus for inking cells and the Triple Head Optical Printer, and his perfection of a sodium traveling matte process for combining live action with animation.[1] Even when he was running his own studio between 1930 and 1936, Iwerks was rumored to have, after the first few years, relegated much of the daily supervision of the animation process to subordinates. In fact, Michael Barrier claims that a Fleischer alumnus, Grim Natwick, "eventually wound up running the studio day-to-day, while Iwerks worked on mechanical improvements in the studio's basement" (167).[2] Yet one of those technical developments would have a marked effect on the reputation of the Iwerks cartoons and would parallel similar developments at other animation studios in the period, most notably at the Fleischer brothers' studio, as we have already seen, and later at Disney. This same technical interest might aid us in better situating his works in terms of American animation's shifting aesthetic in the 1930s, particularly by helping us see his studio's cartoons as symptomatic of a larger struggle in this period between the avant-garde and an emerging realist aesthetic that was closely aligned with the classical narrative mode of live-action cinema—a mode that would increasingly implicate a new sense of animating space.

That key development, of course, was the multiplane camera, a device designed to overcome the essential flatness of the animated image by creating a three-dimensional space in which to photograph the animation cels. Yet it was a development that ultimately brought little success to Iwerks's films, winning them neither great critical accolades nor the embrace of a popular audience. Part of the problem, as the epigraph to this chapter implies and as I sketch out in the introduction, is that the critical community never agreed on the importance of the depth illusion for furthering animation's development, so the value of a device for producing this effect remained an open question. In fact, as we have already seen, many commentators insisted that the real strength of the animated cartoon as it had developed up to this time lay precisely in the stylistic trait that so distinguished it from conventional live-action cinema, that is, its essential flatness. For here was a characteristic that challenged the naturalism of Hollywood narratives and brought the cartoon widespread attention from the era's avant-garde by suggesting that a similar informing spirit was at work. Even Disney's animation was, early on, appraised from this vantage, as being liberated "almost entirely from the restrictions of an oppressive reality" (Kozlenko 246). Yet Disney cartoons, propelled by Walt's growing concern with an illusion-of-life aesthetic,[3] would, as the decade progressed, gradually turn from that essential flatness, first by emphasizing more rounded characters that responded to forces just like real three-dimensional figures, and second by introducing in 1937 Disney's far more complex and capable vertical multiplane camera, a device that would bring the studio an Academy Award for Technical Development. With the success of the Disney cartoons, space would come to the fore and a sense of depth would increasingly become an important measure of animation skill and even quality, at least within the industry, just as the Iwerks studio was releasing its last cartoons in late 1936.

Yet before this point there was, at least in the avant-garde community, a distinct value placed on flatness, owing to the belief that it supposedly signaled freedom from a simple naturalism, and thus from the world of common experience and common values that conventional live-action films reflected. From J. Stuart Blackton's chalkboard drawings that come to life and mutate, to the Krazy Kat and Ignatz cartoons—with their nearly-empty or stylized backgrounds—to Otto Messmer's Felix the Cat, there was the sense that everything within the animated world was essentially the same: graphic representations or simple shapes that were equally available and open to the play of the imagination. Esther Leslie argues that a major attraction of early animation naturally follows from this impression, as it almost explicitly offers to audiences the "dissolution of conventional reality" (149) and so, in a distinctly modernist fashion, makes "the base show itself," signaling that it is subject to question and perhaps eventual change. The protean nature of these early cartoons, particularly their consistent reliance on gags based on multiple and dizzying changes, and their attendant sense of a fundamental impermanence, only reinforce this reading and further hint at links to the avant-garde world. Thus, Leslie describes how Felix the Cat's "permutable world" readily suggests the surprisingly fluid visions produced by the surrealist movement (22). Of course, these early cartoons' frequent transformations—such as Felix's easy conversion of his tail into any tool or device that the narrative situation might demand, or Mickey Mouse's quick adaptation of various farm animals to musical instruments in *Steamboat Willie* (1928) and *The Barnyard Concert* (1930)—follow largely from the very simplicity of the animation, as lines, circles, and basic shapes, unburdened by heft and dimension, easily combined, straightened out, or mutated. But that resulting combination, of a flat aesthetic and a vision of change, results in a sort of formal inconstancy that allows these creations implicitly to both interrogate the cinematic illusion itself and humorously insist on the possibility of change in the world to which the cinema rather obliquely refers. It is these dual capacities that linked early animation to the world of the avant-garde and help explain the level of appreciation that was offered for the styling of the first and more primitive Mickey Mouse and Silly Symphony cartoons—works that were lauded by no less a revolutionary spirit than the Soviet director Sergei Eisenstein[4] and that were fundamentally influenced (and in some cases largely created) by Iwerks.

Certainly, on one level Iwerks's cartoons readily show their own kinship to that combinatory aesthetic of flatness and a transformative, even modernist spirit, and suggest, at least on a very basic level, some awareness of this appeal. And yet stylistically these films were also already beginning to anticipate a shift from this paradigm. The most obvious allegiance to that modernist sensibility shows up in what we might broadly term the mise-en-scène of the Iwerks films, which frequently mirrors the anarchic world of Felix the Cat and of the Fleischers' Out of the Inkwell cartoons. In his Flip the Frog films, made between 1931 and 1933, much of the action occurs on a horizontal plane, as Flip walks or drives a car from left to right or right to left; depth is simply less important than movement within a flat space. And in such a world it seems that almost any inanimate object Flip encounters can easily come to life or change shape, one example being the anthropomorphized autos of

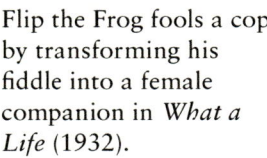
Flip the Frog fools a cop by transforming his fiddle into a female companion in *What a Life* (1932).

The New Car (1931), especially one that dons makeup to allure the new buyer, Flip, and later gets drunk after accidentally lapping up, as if from a dog bowl, spilled bootleg liquor. *What a Life* (1932) seems practically ruled by a logic of metonymy, as a howling dog suddenly turns into a seal barking for a fish, and a "shapely" fiddle case becomes a female companion when Flip tries to fool a cop. And *Movie Mad* (1931) sees Flip trying to sneak into a movie studio by following a fat man, lifting his shadow as if it were literally—as it graphically appears—a piece of carpet dragging behind him, and attempting to hide under it. The simplest impression made by such scenes is that any circumstance, any thing, or any creature Flip encounters is a potential source for a gag, but at the same time they are sketching an engagingly fluid and protean world, one of surprising possibility, much like that found in such key avant-garde films of the era as *Ballet mécanique* (1924), *L'etoile de mer* (1928), and *Un chien Andalou* (1928), and one that suggests a modest modernist element "animating" Iwerks's early productions, just as it did the Mickey Mouse cartoons and the early Fleischer efforts.

Though generally a bit more polished than his Flip the Frog films, Iwerks's Willie Whopper cartoons of 1933–1934 find their essence in a similar protean sensibility, although one that has been elevated to an almost formal level by their concept, as if that very characteristic were being opened up for investigation—and challenge. For the very subject of these films is change, embodied in the most wildly improbable events, typically introduced by Willie asking the audience, "Say, did I ever tell you this one?" It is his conventional prelude to the whopper of a tall tale that follows and that finds its appeal in the extent to which his implied narrative manages to stretch reality, usually through various violations of probability and the laws of nature, opening up a new space for the imagination. One of the few true science fiction cartoons of the era, *Stratos Fear* (1933), nicely demonstrates the general character of these films, even as it also begins to suggest a more problematic attitude that was beginning to surface in Iwerks's efforts. Beginning with Willie's visit to a "painless" dentist, it shows what happens after he is "gassed": Willie seemingly inflates like a balloon, rises from the dentist's chair, bursts through the ceiling, floats into space, and eventually arrives at a strange planet. There he encounters a trio of alien scientists who wield a ray that literally transforms objects—a cow becomes a heap of milk bottles and steaks; a pig is turned into hams, sausages, and footballs (pigskins). Later the lead scientist similarly transforms, becoming a seductive, veiled woman who plies Willie with Mae West's line, "Come up and see me some time," only to return to alien form when Willie begins to succumb to "her" wiles. Willie has, very simply, stumbled into a world of dizzying transformation, one that clearly holds much potential for interrogating the status quo, particularly with its scientists who all too eagerly reduce life to basic commodities.

Yet the film also raises a challenge to that spirit of change, particularly as it develops a parallel fascination with flatness. For as Willie tries to escape from the aliens and their transforming ray, he pulls open a door only to find a blank wall instead of an opening; and when he tries to dive through a window in the background, he bounces back when the "window" proves to be nothing more than a drawn shade, decorated with an image of the sky and covering a blank wall. If everything here is prone to change or transformation, including Willie, who is then captured, it also seems like a world from which there is no escape, since it is almost literally a flat world—a cognate to the animated environments of early cartoons that had rendered such transformations the norm. Only Willie's awakening in the dentist's chair, in another dimension of space and time, just as that ray is being aimed at him, saves him from also being transformed into some unimaginable product, while revealing this world of transformation and flatness to be only a frightening hallucination.

Willie Whopper collides with a deceptively flat space in *Stratos Fear* (1933).

At the level of plot and conception, this film is certainly one of Iwerks's most imaginative, as well as one that suggests some awareness of the character of early animation, and it points up how many of the Iwerks cartoons, with relative consistency, seem implicated in the modernist spirit that Leslie, speaking of other cartoonists of the era, evocatively describes as the "imaginative work of renewal of matter" (96). And yet in its images of Willie bursting through the roof of a building, rising beyond the Earth's atmosphere, and even floating amid various planets, the film also suggests a mindfulness of issues of depth and dimensionality, as if it were deconstructing the conventions of many popular cartoons. Moreover, its plot circuit literalizes the process that Leslie would accuse the Disney studio of, as it manages to "reinstitute the laws of perspective and gravity, and . . . fight against flatness" (121). In effect, it surprisingly pulls back from that "work of renewal," from the spirit of change, and from the flatness that helped generate that spirit, while it also poses a challenge to that spirit, even seems to discern a threat implicit in it.

And indeed, Iwerks's films do increasingly qualify their spirit of transformation, further interrogating the aesthetic that had dominated his earliest efforts. Even in the most anarchic moments of the Whopper series, even as Willie launches into ever greater tall stories, such as the ones about his encounter with the devil in *Hell's Fire* (1934) and his descent to the ocean's floor in *Davy Jones' Locker* (1934), there is always a kind of wink at the audience, one codified in his acknowledgment of the lie, his concluding challenge to the audience in some of the films: "Now you tell one." Of course, that challenge readily opens onto alternative readings: as an effort at pulling back from the preceding anarchic moments, or as a subversive effort at extending the cartoon's work by reminding the audience members of this world's constructed nature and of their own ability to construct one like it—or even better. As we have seen, however, film historians have for the most part tended to read all of Iwerks's efforts, including that recurring coda, in the former way, as a sign of his own simple playfulness, particularly in light of Willie's inevitable return to reality after constructing another version of himself for his listeners, a version at which we are encouraged to laugh. Of course, reality has been enlivened by Willie's often heroic experience, as if the flight of imagination were enough. It seems that Iwerks, rather like Willie, was increasingly being drawn to the three-dimensional world, to the solid world of machine rules and physical laws, as if, even at a distance, he may have been haunted by the spirit of his mentor, Disney, and that illusion-of-life aesthetic that was gradually developing at this same time.

I would suggest that we see Iwerks's development of his multiplane camera precisely in this context, as an effort at exploring how his cartoons might move away from—or develop beyond—the sort of simple modernist construct in which they had early on participated by offering an almost tangible element of depth and substantiality to balance, if not quite overcome, their essential flatness. Certainly the relatively small percentage of multiplane scenes in his films, even given the general effectiveness of his device, suggests that its development could hardly be described as an aesthetic evolution, as a sign of Iwerks's complete embrace of something approaching Disney's illusion of life. In fact, the animation historian Joe Adamson notes how, even after the development of the multiplane camera, the Iwerks cartoons "kept veering from never-never land into the twilight zone. Things get really strange" (qtd. in Iwerks and Kenworthy 131).[5] But what the multiplane device did was to offer a ground for that strangeness, an element of balance that, unfortunately, only made Iwerks's cartoons seem a bit different—neither as challenging as the better "flatland" works nor as comfortably within the pale of the new standard of a conventionalized realism that Disney's far more polished efforts were demonstrating.

Built, according to Jimmie Culhane, one of the studio's top animators, "out of parts from an old Chevy that he [Iwerks] had bought for $350" (Iwerks and Kenworthy 130), the Iwerks multiplane camera was a horizontally oriented device—like that of the Fleischers but in contrast to the later Disney vertical mechanism—that simulated depth of field by placing the animation cels in vertical holders along various fixed planes in front of a stationary camera. Both simple and practical, the device produced a striking sense of dimension, although one that was never quite as impressive as the Fleischer Stereoptical Apparatus, with its miniature sets and three-dimensional props,[6] nor as well integrated into the plots or themes of Iwerks's films as we later find in a Disney cartoon like *The Old Mill* (1937) or a feature like *Bambi* (1942). The opening of *The Old Mill*, for example, is built around a series of track-in shots that maximize the new Disney device's ability to move the camera toward its layered animation cells, creating a sense of movement into the world of the various animals that have taken over an abandoned windmill. The privileged and intimate vision that results forecasts the effect that Disney would later capitalize on in the live-action format of its True-Life Adventure films, when it would exploit the capacities of a variety of new technologies, most notably the telephoto and zoom lenses, to allow the audience to feel an unusual intimacy with and a part of the natural world.

The Iwerks cartoons produced after the introduction of his multiplane camera, though, offer nothing quite comparable, and indeed, much of the most obvious use of the device seems pedestrian and unimaginative. For example, in *Mary's Little Lamb* (1935) we see Mary and her lamb in the foreground, dancing on the way to school, moving from left to right against a deep background of countryside. Since this film is essentially a remake of an earlier Flip the Frog cartoon, *School Days* (1932), in which we find almost exactly the same scene, as Flip and his dog frolic on the way to school, the use of depth seems particularly uninspired, almost as if it were being used primarily to distract audiences from the recycled narrative—and indeed from what appears to be some recycled animation footage here. And it is the pattern of application we find repeatedly in Iwerks's various ComiColor shorts, especially in a string of 1934 efforts, such as *The Valiant Tailor, Don Quixote,* and *Jack Frost.* Each narrative uses the multiplane camera sparingly, typically by exploiting the narrative opportunity to have a character, usually brightly colored, move horizontally across the frame, that movement typically set in contrast to a deep background that is drawn and colored in a pastel, soft-focus style to increase the depth-of-field illusion. In this regard, then, the relatively late ComiColor short *Mary's Little Lamb* suggests little development of the possibilities opened up by the multiplane camera since Iwerks had first introduced it in the previous year's *Headless Horseman.*

Yet one of the cartoon's more interesting variations on this effect is noteworthy. It involved imposing a static image in the foreground, in such a way that it masked a small portion of the frame. We see this approach in *Mary's Little Lamb* when the schoolchildren watch a series of song-and-dance performances. Having established the children as audience, the cartoon then depicts the performances in the middle and back of the frame, while black silhouettes of heads and shoulders occupy the frame's lower margins. Simply achieved, this technique neatly combines flatness and depth; in fact, it uses the former to enhance the latter effect, as if it were trying to strike a bargain between two guiding spirits. By no means a novel effect (recall Winsor McCay's similar use in *Bug Vaudeville*), it was achieved by placing black cut-outs along the lower border of the frame to create a stark contrast between a dark foreground and light background, thereby suggesting varying lighting levels and effectively "throwing" the eye deep into the frame.[7] A version of this approach does prove more successful in building the eerie effect of

The Headless Horseman's (1934) conventional multiplane effect: Ichabod Crane rides across a deep-set landscape.

122

Ichabod Crane's ride across a night landscape, done largely in silhouette, as he anticipates a ghostly visitation in *The Headless Horseman*. Yet even here the essential dynamic of the scene remains unchanged, as Ichabod basically rides horizontally across the frame in the sort of conventional depiction of action that typifies most cartoons of the era, as well as Iwerks's efforts from both before and after the introduction of his multiplane device.

What is more interesting in *The Headless Horseman* is not so much the use of the multiplane camera as the multiple efforts with other, complementary techniques of depth illusion, suggesting that this cartoon, as the first of Iwerks's multiplane films, might well have been pointedly designed around spatial concerns, as a determined effort to leave flatland behind and to visualize space itself. For at almost every turn in this film we encounter a design scheme different from those that typify many of the earlier Iwerks efforts, one that, while infrequently involving the multiplane camera, employs a host of visual cues to suggest a three-dimensional world: action is arranged to move between foreground and background, compositions are designed at an angle to create a visual dynamic for the image, and visual effects—including shots within shots—suggest different levels of reality in the narrative. The combination of such techniques hints of an effort at trying to explore and exploit animating space itself, thereby creating a different realm of animation, a kind of multiplane world.

From its opening *The Headless Horseman* stylistically suggests this possibility of difference, as much of its world is depicted on an axis diagonal to the frame. An establishing shot opens the narrative, showing the schoolhouse in which Ichabod Crane teaches set at a 45-degree angle in the frame; one path leads from the school to an outhouse back left, and another path leads into the right foreground, effectively tracing a compositional line from left rear to the right front of the frame. A cut to a long shot of the schoolhouse interior repeats but reverses that compositional principle, as we see Ichabod in the right rear of the frame with his desk set at an angle and the students' desks angled into the left foreground. A subsequent scene as Ichabod prepares for Katrina's party is similarly composed on a diagonal, two walls angling into the background, forming a triangular composition, much like that used in the opening introduction of the central characters (as triangle insets are used to depict each character). And this principle then recurs as Ichabod enters Katrina's house, not simply from left or right, but from a door again set at an angle, which enables the characters to move diagonally between background and foreground, thereby more effectively measuring space for the audience. Subsequent shifts in this scene amplify that sense of space, as dinner is announced from the background of the frame, prompting everyone to rush from foreground to background and crowd through the dining room door; and when Ichabod is eventually thrown out of Katrina's house for trying to kiss her, it is from the background to the foreground, where he becomes a silhouetted figure against the brightly lit house, so that the lighting scheme enhances the depth illusion. At its conclusion, the narrative depicts a church steeple and church bells announcing Katrina's wedding to Brom at an angle in the center of the frame, and it finishes with the wedding scene composed in depth: Katrina and Brom in the foreground and guests arranged in church pews leading into the background. Suddenly interrupting the ceremony, however, is a mysterious headless figure who emerges from that deep background, scaring off the bride and groom in the foreground, revealing itself as Ichabod in disguise, and thereby suggesting a kind of unexpected "depth" of knowledge in this otherwise simplistic and dimensionless character—an understanding that allows him to replay the joke previously played on him by Brom. Other than in this scene and when the partygoers run from background to foreground to squeeze through the dining room door, these compositional patterns do little to support the humor of the film or to advance the narrative, nor are they particularly innovative. In fact, we earlier noted some of these same patterns at work in *Bobby Bumps Starts a Lodge* (in chapter 1). They project a consciousness of the space of animation, however, a space presented as substantial, realistic, and narratively functional, as if to lead up to and support the similar effects achieved by the multiplane camera elsewhere in the film.

To somewhat mixed result, the film also employs a variety of graphic effects that build another level of dimensionality here. It uses, for example, several wipes and irises that inject a kind of visual dynamism, although they also tend to bring to the surface the sense of a constructed and protean world. Triangular insets introduce the central characters and visually reach across the landscape depicted at the start of the film, and later diagonal wipes repeat this visual pattern, although merely to suggest shifts in scene. To more effect, the narrative employs several circular inset shots to depict Brom's thoughts when he is introduced to his new rival, Ichabod. Though the enclosed images of a snake, skunk, and jackass suggest another level of depth, an unspoken psychological dimension, and the manner of their insertion again injects dynamism into what would otherwise simply be negative space, they are ultimately the stuff of flat cartoons, closely recalling the word balloons and common graphic effects of the comics, of an all-too-familiar flat and even static form of animation.

The centerpiece of three-dimensionality, though, is clearly the scenes introducing and demonstrating Iwerks's new multiplane technology. Early on the cartoon uses it in conjunction with a simulated tracking shot in the schoolhouse, as the camera seems to move around Ichabod to reveal that he is reading about the legendary headless horseman while his students are doing their lessons. It is a surprisingly effective as well as innovative shot, since the tracking motion, when combined with the multiple planes of the composition, seems to occur within real space and to offer an insight into Ichabod's character, suggesting that he is a three-dimensional figure with secret if unmotivated interests. Yet the following scenes do little to develop this potential. After the schoolhouse scene the multiplane effect occurs three times in quick succession, and each instance follows the same simple pattern: a messenger rides to Ichabod with Katrina's party invitation, moving left to right against a three-dimensional landscape; Ichabod rides to Katrina's party, moving right to left against that same landscape; and Brom gallops past Ichabod, also moving right to left, with the same soft-focused landscape forming the background. These scenes effectively suggest motion through space, but it is largely movement for the sake of movement, since the action could more easily have been handled with jump cuts. This movement anchors the story in a mundane reality rather than building any sort of narrative complexity. A similar pattern also forms the climax of the narrative, as Ichabod rides horizontally, his image silhouetted in the foreground against a dimly lit landscape and fence. The appearance of the headless horseman has some dramatic effect, but the horizontal action mitigates that effect, since he appears as a shadowy figure riding behind and then chasing Ichabod against the same dimly lit landscape. The depth illusion in these scenes is minimal, particularly during the chase, since there is little complication to the action and the plot dictates that it occur largely in shadow. In only one other instance does the multiplane method show to some effect—when at Katrina's house a partygoer begins telling the story of the headless horseman in front of a fireplace. With the fireplace and fire done as a separate plane in the deep background and the party guests gathered in the foreground, the scene allows for valuable light and shadow effects, while providing a very real dramatic space to suggest how this specter was influencing the listeners' imaginations; it is a vision that the film even injects into that space through another inset of a silhouetted horseman that the audience has now imagined. In this instance the film effectively employs that real space provided by the multiplane camera to link the real and imagined worlds, but this sort of dramatic contribution is otherwise generally missing here.

Missing too is any evidence that the Iwerks films further developed or successfully exploited such possibilities. Though the ComiColor shorts of 1936, works like *Ali Baba* and *Happy Days,* clearly show that more attention was being paid to physical details and to lifelike animation than we find in the earlier films, they also make little use of the multiplane camera, save in the presentation of backgrounds, particularly in the studio's last effort, *Happy Days*. When the Forty Thieves attack a town in *Ali Baba,* for instance, the action is presented largely as diagonal movement across the frame, from background to foreground, using screen space but suggesting its depth only in a conventional manner and essentially substituting frenetic motion for a three-dimensional effect. And at the same time, these films still offer some throwback elements to the world of flatness and transformation, as when in *Ali Baba* a camel's hump opens up like a car hood and a water hose is inserted to fill up its "tank"; and in *Happy Days* a group of boys make fun of a military hero's statue, prompting it to suddenly come to life and blast them with a stone canon, the shell of which anthropomorphizes, revealing an angry face as it chases them and shoots out, in turn, each tire on their car. In general, though, these late films are marked neither by advanced techniques of realistic animation after the Disney fashion, nor by a consistent effort to explore and exploit animation's early strengths—"motility, change, movement, and its ability to be everywhere and anywhere at

Happy Days' (1936) frightening vision of transformation as a canon shell comes alive.

once," as Leslie effectively describes it (39). Demonstrating little aesthetic consistency, they are, quite simply, rather plain affairs.

The aim of this overview has not been to suggest that the films produced by Iwerks's studio were important steps in the development of a realist aesthetic or to argue that Iwerks was himself a kind of misunderstood or underappreciated avant-gardist. Rather, I have tried to focus on the middle ground implied by such perspectives, one wherein we might find a better sense of why his films failed to catch on and a clearer measure of his place in American animation history, perhaps as a figure who helps cast in relief the developments then occurring on a more ambitious level at the Fleischer and Disney studios—hence his chapter placement here linking those two studios. Michael Barrier suggests that there were two different pulls at work in Iwerks's career, that Iwerks "asserted himself most forcefully . . . by insisting on a sort of mechanical perfection" (167), but that artistically his films were "locked in time," and that Iwerks himself was unable to break free from the earlier styles for which he had been so lauded (165). The fact that the Iwerks studio lasted only from 1930 to 1936 is some testimony to that view and certainly a reminder that audiences never quite warmed to its products, such as his weakly conceived and constantly revisioned figures of Flip the Frog and Willie Whopper. Iwerks was by no means committed to a figural cartooning, nor did he ever determine how best to exploit the spatial properties of his art. But in those films we do get a sense of an increasing awareness of and an attempt to work out the problems involved in animating space.

In fact, we might suggest that weak audience response to Iwerks's films at least partly follows from what is implicit in those different pulls Barrier notes and what has never really been articulated, that is, the films' mixed stylistic message, as they seem engaged at one level—and probably quite unconsciously—in pursuing "the objective of modernism," for which many other cartoons were at the time being lauded, including those of the Fleischers, and on another in exploring new standards of realism, similar to that developed more successfully in Disney's work. In effect, they seemed to be caught in a kind of paradox, variously working at both flattening out *and* fleshing out their animated worlds, which resulted in a mixed product that inevitably sent mixed cues to an audience and troubled their response. But it is that very mixture that also argues for their usefulness in putting the two leading animation studios of the era, Fleischer and Disney, into better perspective.

The problematic nature of these films is also noteworthy given the period, for they appear—and disappear—at a time when modern culture was beginning to witness what Paul Virilio has described as "the advent of the logistics of perception," that is, a developing emphasis on creating a kind of machinery for standardizing, enhancing, and even controlling vision, or as Virilio puts it, "cinematizing" reality (*Vision* 12). That logistics would, in a variety of ways, help push realist tendencies, in part because it would become central to the practical waging of the world war that was already on the horizon in the mid-1930s, a great drama in which even animation would come to play a valuable role through its use in the production of training and propaganda films—in both of which a semblance of realism would prove highly valuable. Certainly Iwerks's fascination with the machinery of film would position him to be a contributor to such developments, to a world in which perspective, line of sight, and depth cues would play crucial roles. In fact, once he had returned to within the Disney orbit in 1940, he would help advance that logistics by contributing to the studio's new hybrid animation program, helping make possible one of its most famous propaganda efforts, *The Three Caballeros* (1945).

Yet, ironically, that very move would bring Iwerks's efforts full circle. For that hybrid work inevitably harkened back to similar efforts in the Fleischers' Out of the Inkwell cartoons, Walter Lantz's Dinky Doo-dle shorts, Disney's Alice comedies of 1923–1927, and various other early works that, in blurring the boundaries between the real and the constructed and in foregrounding reflexive effects, celebrated film's power not so much as a representational form but as a fantastically creative and transformative medium. In fact, this sort of foregrounding, particularly of the very mechanism of reproduction and representation, is precisely what we find in such avant-garde efforts as *Ballet mécanique* and Walter Ruttman's animated *Opus* films of the 1920s—works that testify to the avant-garde's fascination with the mechanics of reproduction, while also drawing out of that concern some very unnaturalistic and unrealistic effects. Though Virilio has suggested that the result of the cinematizing process is that we could all become, as he puts it, "victims" of a movie culture, bound to the specific sort of vision allowed us by the ongoing "industrialization of perception" (*Vision* 79), it seems that Iwerks could sidestep that fate—if not subvert it, in the avant-garde fashion—only by becoming a master of those mechanics. It is a move that we see forecast in the 1930s when, even as he was drawn toward the realist realm and, through his mechanical endeavors, contributed to that "industrialization," he was still mining that world of flatness and transformation for some wonderfully imaginative effects. Yet the cartoons that his studio produced could never quite negotiate this double pull, just as they could not help reflecting a similar vacillation in the culture: caught between worlds, between styles, between notions of what our cultural works might do, able to point to the potentials in both of these approaches but never able to fully exploit either. Despite Iwerks's own talent, his could eventually be only a plain cinema.

6

LOOKING IN ON LIFE

Disney's Real Spaces

Both the Fleischers and Ub Iwerks, throughout their studios' productions, veered from a flatland aesthetic, with its attendant emphasis on amazing transformations, to an approach to animating space that seemed to aim at reproducing a conventional three-dimensional realm. Save in a few scattered instances, though, neither ever truly explored or developed the sort of modernist space that Anthony Vidler describes and that is so effectively imaged in cubist painting, expressionist film, and the modernist structures of a Frank Lloyd Wright—a space of surprise, distortion, and warping that we find repeatedly in the work of Winsor McCay and often glimpse in the first Mickey Mouse cartoons. And yet it is the Disney studio that typically drew the most criticism for this sort of tendency, that most crystallized critical commentary, perhaps because of the very promise that had been recognized in Mickey's early turns or because of the very clear sense of a developing studio aesthetic, one that in various ways recalls the world of classical Hollywood narrative. That aesthetic has often been associated with Disney's own creation of an elaborate multiplane animation camera that seemed to enthrone not modernist space but the sort of conventional realist space on which the other, ultimately less ambitious studios—the Fleischers' and Iwerks's—had also in their own ways come to focus.

The Disney multiplane camera was, of course, a far more complex and expensive device than those created by the studio's competitors, and it quickly achieved higher visibility by helping the studio win an

131

FIG. 1.

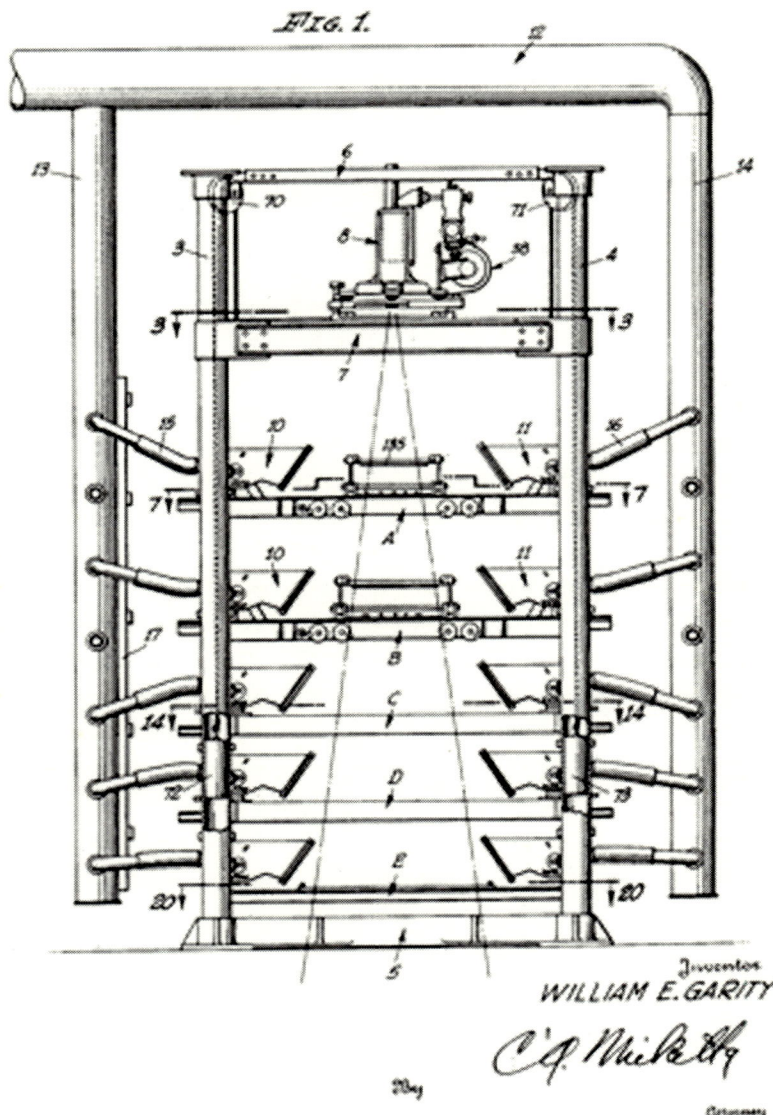

Inventor
WILLIAM E. GARITY

The Disney patent description of its multiplane camera.

Snow White meets her prince in a deep-space composition.

Academy Award for the first cartoon shot with the device, *The Old Mill.* Though certainly welcome, that industry recognition only underscored for many the extent to which the Disney studio, long existing on the margins of the film industry and almost constantly on the verge of bankruptcy, had become accepted, part of the mainstream, and, in the eyes of many, thoroughly conventional. And *The Old Mill* was essentially a trial run of this new technology, just a first step in advance of its use in *Snow White and the Seven Dwarfs,* which would also win an Academy Award, earn large profits, and be hailed as a landmark film, both for its status as the first American feature-length cartoon and for its own realistic effects. The critical climate, however, would quickly shift. By 1941 Siegfried Kracauer, a key theorist of cinematic realism, criticized the Disney films precisely for the way they had begun to "imitate the technique of the realistic films" by emphasizing three-dimensional space, camera movement, and characterization. In a declaration that suggests his preference for early animation's avant-garde spirit (if not for its equally inherent spirit of imitation), he argues that the cartoon should work differently from live-action film, that it should emphasize "the dissolution rather than the reinforcement of conventional reality," since "its function is not to draw a reality which can better be photographed" ("*Dumbo,*" 463).

And of course, photographing reality—or at least a Disney-style reality—seemed very much the point of the new multiplane camera that was crafted by William Garity, then head of the studio's camera department, and Roger Broggie of its machine shop. Developed as a vertical apparatus, in contrast to the horizontal ones created by the Fleischers and Iwerks, the Disney multiplane device consisted of a camera shooting down through four horizontal planes, each of which could be moved and lit independently. The spatial separation that was fundamental to using those different planes helped overcome the silhouette effect that often came from stacking cells on top of each other, and the independent lighting of the planes reduced the problem of color shift that commonly afflicted cels in the lower levels of an animation stack. Just as important, movement into or away from the image could produce a natural sense of parallax, since relative distances from the camera could be altered for each plane, thereby more genuinely simulating our normal visual experience. The overall effect of the new device was to produce sharper, brighter images, while offering the visual separation of live-action photography and conforming to natural laws of perception. Seen solely in these terms, the Disney multiplane camera indeed seemed designed to support a generally realist thrust, perhaps even the Bazinian "myth of total cinema" (22).

And yet, in practice the Disney illusion-of-life aesthetic was never quite aimed at producing a reality that could "better be photographed." As the Disney animators Frank Thomas and Ollie Johnston have recalled, there was "some confusion among the animators when Walt first asked for more realism and then criticized the result because it was not exaggerated enough." The reason, they submit, is that when he asked for realism, Disney actually "wanted a caricature of realism," an effect that might be achieved by combining "believability" with "exaggeration" (65–66). In light of this combinatory emphasis, it should be no surprise that the multiplane camera, for all its realistic effects, did not alter the fantastic elements from which the cartoons still drew their primary attraction, nor did it make the images themselves truly lifelike. Rather, it allowed Disney's animators to set their fantasy subjects—their talking deer, dancing trees, living wooden puppets—within more realistic spaces, while also allowing them to approach those subjects *as if* they were real and *as if* the characters inhabited a three-dimensional environment. In turn, that placement allowed audiences to accept more readily Disney's caricatured figures, and those figures to retain their fantastic appeal. Moreover, because of the multiplane camera's ability to move fluidly into those worlds and around the characters and to explore those fantasy realms, audiences could see these creations as linked to yet extending beyond the real world—making a connection that might even allow for an interrogation of the real in a way that Disney's critics of this period seldom acknowledged.[1]

Though that trial effort, *The Old Mill,* is certainly aimed at showing off the capabilities of the new multiplane camera—perhaps even at demonstrating just how much more capable it was than the competing Fleischer mechanism—it is also a sharp departure from other Disney Silly Symphony cartoons. Right from the start it seems almost insistently nonfigural in the way it introduces conventional Disney animal characters and then quickly passes on to others—a spider, ducks in a pond, a family of bluebirds, a nest of mice, two doves, an owl, a flock of bats—in short, the *world* of nature. Though the narrative will, at some point, eventually return to each of these, the real point of the introductory sequence is not to prepare for the introduction of characters, but rather to measure out space, and particularly the space that each figure or group occupies in or around the "abandoned" mill. A constantly tracking camera allows us the pleasure of discovering each group, noticing how the various animals fit into the mill, and helping us understand the importance of this physical space, as a constructed, seemingly useless human space is revealed to be a kind of natural habitat, a sheltering space for the great variety of creatures the cartoon catalogues.

The resulting story—what there is of it—focuses precisely on the

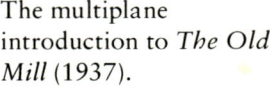
The multiplane introduction to *The Old Mill* (1937).

relationship of constructed and natural spaces when a storm suddenly strikes. Frogs in the millpond simply dive into the water to escape the storm, while the bats fly to safety. Those that cannot flee, though, such as the mother bluebird who stubbornly sits on her nest to protect her eggs, and the family of field mice, rely on the dilapidated mill for protection. In fact, the impact of the storm is largely measured not through the elaborate multiplane shots but with a montage that repeatedly alternates between the creatures huddled inside the mill and images of the mill's exterior as it is buffeted and torn by the furious storm. Once the storm passes, the creatures inside are, one by one, shown to be safe, and others return to its shelter; the film concludes with multiplane effects that again measure the space here, in the process reminding us of the connection between natural and constructed spaces, and underscoring an especially appropriate point for this sort of film: how much of importance typically escapes our vision. Through the agency of the multiplane camera *The Old Mill* does not merely set about reproducing a three-dimensional space; it tells a story about our need to see better, to look more deeply into those contiguous spaces that we take for granted because they do not seem to be inhabited. It is a point on which Disney would later build one of its most successful series of films, the True-Life Adventure documentaries, and one that would resonate in one of its most highly praised animated features, *Bambi* (1942).

Of course, the discourse about *Bambi* has most often centered on its level of realism. One often-recounted story recalls how, in working on the film, the artist Rico Lebrun, who had been hired to instruct the animators "in the finer points of animal anatomy," became "obsessed" with dissecting a dead fawn, to the revulsion of his animator-students (Watts 177, Gabler 320). More broadly, Disney clearly cultivated an element of naturalism, as evidenced by the creation of a studio menagerie of live animal models, the use of "hundreds of specially commissioned wildlife photographs," and Disney's sending a group to the Maine woods for several weeks to study the animals and their habitat (Watts 68). And Walt Disney publicly encouraged that line of thinking, as he proudly described the studio's efforts "to get closer to nature" by resorting to naturalist cameramen and location study in the hope that his artists "might get something unique" (De Roos 56). That discourse, however, would ultimately play into those critiques that saw such efforts, along with the use of the multiplane camera, as testimony that the Disney studio had obviously lost its way, producing works that, because of their realist impulse, were too much like the world of live-action features. It is an attitude that we see reflected in Manny Farber's scathing review of *Bambi*, wherein he describes the film as "an affectation of reality, like a Maxfield Parrish painting" (91), and in Siegfried Kracauer's later dismissal of it as "sham nature" (*Theory* 90).

Yet Leonard Maltin's more measured description of *Bambi*'s style as a "compromise between an artist's fancy and a naturalist's authenticity" (*Of Mice* 66) suggests that there is something more at work in the film, something other than merely a naturalist's impulse. Curiously—for a Disney production—it is actually a film of *many* styles, one that calculatingly draws on multiple animation traditions. Since the project was approached in a different way from most Disney films, that is, since the studio "cast" the animators by sequence rather than by assigning each to a specific character, *Bambi* almost inevitably involved a broader range of styles.[2] For example, in an effort to meld a level of realistic treatment with the mannerism of the Felix Salten work on which the film was based, the artist Tyrus Wong was assigned to the film; he brought an "oriental tradition" to the production that is particularly evident in the forest backgrounds (Thomas and Johnston 192). To depict the onset of the fall season, the Disney animators relied on an impressionistic cascade of multicolored leaves. To inject a more dramatic feel, the fight between Bambi and another male deer was staged entirely as a dark silhouette scene, the characters indicated only by the use of "rim lighting" (Thomas and Johnston 483). The forest fire was done in a pointedly stylized manner—in fact, Maltin terms this section "*too* stylized" (*Disney Films* 56); the colors here and in the sequence where Bambi must fight off a pack of hunting dogs are highly exaggerated. And as Frank Thomas and Ollie Johnston have pointed out, throughout the production the background painters were instructed to make their paintings "reflect the overall mood rather than show blades of grass" or other fine naturalistic details (250). The cumulative effect was less to sustain a realist vision than to allow the visual style itself to carry much of the action and to articulate feeling, theme, and shifts in time.

And the multiplane camera was employed largely to support that approach, to turn our manner of seeing events into one of the film's key concerns. For even as *Bambi* evokes the natural cycles of life and death and of the seasons, even as it presents, thanks to the painstaking research that went into its preparation, natural animal behaviors and movements, and even as it stages several scenes in layered depth, it also underscores the very difficulty of ever viewing that natural world clearly, of entering into these spaces and fully understanding the animal realm. As an example, we might consider *Bambi*'s opening sequence, which is an extensive multiplane creation. The film begins with an elaborate tracking shot, as the camera moves from left to right across the thick mass of a forest, momentarily pausing at a break in the cover to move in, and then continuing its horizontal tracking, past branches, leaves, tree trunks, and vines. The opening is, in fact, composed of a series of such movements that slowly and gradually takes us deeper and deeper into this world, all the while visually reminding us how difficult it is to penetrate this space, to open it up to and for our intrusive eyes.

Eventually the halting movements across and then into the frame and forest bring us to a slight clearing where some of the creatures have gathered to share the news about the birth of the "new prince," Bambi. Here and shortly after, when we approach another clearing, the bower where Bambi's mother shows him to the assembled wildlife, we get a sense of an *intimate* world, of the private space of the animals into which we have been allowed to enter, thanks to the multiplane camera and its constantly tracking, penetrating movements. Those movements, along with the sense of a consistently barred, troubled, or problematic perspective that they foreground—owing to the branches, leaves, and vines that seem constantly to block our view—take on added resonance for the narrative when Bambi's mother, before she is shot, warns her young son, "Humans are in the forest." The multiplane effect then evokes something more, the stalking eye of the hunters who bring death and destruction to this world, thanks to the forest fire they accidentally start. Able to provide a privileged access to the intimate, embowered spaces of the forest creatures, while also suggesting our own intrusive and even dangerous presence in these spaces, the multiplane camera contributes substantially to the thrust of this film, perhaps even helps give reason to the varied stylings we previously note. We better understand the difficulty not only of seeing into but of *understanding* this world—an understanding that, because of our very nature as "humans

. . . in the forest," we have difficulty with and that might be approached or suggested only through a great variety of effects: realistic stylings, silhouettes, impressionistic effects, exaggerated colors and lines, and the like. Thus, far from a realistic film, from a narrative leaning toward Bazin's "myth of total cinema," *Bambi* seems concerned with underscoring just how difficult it is to depict these other spaces that abut the normal human world, and ultimately to understand and fully appreciate them.

In this respect, the film seems a most revealing demonstration of the way that Disney came to use its multiplane device most effectively, and to some extent of a conflicted style that would increasingly become a studio hallmark. Hardly just a way of measuring dimension or producing parallax, the apparatus gave the studio and its animators new ways of investing space with meaning, of balancing it against the lure of character, as we see in *The Old Mill*, and even of carrying a thematic weight, as *Bambi* suggests. Of course, at the same time it produced a more natural sense of space, making the sort of transformations and exaggerations of earlier animation, including those of the early Mickey Mouse cartoons, seem wildly out of place, particularly given ever more realistic character animation. Yet it marks, I suggest, a kind of transitional point for Disney animation—a point at which its modernist impulses were not so much tamed by a conventional realism as already seeming to be looking beyond, trying to locate ways of moving through that conventionalism that had been developing at the studio and finding the sort of combinatory approach that Walt Disney instinctively desired but could never quite explain to his artists. Animating space itself was a key to the studio's conflicted style, producing an almost tangible dimensionality in films like *The Old Mill*, *Pinocchio* (1940), and *Bambi*, yet also mocking the conventional, as we see in some of the Mickey cartoons from the late 1930s, particularly *Mickey's Trailer,* and underscoring how difficult it is to penetrate or truly understand the natural world in *Bambi*.

We can gain an even better sense of the progress of this conflicted approach and its links to developments in animating space by examining Disney's hybrid films of the 1940s, a type that would, for a period, dominate Disney feature production. Midway through its narrative, one of these films, *Fun and Fancy Free* (1947), offers its audience a most striking situation—and a revealing technical achievement. Jiminy Crickett of *Pinocchio* fame jumps up on a window frame and looks out across a yard, various shrubs, and a street to a house in the deep background, situated apparently amid the Hollywood Hills. He then moves into these multiple planes of visual detail, across this strikingly three-dimensional space, to find himself outside that house and peering through its picture window. Yet while the house frame itself is animated, the interior he glimpses is actually a live action scene: a party involving a little girl, Luana Patten, the ventriloquist Edgar Bergen, and two of his dummies, Charlie McCarthy and Mortimer Snerd. That movement deep into the frame—an artificial three-dimensional movement here rendered all the more effectively by the use of the Disney multiplane camera—stops with a real three-dimensional scene, the framed image of the live actors (and not-so-live dummies), as if the animated scene had somehow produced the live action, as if the window scene were a kind of 3-D movie projected for the animated 2-D character, and as if *our* world constituted the entertainment for the cartoon one. It is a scene that some might see as metaphoric of the trajectory Disney animation followed, as its animated figures, impelled by technology like the multiplane camera, constantly seemed to edge closer and closer to the reality of live-action cinema. Yet something more—and more revealing—is at work in this generally pedestrian postwar Disney effort. With this opening *Fun and Fancy Free* inverts the usual visual and narrative situation, as character (Jiminy Crickett) becomes secondary to the spatial arrangement, live action ultimately serves animation by framing the two animated stories that make up the bulk of the film, and that frame provides an unexpected reflexive thrill by highlighting the technological "trick" of its hybrid technique. In the process that reflexivity also casts in relief the complex way in which space was coming to function in the development of Disney's animation aesthetic.

Throughout much of its early history, Disney animation was, as Timothy White notes, "almost universally praised . . . by the public, popular journalists and critics, and even academics and 'serious' artists" (4). It was lauded not only for its initially anarchic, free-spirited mouse, but also for the way it broke the boundaries of conventional narrative and linked to the world of avant-garde art; Walt Disney himself was even compared to the surrealist artist Salvador Dalí (Leslie 217).

Disney animation was showcased at the First Moscow International Film Festival in 1935 and enthusiastically supported by Sergei Eisenstein because of its revolutionary spirit, particularly its capacity for "freely reimagining" the world "according to fantasy and will" (qtd. in Leslie 231). Yet as Disney moved toward the development of its illusion-of-life aesthetic, as it introduced the elaborate multiplane camera, and as it brought various lifelike principles into its animation, critical opinion began to change. Paul Wells has renewed this charge, arguing that though "Disney made animation a credible art-form," he also "veiled the capacity of the form to more readily exhibit its subversive credentials" and thus demonstrate its complexity. That effect followed, he offers, from a studio style that, while "endorsed" by a cross section of American culture, seemed to break with the transformative and self-conscious or reflexive spirit widely found in earlier animation (45).

Yet that break, as our discussion of Mickey Mouse has already forecast, was hardly as definitive as these commentaries suggest, for during and immediately after the war years we find evidence of Disney's repeatedly trying to regain some balance between those realistic and subversive possibilities that, we often tend to forget, are *both* intrinsic to animation, as well as to create the sort of reflexive flourishes that we see surprisingly foregrounded in the otherwise conventional film *Fun and Fancy Free*. The efforts of this period, I suggest, point to an increasing interest in recouping something of that modernist attitude, or at least finding some accommodation between what Disney had been and what it was becoming—or perhaps with what animation itself was becoming as a result of new cultural and aesthetic pressures. Certainly, *Fantasia* (1940) hints of this ambition with its effort at forging a link between classical music and animation in a nonnarrative format. But that effort to retrieve an avant-garde spirit shows most clearly in another sort of film that would, for a time, dominate Disney's efforts and that has, unfortunately, usually been seen in a much different light, in fact as but one more symptom of the studio's falling off, and particularly of the realist thrust that Kracauer and others lamented. In the late war and postwar era the studio sought, for various reasons, to combine the attractions of its multiplane camera with one of the earliest approaches to cartooning, hybrid animation, a combination of animation with live-action figures that, as we have seen, was employed in the Fleischer brothers' Out of the Inkwell series, as well as in Disney's own Alice comedies of the 1920s.[3] But hardly a retrograde turn, the use of that approach in the films of the 1940s reveals an increasingly complex concern with space, one far more modernist than most critiques have acknowledged, but also one that looks toward different spatial attitudes that would become widespread in the later postwar years.

The following discussion, then, considers how a number of Disney's hybrid feature films from this era directly address the shifting issues of space bound up in their creation, particularly the space of spectatorship, which, though typically omitted from classical film narrative, is commonly implicated in modernist texts. As a lead in this direction we might once again turn to the work of Anthony Vidler, particularly as he describes the modernist introduction of space as a kind of constituent element of consciousness. Thus, he describes how the twentieth century introduced, along with its insights into psychology and culture, a hybrid between physical and psychological notions of space that modernist artists would try to evoke because of the way it "elides the boundaries of the real and the unreal in order to provoke a disturbing ambiguity" (*Architectural* 11). As part of this new sensibility, space was no longer perceived to be just a "stable container" or objective and measurable dimension of human experience, but "a product of subjective projection," an inconstant and shifting realm (*Warped* 1). And because of that subjective dimension, this new warped space posed a fundamental challenge for a conventional point of view since it "put the assumed stabilities of the viewing subject into question" (*Warped* 10). That sense of instability obviously colors the hybrid animation of both the Out of the Inkwell cartoons and Disney's Alice shorts, both of which depend on a dreamlike blurring of the boundaries between the real and the imagined and, to some extent, between the audience and the action. But it is an effect that would resurface and wield a telling influence over Disney's feature efforts done in that same vein during the 1940s by persistently troubling what many would see as their realist bias.

Of course, in animation's early days the hybrid approach was partially motivated simply by the need for various economies of production, the most obvious of which was that, by incorporating live-action elements, animators had to draw fewer images, thereby reducing costs and, in some instances, speeding up production. And in the 1940s such economies again became attractive, particularly at Disney, since budgets had become tighter, many skilled animators had been lost to the war effort, and the studio had committed much of its remaining resources to producing training and informational films for the government. In place of its labor- and cost-intensive full-length animated features of the prewar years, Disney developed a hybrid formula that would dominate its production for much of the decade, which resulted in such feature films as *The Reluctant Dragon* (1941), *The Three Caballeros* (1945), *Song of the South* (1946), *Fun and Fancy Free, Melody Time* (1948), and *So Dear to My Heart* (1949), among others. Often weakly constructed, these "package pictures," as they were known within the studio because of the way they packaged together various short cartoons, were typically episodic, often depended heavily on musical numbers, and used live-action scenes to link their animated sequences—or animation to link their live-action elements. Yet despite the live-action material, within the studio they were seldom considered to be particularly realistic or conventional efforts; rather, the veteran Disney animators Frank Thomas and Ollie Johnston recall that these projects were typically approached as "a showcase for . . . experimentation" (511).

The films were marketed in that same light, as distinctly innovative stylistic efforts, in keeping with the studio's growing public reputation for technical advances. Thus, the original theatrical trailer for *The Three Caballeros* describes its combination of live action and animation as "the newest thing to hit the movies since talking pictures came in." And an obvious publicity piece, a behind-the-scenes article in *Popular Science* preceding the film's release, refers to it as "another surprise from the Disney bag of tricks" ("How Disney" 107). Certainly there was something new to its techniques, particularly to the creation of a three-dimensional illusion in this and the following hybrid efforts. To create the complex imagery in *The Three Caballeros*, the studio claimed that it combined three photographic processes: the multiplane camera, a front-projection technique using the multiplane apparatus, and a new rear-projection process—offering a new level of interaction between the live-action and animated worlds and further eliding "the boundaries of the real and the unreal." What the *Popular Science* article failed to describe was its use of a new optical printer developed by Ub Iwerks that could seamlessly matte the animated figures into the live-action world, eliminating the image softness, graininess, and distortion that previously plagued hybrid scenes (Kaufman, *South of the Border* 203–4).

In spite of that technical complexity, critical response focused mainly on the situations created by its mixture of cartoon and human characters, that is, on what might be broadly termed figural relationships. One critic slams the film for its narrative, calling it "impossible to understand" (Brown 23), whereas the *Time* reviewer, commenting on Donald Duck's romantic pursuits of several live-action women, attacks its "alarmingly incongruous case of hot pants" ("*Three Caballeros*," 92). Even one of the most perceptive responses, that by Barbara Deming, quickly shifts from noting that its "techniques are mixed incongruously" (228) to suggesting that in the narrative Disney has "wrought something monstrous" (226) by placing Donald within a human world, one in which "boundaries fall apart" (229). Putting aside that spatial observation, though, she emphasizes her disappointment at Walt Disney's own "artlessness," his growing tendency to mirror the attitudes and values of his culture—one for which boundaries and certainties of every sort had indeed begun to disappear. Thus, she reads *The Three Caballeros* within the cultural context of late World War II America, a world wherein "values . . . are in conflict and in question," and she attributes both its stylistic and its thematic "incongruities" to the "nightmare of these times" (226).

Of course, Deming is correct with respect to "these times," as well as with the blurred boundaries they were producing. In keeping with the cultural situation created by the war, *The Three Caballeros* had been conceived as a film that would encourage a new level of inter-American friendship.[4] Yet it approaches that task in a way that surprisingly links its geographical concerns with the issues of space bound up in its complex creation, particularly the space of spectatorship. In fact, *The Three Caballeros* almost immediately strikes this note, as it begins with Donald Duck opening several presents from, as a card says, "his friends in Latin America," the first of which contains a movie projector, a screen, and several films. As he then runs these films, Donald immediately resituates himself from the status of a cartoon subject and inhabitant of the conventional space of animated narrative to, like Jiminy Crickett in *Fun and Fancy Free,* an unconventional spectator, in fact, a moviegoer himself. Here he looks into another world (south of the border), as if suddenly aware of a different space that these cartoons (or his *own* cartoons, for that matter) might make manifest, certainly a space of decided difference for America in the 1940s. These films and his status as viewer allow the thoroughly American duck to stake out a new territory, one in which he can unconventionally "meet" his friends from South America and see, apparently for the first time, the continent's varied realms, as well as some of the rara avises who inhabit them. At this point we can begin to glimpse how the film's key strategy, its paralleling of America's awakening to Latin America's importance with Donald's discovery of his new friends, coincides with its stylistic ambitions: its showcasing of that other, fantastic or warped space that animation exploits and makes available for our experience here, as well as Disney's own reawakening to and reexploration of the possibilities inherent in such cartooning.

The film's two other main stylistic turns further develop this stylistic "story," first by linking Donald to a pointedly nonrealistic style of animation, and then by juxtaposing him with real humans in the film's showcase hybrid scenes—those on which most critical commentaries have focused.[5] Though the two brief cartoons Donald watches, about Pablo the penguin and the Argentine boy Gauchito and his donkey-bird, are done in the typical Disney style of the period—soft, rounded figures set in a recognizably realistic context, and the exaggeration of specific traits or features to emphasize personality—both are really about aberrations, departures from the norm: a penguin who wants only to find a warmer place to live and a donkey with wings, both suggesting Latin America's exotic nature. Those strange stories, along with the opening of a second box, lead us away from a conventionally realistic and "cute" approach, as they bring the boisterous Brazilian parrot Joe Carioca, a pop-up book offering images of his country, and an invitation from Joe to go with him to Brazil, immediately introducing a shift in both style and content—as if the film were pointedly leaving behind conventional Disney animation and especially its typical spatial styling. For Joe suddenly and surrealistically multiplies, transforming into a row of images recalling the popular "Brazilian Bombshell," Carmen Miranda, all beckoning seductively to the duck and effectively exploding the sense of conventional personality. When Donald follows these fantastic images *into* the book, into a most unexpectedly "deep" composition, not only does he become a viewing subject—or tourist—within a pointedly viewed world—that of the picture book—but the visual style also radi-

The hybrid technique of *The Three Caballeros* creates various comic combinations of the human and the animated.

cally changes. For as he literally hops onto a train depicted on one page, the images become flat and hard-edged (the train even has one square wheel) and the color scheme over-saturated, all characteristics of Artistic Supervisor Mary Blair's distinctive style, which was, as John Canemaker has observed, "the polar opposite of the representational 'illusion of life'" aesthetic that had become associated with Disney in this period (ix). It is, very simply, a movement in depth where there *is* no apparent depth, a strike at the conventions of representation, and a reminder of the ways in which animation might open onto unexpected spaces and other worlds, thereby subverting our usual realist expectations.

That movement *into* a seemingly two-dimensional world rather surprisingly opens the door to another kind of spatial experience, the three-dimensional one of the hybrid scenes that dominate much of the rest of the film. These scenes, which employ both the front- and rear-projection techniques noted above, repeatedly involve Donald interacting with live characters—Aurora Miranda (posing as a cookie seller), a group of bathing beauties at the beach,[6] the popular Mexican singer Dora Luz, and the dancer Carmen Molina. In fact, the duck pursues the human women in each of these scenes, suggesting the sort of impossible sexual involvement that disturbed some viewers expecting the usual Disney fare and which precipitated several protesting reviews. Yet those pursuits are not the ultimate point here. Donald's repeated and comically underlined frustrations, which were by this time part of his well-established charac-

Aurora Miranda enters the animated space of Donald Duck and Joe Carioca in *The Three Caballeros* (1945).

ter, should have told audiences as much. Rather, these encounters are all about border crossings or boundary blurrings, about discovering the beauty, talent, and wonders of another world, about moving out from the secure space of the conventional spectator (implicitly, America's prevailing stance toward its "exotic" southern neighbors) to enter another space that beckons to us, as Carmen Molina repeatedly does to Donald. Those encounters, punctuated by all manner of quickly changing and reflexive images—Dora Luz as an image in Donald's eye, Donald transformed into the shifting lines of a film sound track, dancing cacti taking Donald's shape, and all parodying Busby Berkeley's spatially impossible, proscenium-bursting, self-conscious musical numbers—work very much in the tradition of the avant-garde to interrogate our own space, our own carefully bordered world, as well as our own cultural insularity. In so doing they pointedly emphasize one of this film's underlying impulses, its effort to recuperate an element of that earlier avant-garde spirit, the seeming abandonment of which had brought much criticism.[7]

Released the next year, *Song of the South* seems less marked by that spirit of "experimentation," less an obvious effort to recall the avant-garde tradition, although its key focus is also on fashioning a new vantage, in this case for young Johnny, its central character. And here too the film's stylistic experimentation, involving a greater emphasis on purely live action and nearly seamless transitional hybrid scenes, drew less attention than its cultural content—its racially charged adaptation of Joel Chandler Harris's Uncle Remus tales. A Disney poster for the film describes its combination of live action and animation as "An Epochal Event in Screen History," but the *Time* reviewer focused largely on the Uncle Remus character, a figure "bound to enrage all educated Negroes, and a number of damyankees" ("*Song*" 101). And that response was consistent with a marked change in critical perspective on Disney, as postwar commentators began to shift focus from aesthetic issues to what Eric Smoodin terms "broader ideological ones"—questions interrogating Disney's implicit attitudes toward nationalities, gender representation, and race (104). In fact, Smoodin insightfully suggests that this shift may ironically have been abetted by "the inclusion of more realism—both drawn and live-action" in the Disney films (106), as if the turn to hybrid techniques had cast these ideological issues into relief, even made them almost unavoidable.[8]

And perhaps they were unavoidable, given the flimsy live-action story with its separating husband and wife and the son who turns for consolation and guidance to Uncle Remus, a figure vaguely linked to the grandmother's plantation. Because it is weakly plotted, context becomes all, and that context, particularly the sense of place, is that of a rural plantation, peopled with servile blacks and a benevolent white mistress, and apparently isolated from the conflicted realities of its post–Civil War South setting. Though it seems a context that the studio sought to frame not so much nostalgically as almost abstractly, as a kind of historical never-never land, the cultural weight of the live action undercuts the appeal of its hybrid scenes and their alternative stylistic thrust. The narrative, however, pointedly establishes that this world is meant to be an escape from the real, a place where Johnny and his mother go to get away from some vaguely described unpleasantness back home in Atlanta, where "everybody's mad about what Daddy writes in the newspaper." It seems the family is being split because the father is challenging the status quo and, despite his wife's pleadings, is determined to go back and face that situation after safely depositing his family in this country backwater, in the safe isolation he experienced as a child. Thus, Johnny finds himself in a home that is not his home, one filled with problems that he too cannot avoid—a bitter and overprotective mother, two harassing neighbor boys, and a bull that nearly kills him. Neither the hybrid scenes nor the animated tales of Brer Rabbit, however, satisfactorily resolve these concerns of place and space, bring Johnny to an acceptable home, or link the space of the imagination, represented by Uncle Remus's tales, to that of the real world, embodied in his parents' and the postwar South's troubles. In short, though Uncle Remus tries to shift the child's way of seeing this world and though the film suggests our own need to change perspective, to challenge a conventional point of view, even conventional racial attitudes, the real world remains very much with us.

Yet emphasizing the links between the animated and real worlds, what we might term a *reciprocity* of space, seems like the film's key concern, as its opening and the various packaged cartoon episodes suggest. *Song of the South* starts with an image of the interior of Uncle Remus's cabin, lit so that we cannot be sure if it is real or animated, and accompanied by his voice setting out a coda for the film: "Just 'cause these here tales is about critters like Brer Rabbit and Brer Fox, that don't mean they ain't the same like can happen to folks. So them that can't learn from a tale about critters just ain't got their ears tuned for listenin'." It is a warning, of course, to "tune" our ears—and eyes—correctly for what follows, so that we can better appreciate the correspondences between the animated and the real, the worlds of "critters" and "folks," and also better understand the rather hazy boundaries between the two. The subsequent hybrid scenes, easily some of the studio's most successful efforts in this area, underscore that linkage in their nearly seamless nature. When Uncle Remus walks from the background to a mid-frame fence rail and leans on it to talk to an animated Brer Rabbit in the foreground, it is almost impossible to tell where the real rail ends and the animated one begins. But that blurring of boundaries was an integral part of the film's visual design scheme; as Thomas and Johnston explain, "The 'real' parts were only theatrical sets . . . and had been designed with flat surfaces and simple shapes so they would match the drawings that had to be part of the whole composition" (524–25). When Brer Rabbit subsequently jumps onto the mid-frame fence and then beyond it, into the "real" area occupied by Uncle Remus's body, he not only underscores that careful matching, but also prepares us for the narrative exploitation of what is essentially a new sort of space, since he then hops into the background, the area from which Uncle Remus had emerged (thus previously testifying to its reality), and in the process takes us into a

Uncle Remus interacts with cartoon characters in *The Song of the South*'s (1946) combination of stylized sets and animation.

fully animated shot, into the cartoon story wherein, just as he determines to leave his home behind, he finds himself caught in Brer Fox's trap and must use his wits to escape. It is, of course, a variation on Johnny's own plan to run away, as Uncle Remus's moral underscores: "You can't run away from trouble. There ain't no place that far." But just as important, it speaks to our situation as well, as we find ourselves, albeit pleasurably, also caught up in a trap, that of the film's hybrid scheme, which has made it practically impossible to parse out real space from animated. And within that subtly subversive trap, within this new space, we are essentially compelled to make the connections between the realms of "critters" and "folks," and to begin to see our world in a very different way.

That design scheme, along with its implications, carries through the rest of the film's hybrid scenes, as borders constantly dissolve and the real and animated spaces become contiguous and mutually interrogating. For instance, leading into his tale of the Tar Baby, Uncle Remus appears walking from deep background into an animated foreground, where he encounters Brer Rabbit. In fact, Brer Rabbit hops all around him, over and under various fences, and, at one point, even from background to foreground *through* Uncle Remus's legs, before Uncle Remus stops to fish and casts his obviously animated line into an animated pond in the foreground, a move that, through a dissolve, casts *us* into a fully animated sequence wherein Brer Rabbit heads down the road and falls into Brer Fox's Tar Baby trap. The introduction to the tale of the Laughing Place is more abrupt, but the link is no less pointed. In this case when a crying Johnny comes to Uncle Remus for consolation, a close-up of his sad face simply dissolves into the image of Brer Rabbit, also in a sad state—tied up by Brer Fox and Brer Bear, who are about to roast him. Yet the conclusion of this tale more emphatically links the animated and live-action worlds, as Brer Rabbit, laughing at Brer Fox and Brer Bear, throws handfuls of leaves into the air, and, through a dissolve, those same animated leaves seem to bridge worlds, as they come down all around a similarly laughing Uncle Remus who assures his listeners, Johnny and his friend Ginny, that they too have a "laughing place" somewhere. The film ends on a similar note, as Uncle Remus, Johnny, and Ginny walk down a road, are soon joined by a variety of animated animals—all of whom cast realistic shadows and interact with the live actors—and eventually move into a landscape that dissolves into a perfectly matched animated one, recalling the opening shot of Uncle Remus's cabin and complete with the naturalistic depth effects created by the multiplane camera. The animated world, the world of the imagination, it seems, easily opens up new space to those willing to shift their perspective, or as Uncle Remus says, become "tuned" to it, as the concluding transformation from real to animated suggests that *we* are by this point.

The film, however, clearly offers a kind of forced jointure, one we are cast into like Uncle Remus's fishing line or caught up in as if in Brer Fox's trap, something constructed by the skill of the storyteller—Uncle Remus—as well as by Disney's skilled animators and technicians. The reflexive dimension of the narrative is simply inescapable. The real spaces here—of far away and trouble-bound Atlanta, of the grandmother's elaborate plantation house, of the meager cabins and campfires of the black workers, of the poor white sharecropper's cottage occupied by Ginny and her family, of the bull's pasture—are pointedly distinct realms, separated by physical distance, by real-world troubles, by social taboos, even by fences. And crossing those spaces, as Johnny does when he ducks under the fence surrounding the bull's pasture, only invites trouble—in fact, nearly gets him killed. *Song of the South,* for all its technical accomplishments, never quite manages to reconcile these real-world borders with the boundary-busting spirit of its hybrid scenes and, as a consequence, for all its ambitions never escapes the ghostly anxieties bound up in the different spaces it depicts—never escapes *reality itself.* And as this film's subsequent history tells us, the studio's efforts at boundary crossing, despite what were probably good intentions, only invited troubles for it.

Still, *Song of the South* seems to be working out, if somewhat unconvincingly, the essential Disney concern of this era and one not too far removed from the modernist project: to demonstrate that there is another, more promising world alongside our own, if only we can shift perspective to see it. Not simply our own "laughing place," it is the space of the imagination, inviting us, in at least a nod toward the avant-garde tradition, to compare its topography to that in which we live—here shown as a world of fences, economic barriers, racial prejudice, and cultural boundaries, all of which the film invites us to challenge. And that project continued in *Fun and Fancy Free,* although it is approached differently, almost perfunctorily, as if Disney had by this time begun to recognize how nearly impossible it was becoming to mix that modernist impulse with its illusion-of-life aesthetic, at least within a feature context. Despite the reflexive framing scenes we earlier describe, this film is, on the whole, far less "experimental" than the hybrid types preceding it. And the critical reception only confirmed that this formula was not going to work for a changing postwar audience. In fact, Stephen Watts characterizes the response to this film as "outright hostility" (250); the reviewer for the *New Yorker* saw it as evidence that the studio in this period seemed to be "determinedly aiming at mediocrity" (21).

Yet *Fun and Fancy Free* hardly merits that charge of "mediocrity." Though it packages two conventional—and conventionally realistic— cartoons, it does so with that clever reflexive twist of the animated Jiminy Crickett looking in on the live-action human world, prodding us to reassess the normal spectator-spectacle relationship. In fact, the film frames much of its "package" with similar effects. To introduce the first cartoon sequence, the story of Bongo the bear, Jiminy makes his way through an apparent jungle, actually an indoor plant display whose nature we cannot make out because we see it from up close and thus lack perspective and a sense of scale. We recognize it only when, in a long shot, Jiminy catapults himself from an animated plant leaf into a hybrid scene of a real room and a shelf of real books, whose titles he

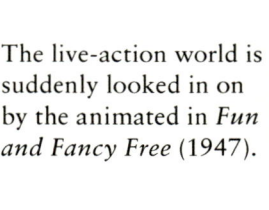

The live-action world is suddenly looked in on by the animated in *Fun and Fancy Free* (1947).

then inspects—titles like *Misery for the Masses* and *Anatomy of Melancholy*—before launching into the narration of a very unmelancholy cartoon about the bear who manages to escape from the gilded prison of his life as an exploited circus performer. Following the second cartoon segment, the story of Mickey, Goofy, and Donald ascending a beanstalk to find wealth, only to be pursued by an angered giant, another sudden spatial shift occurs. As we return to the live-action party, Edgar Bergen, Luana Patten, Charlie McCarthy, and Mortimer Snerd discuss the story, obviously missing its subversive implications, decide that it is, after all, just a "figment of the imagination," and thus reassert a boundary between the real and the imagined, just as the adults repeatedly try to do in *Song of the South*. But at that point, the roof of the house—now animated—is lifted off by Willie, the cartoon story giant, who peers in, excuses himself, and then heads off into the landscape to continue "looking for a little mouse," as he announces. The boundary between animated and live worlds having literally been lifted away, the film then closes with an extreme long shot of the famous Hollywood sign blinking in the background and Willie, the animated figure, continuing his search in this tentatively "real" environment and leaving us with a very different perspective on our world: not just the narrative sense of how difficult it is to find freedom or wealth here, but, given this new sense of space and the obvious constructions of Hollywood, a stylistic reminder of how elusive the real is, and how *illusive* all

153

that movie culture constructs for us also is. Certainly a clever ending and one consistent with the other reflexive framing scenes here, it nevertheless feels a bit like a trick that has too little connection to the two framed stories, much like the opening images of Jiminy Crickett. It simply catapults us into a hybrid world and forces us to acknowledge the relationship of real and fantastic spaces, even as it allows that such connections are part of an increasingly cinematized world.

Yet this acknowledgment may be the most important element of the conclusion, since it obviously emphasizes the way in which all these hybrid efforts, in various ways, seek to mine one of the underlying appeals of animation. As Michael O'Pray has argued, "In animation, at its best, we thrill to the means of representation and not only the representation" (201), and here the "thrill" bound up in the artistry of these films is constantly underscored. Despite that element of self-consciousness, these films also have another sort of fallout that might shed some light on their relatively weak or troubled receptions. For in different ways they also subtly undermine another pleasure of the animated spectacle by reminding us of a problem implicit in those different spaces, one made quite explicit in the middle of *Fun and Fancy Free,* as the animated viewers—Jiminy and Willie—also call into question the substance of our own space, thereby qualifying our satisfaction in a key part of the animation experience. O'Pray adds that a "desire for omnipotence" is also central to animation's satisfactions, as it demonstrates "that the skill and virtuosity involved in form is supreme" (200)—and human. The reflexive impulse here, however, ultimately threatens to empty out the whole process of representation, to show it all to be a kind of game.

Though this revealing of film's own power of illusion recalls something of the modernist agenda, it also points to a sort of functional paradox inevitably bound up in these films that many saw simply as new efforts at approaching the real. Thus, Watts sees the hybrid films as evidence of Walt Disney's "desperate search for direction" in the postwar era (250), but we might view them more as a revealing gauge of his studio's efforts at working out the apparent contradictions between the realist and avant-garde trajectories in which it was involved, or perhaps even more tellingly, between a troubled modernist attitude and an emerging one with which Disney was not quite ready to engage. For all of those efforts to dissolve boundaries, to "cast" one space into another, to "catapult" from one realm to another also suggest the sort of "space compression" that David Harvey sees as a hallmark of a developing postmodernism (305).[9] However, once generally committed to a more naturalistic studio style and to feature film production, Disney was—despite a number of efforts—never quite able to find a formula for recouping that experimental spirit, or to map out a path to the other kinds of space that would increasingly characterize contemporary animation and that would be more effectively addressed by a number of other animation studios.

7

WHAT'S UP—AND DOWN—DOC?

Warner Bros., Chuck Jones, and Abstract Space

Though for many people in the 1930s and 1940s Disney was the standard by which animation was judged, Warner Bros., with its Looney Tunes and Merrie Melodies cartoons, would increasingly challenge that preeminence in the post–World War II era. In fact, as Timothy White chronicles, the widespread praise of Disney animation, largely for its "level of sheer craftsmanship" (40), began to wane precisely as the Warner Bros. stable of characters—Bugs Bunny, Daffy Duck, Porky Pig, and many others—developed and began to win a popular audience. But that popularity was due to more than just the nature of those figures, which were noticeably more frantic, more anarchic, and ultimately funnier than Disney's. They were characters that inhabited a very different world; as Barry Putterman has observed, it is a "noticeably nonnaturalistic" environment (33), one that could never be confused with the supposedly realistic spaces for which, as we have seen, a number of commentators had already begun to criticize Disney. Yet that "nonnaturalistic" epithet only begins to suggest the nature of the difference here. In the Warner Bros. cartoons, particularly those of the late 1940s and the 1950s, we see animating space itself undergoing a radical change; in some cases, as in the celebrated Daffy Duck cartoon *Duck Amuck* (1953), it becomes completely unstable and even seems to disappear, at one point leaving Daffy lost and purposeless in a plain white frame, but in the process opening up a new level of meaning for the cartoon.

White suggests that the shift in critical estimation ultimately owes much to the rise of European art films in the 1950s and 1960s, with their own radically different treatment of character, but a more complete assessment would need to take into account the rise of—and increasing cultural fascination with—what Amid Amidi terms the "cartoon modern."[1] Certainly the art film, as typified by such works as *L'Avventura* (1960), *Last Year at Marienbad* (1961), and *My Life to Live* (1962), would often present characters as ciphers and space as an almost abstract rendering of lines and surfaces, while reflexively shooting holes in conventional cinema's reality illusion. And the Warner Bros. product, especially the cartoons created by Chuck Jones, played with many of these same effects. Yet they were doing so and already attracting attention with their deliberately designed worlds and their "more stylized, often abstract approach to movement" (Amidi 10) before many of the European auteurs of the New Wave had even begun to work in film.

Often associated more with the work of United Productions of America (UPA) and its briefly popular Gerald McBoing Boing and, later, its Mr. Magoo films, cartoon modern drew heavily on a variety of earlier art movements—cubism, surrealism, expressionism—all of which in various ways had launched assaults on conventional realism and its common spatial illusion. There was a sense, as Amidi suggests, that in much animation, but especially that emanating from the Disney studio, the drive for such realism had been at too great a cost, that it had eventually "trumped the graphic possibilities inherent in the art form" (9). By adapting principles drawn from these art movements and even pushing their potential, however, animators hoped to reconnect with this neglected graphic vein, not only opening up new spaces after the fashion of the modernist project described by Vidler and others, but virtually exploding the conventional space of animation.

In the new, graphically driven cartoons that resulted—the work emanating from UPA, much of the Warner Bros. output during this period, and even some of Disney's efforts, notably cartoons directed by Ward Kimball—we can easily see the influence of this stylistic turn. Characters become line-drawn caricatures, traditional perspective practically disappears, and various elements of the designed mise-en-scène seem to vie for attention with the often motionless or limited-motion characters to which the animation studios were increasingly turning. Though in these efforts space never quite "vanishes," as Paul Virilio puts it (*Lost* 34), it does seem to become practically hidden within the larger design scheme, or radically "collapsed," as David Harvey proposes (293). Chronicling this changing nature of spatial representation in the late modern period, Stephen Kern describes how negative space—the space of background, of contrast, of "negative" function—became for many artists "positive negative space," as space took on "a positive, constitutive function" (153). In a similar vein and speaking to a slightly later period, Amidi suggests that in cartoon modern "emptiness had become a positive value" (11).

As an initial illustration of this development of designed space, we might consider one of the most celebrated Warner Bros. cartoons of the postwar era, *What's Opera, Doc?* (1957). This Chuck Jones effort opens its send-up of classical opera with a radically stylized imagery, as splotches of blue and black intersect with angular lightning bolts, which eventually form an abstract landscape of jutting mountains set at odd angles. Against a central jagged peak, we then see a massive shadow of a helmeted figure with arms outstretched, dominating the "landscape" and suggesting, along with the opening's heroic Wagnerian music, that this wild mountain is a very appropriate measure for this equally majestic character, one whose imposing size we can gauge only by this menacing shadow projected into the frame's depth. Of course, no Warner Bros. cartoon, particularly in its "golden era" of the 1940s–1950s, would ever have allowed such inflated expectations to stand for more than a moment. And this awesome imagery is simply the first of many visual gags here, as we see when the "camera" booms down to a very small figure of improbably heroic nature—Elmer Fudd—who has cast this giant shadow, a figure further dwarfed by the armor he wears, including a "magic" helmet that swallows his head and neck, rendering his usual egg-shaped cranium pointy-headed, as if in mocking honor of the film's elevated subject matter. Yet this elaborately constructed opening offers more than just a series of visual surprises and puns. Here space itself becomes dramatic and fools the eye, whereas the figure seems almost an

In *What's Opera, Doc?* (1957) Chuck Jones offers audiences a radically stylized imagery.

afterthought, a punch line. It is an effective inversion of expectations, but one that points toward the role that space had come to play in the studio's cartoons, and particularly the extent to which its best cartoons, with their stylized and constructed spaces, were beginning to situate themselves between an older modern and an emerging postmodern aesthetic.

Part of that situating is immediately apparent in this opening scene. For it not only plays with—even as it quickly deflates—our visual expectations, but also depends on our expectations of depth to construct its gags. Esther Leslie has observed how the modernist impulse resulted, across a wide range of the arts but especially in animation, in various efforts "to depict flatness and loss of volume. . . . The surface overlays the content, form is torn into deformation, and, frequently, colour glares out instead of delighting in delicate modulations of hue" (50). Yet in its efforts to approach the look of a realist art and to model itself on the conventions of classical film narrative, animation had in various ways—through multiplane camera devices, increased emphasis on perspective, the widespread adoption of the Technicolor process, and a focus on personality animation (on "depth" of character)—moved away from what she generically labels flatland. And Warner Bros. was, for much of the 1930s, no different; in fact, as Gene Walz has shown, like most other animation units in this period, it apparently "accepted the challenge of conforming" to a style that had become primarily associated with the industry leader, Disney, even modeling some of its characters on ones created at Disney.[2]

Yet as is quite obvious even in the much later Warner Bros. effort *What's Opera, Doc?* that movement was hardly permanent. For here we quickly recognize that the depth producing Elmer's giant shadow is simply a trick, just one element in a mechanism that works with conventional perspective to construct a most misleading "reality" and, more important, an effective joke *about* that reality. The otherwise flat, even self-conscious graphics of the composition point to an interesting dynamic between the conventions for producing a three-dimensional world and an insistent two-dimensionality—a dynamic that we might see as a hallmark of late Warner Bros. style, and especially of the work of what many consider its preeminent stylist, Chuck Jones.

Though there is much of flatland about *What's Opera, Doc?* we should also note that there is another sort of offscreen space—and depth—implied here but omitted in this initial description. As the very title *What's Opera, Doc?* hints, and as a long tradition in Warner Bros. animation might lead us to expect, the cartoon is ultimately *about* performance: a radically condensed version of Wagner's *Ring of the Nibelung*.[3] Even the film's final lines hint of this impression, for as Elmer carries Bugs Bunny's seemingly lifeless body into the background—an injury he has caused by calling down lightning on the "wascally wabbit"—and is himself apparently carried away by operatically exaggerated emotion at this loss, the rabbit suddenly comes back to life, turns to the audience, and notes, "Well, what did you expect in an opera, a happy ending?" That final acknowledgment of an audience, that address to the offscreen space that it—and we—implicitly inhabits, recalls a great many Warner Bros. cartoons that not only present their stock characters as performers, but also depict, often as silhouetted onlookers or as a vague mass of unmoving figures, a diegetic audience for their performance. In *Rhapsody Rabbit* (1946), for example, Bugs is repeatedly interrupted as he begins a piano recital by a coughing audience member, never seen but pointedly situated in what the cartoon establishes, through its emphasis on the stage proscenium, as the space occupied by the concert audience. His patience with the cougher worn thin, Bugs pulls out a pistol, aims into that offscreen space, and shoots the

offending spectator. In that reflexive play between the performing character and audience, and thus in that comically violent effort to maintain
the barrier between the onscreen and offscreen worlds, *Rhapsody Rabbit,* like many other films, including *A Corny Concerto* (1943), *Stage
Door Cartoon* (1944), *Hair Raising Hare* (1946), *Rabbit of Seville*
(1950), and *Show Biz Bugs* (1957), draws out the humorous potential of
those two spaces, and particularly of the manifest differences between
them. In effect, it admits difference, while establishing its narrative
action, in a postmodern fashion, as a kind of game played with the reality illusion that is at the heart of all film, including animation.

Yet with *What's Opera, Doc?* that sense of difference, along with
the audience itself, practically disappears, leaving us in an abstract
world. And that absence is significant, for the audience depicted in such
films does more than, as Hank Sartin suggests, "provide . . . a diegetic
relay for our pleasure" (74); it also produces its own sense of reality, the
reality of a performance that is underscored by the constructed depth
between the narrative action and the onscreen audience. With that audience's absence here, we better see the stylistic trajectory of later Warner
Bros. cartoons, as depth flattens out, the artifice of the stage becomes a
primary reference point, and performance collapses into the narrative,
at least until Bugs's final—and unmotivated—look of outward regard
and closing line that construct us in the place of that usual onscreen
audience. Hence, an improbable topography (like the starkly conceived
mountain backdrops), exaggerated figures (such as the horse with bul-
bous flanks and stick legs), stylized actions and mock motivations ("Kill
the wabbit! Kill the wabbit!"), and (badly) sung dialogue all form a kind
of coherent, if pointedly pastichelike and decidedly comic, "reality."
The game is everything here, as the cartoon's primary point of reference
becomes artifice itself—the worlds of opera and ballet most obviously,
but also other films, as the title's play on the character of Bugs Bunny
immediately suggests, as well as Chuck Jones's assertion that *What's
Opera, Doc?* was, after all, just a thinly veiled "satire of *Fantasia*"
(Furniss, *Chuck Jones* 112), after the fashion of the studio's earlier film
A Corny Concerto. As a result, even though this film stylistically seems
to revisit the formal flatness of much earlier animation, suggesting its
kinship to a cinema wherein "everything in the drawn world is of the
same stuff" (Leslie 23), it also finally winks at that modernist vision, as

it tries to establish not only a different sense of space, but also a different use for that space.

The real claim of this film, as well as of Jones's other late work, I suggest, is its emerging postmodern aesthetic. It is one wherein the animated image does not simply strike at the natural, at the representational—or, perhaps more accurately, at the conventions of representation both within and outside the cinema—but suggests that the natural is always largely an effect or a gag waiting to be seen, part of the larger "set" in which our lives, no less than those of the cartoon characters, are played out. In such a context, depth, that early yardstick of the two-dimensional world's yearnings and failings (depending on one's ideological vantage), becomes not just an effect, but also what might be described as a kind of affectation, an important dimension of the larger gag, as Warners' cartoon efforts—if not as a house style, then as a recurrent and in Jones's work a dominant pattern—would increasingly demonstrate.

To better map out this trajectory, we might first consider Friz Freleng's *You Ought to Be in Pictures* (1940) because of the unique way, for Warner Bros. cartoons, that it tries to situate its narrative between different levels of reality by combining live action with animation. It is a singular effort at employing the hybrid cartoon style that we have already observed in the work of the Fleischers and especially in the Disney package features of the 1940s; moreover, it marks a clear shift from the dominant Warner Bros. animation style of the previous decade —a shift anticipated as well by another graphically inventive film, Bob Clampett's *Porky in Wackyland* (1938). In *You Ought to Be in Pictures* two of the studio's "stars," Porky Pig and Daffy Duck, who would increasingly be paired in cartoons, maneuver for better roles in both cartoons and live-action features, as the action takes place within the real offices of the producer Leon Schlesinger and on the lot of the Warner Bros. Studio. The cartoon actors' interactions with the animators, a studio guard, and especially Schlesinger himself play up their own claims on solidity, even as the film's comparison—and suggested equation—of animated and live-action films places both within a larger fantasy context.

In discussing this film, Leonard Maltin notes an interesting psychological dimension it implicates, as he suggests that *You Ought to Be in*

Pictures "capitalizes on the wonderful fantasy" involved in all animated cartoons, that is, on a collision between things and characters that we know are not real and our own inherent pleasure in, even our desire "to suspend logic and believe, even if for just a few minutes, that they exist" (*Of Mice* 238). In this instance, the film enhances this appeal by high-lighting it, by acknowledging it, thereby undercutting any audience pro-test. In fact, belief—and the willing suspension of disbelief—is everything in this cartoon. We want to believe in the characters, in this case, Porky and Daffy, and the live-action characters in the film, including Leon Schlesinger, support that desire by manifestly believing in and interact-ing with them. In support of that illusion, a Warners director, inter-rupted while shooting, chases Porky off his soundstage; a security guard bodily throws Porky, along with his car, off the Warner Bros. lot; and Schlesinger holds these characters under contract, just as the studio does stars like Errol Flynn and Bette Davis. In similar fashion, we want to believe in the world of the movies, even though it is manifestly a world of artifice, convention, and generic storytelling—all characteristics cited within this cartoon narrative. And that belief is affirmed by the ani-mated characters who also believe in it and are attracted, just as audi-ences are, by the glamour and power of the movies. Thus, Porky is easily lured by the prospect Daffy dangles before him, of "a job in features, as Bette Davis' leading man, at three grand a week," although once he experiences some of the dangers of the lot, including getting caught up in a live-action western land-rush scene, he seems to find their reality a bit too much for him and rushes back to the relative safety—and visual simplicity—of his cartoon world.

What may be the most important element of belief here, though, is Daffy Duck's understanding of the *power* of these beliefs, of the hold that these illusions have on us all. For the plot, what there is of it, simply turns on Daffy's easy ability to manipulate Porky's gullibility—convinc-ing him to have Schlesinger tear up his contract so that he might pursue bigger opportunities in live-action films—while Daffy, in turn, tries to convince the producer that he should be cast in bigger things, better roles, have a more prominent place in this world of Looney Tunes illu-sions. That turnabout is, of course, quite in keeping with his "daffy" character, a figure who is, as Michael Barrier styles him, "sane-but-hysterical" (463), often scheming but at such a high pitch that his

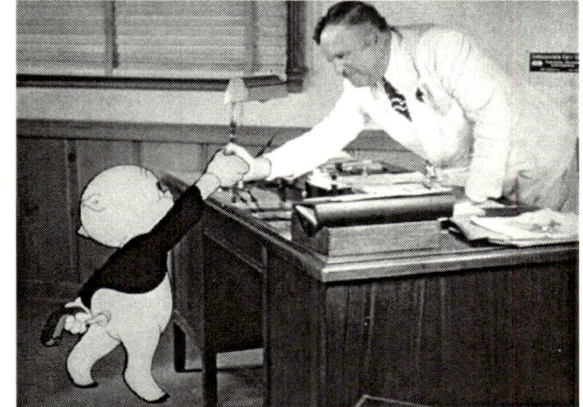

Porky interacts with his "boss," Leon Schlesinger, in *You Ought to Be in Pictures* (1940).

schemes always seem beyond belief, as if he inhabits a quite different reality. But his ability to "sell" those schemes, to continue constructing a reality and promoting belief in it, lasts to the very end of the cartoon. For even after Porky has seen through his manipulations, reaffirmed his contract with Schlesinger, and beaten the duck for his trickery, he persists in offering one last hot tip to Porky, this time for a possible starring role with the even more unlikely Greta Garbo.[4] That persistence certainly comments on a foolish consistency in Daffy's character—the very stuff of most cartoon characters—but it also points to our own tendency to cling to those illusions, our readiness to buy into the world and the fantasies that the movies construct for us.

Of course, the film's ultimate argument for belief, especially for belief in its peculiar sort of reality, rests in its hybrid approach, which allows it to forge a convincing interaction of animated and live action, using the real people, locations, and events to cast its actually scant cartoon elements into a seemingly three-dimensional world. In a nod to an early tradition of cartooning, the film initially offers a shot of an animator's hand sketching Porky to establish a stark distinction between the real and the animated. It quickly becomes apparent, however, that the hand itself is nothing more than a cutout, a photograph of a real hand that is being animated along with the successively more complete images of Porky, suggesting not just his animation, but also a level on which both drawn and live are similarly constructed, equally "drawn" from nothing. And it is a suggestion reaffirmed by a variety of subsequent scenes: the cartooning of the live-action animators who—with a call for "Lunch!"—all crowd out of a single studio door in speeded-up action, much as cartoon characters might; the shots of Leon Schlessinger's office, on the walls of which we see framed portraits of both drawn and real figures; the caricaturing of the studio guard (played by the cartoon story man Michael Maltese), who is given an exaggerated and not-quite-synchronized voice by Mel Blanc, the cartoon voice artist; and the scenes on the Warner Bros. lot, where Porky watches the production of the highly artificial world of a Busby Berkeley–style musical. All emphasize that in the "Home of Looney Tunes/Merrie Melodies"—as the first shot informs us—we should expect to find no easy distinction between the drawn and the live. "Real" space and animating space prove equally elusive and illusive.

In fact, *You Ought to Be in Pictures* repeatedly uses one of its hybrid elements—either the animated or the live-action image—in isolation to argue that we accept the reality of the other. Porky's interaction with the Warner Bros. studio guard, for example, consists mainly of a series of subjective and reaction shots, as in successive shots each figure looks in the direction of and addresses the other, their respective eyelines conventionally fixing the presence of the other for subsequent shots, underscoring the way in which cinematic conventions effectively construct for us both spatiality and a nonexistent reality, and thus the extent to which we buy into those conventions. And when Porky returns to the cartoon studio and proceeds to repay Daffy for his trickery, it occurs in an interior office space, just off camera, and is measured out for us by solid objects. Various papers, a notebook, and a chair come flying out of that office, as the real testifies to the unseen cartoon violence, allowing this offscreen, insubstantial action to transpire in what we accept to be real physical space.

If *You Ought to Be in Pictures* opens up an interesting avenue for interrogating the space of animation—well preceding Disney's more mature and ambitious projects in this hybrid vein later in the decade—then it is a path that Warner Bros. never really pursued, at least until the studio became part of the larger Time-Warner media conglomerate and began plundering its past to produce a series of homogenized hybrid efforts such as *Space Jam* (1996).[5] Other cartoons, however, would exploit its ground situation, reflexively focusing on the nature of animation and depicting the studio's stock characters as quite conscious of their place as constructed figures living within a constructed—and easily erased—world. The most imaginative and probably most famous of these is Chuck Jones's *Duck Amuck,* which presents Daffy as a figure frustrated because he is completely at the mercy of an unseen cartoonist who quickly shifts and eventually removes backgrounds, leaving him in a stark white space, implicitly the paper of a cartoonist's sketch pad, or who erases sections of his body and then draws new, mismatched elements, turning him into various surreal hybrids. The godlike figure who imposes all these transformations remains out of frame, unseen until the final shot, when a pull-back reveals this tormentor-creator to be not a live-action animator but his colleague and competitor, Bugs Bunny. Creating a kind of *mise-en-abyme,* Bugs turns to the camera and admits his agency—and implicitly his own greater level of reality—with a winking "Ain't I a stinker?" Yet Bugs's reality proves no more substantial when he suffers from similar indignities in the later *Rabbit Rampage* (1955), which presents the rabbit as equally at the mercy of a cartoonist's whims. But as *What's Opera, Doc?* has already reminded us, this sort of reflexive development consistently proved both an inspiration and focus for Warner Bros. cartoons, as performances, impressions, asides to the audience, and even depictions of audiences figure into so many of these efforts, all by way of presenting the world, the space of animated action, as insubstantial, as little more than a movie or stage set.

Moreover, that reflexive impulse itself opens up an interesting approach to narrative space within these films, as the areas occupied by both the diegetic audience the cartoons often depicted and the film spectators who are just as frequently addressed via signs and character asides become analogous to the space of the narrative action—even its constantly transmuting space in *Duck Amuck*—producing a kind of uncanny sense of space. But another reason that reflexive dimension came to seem so appropriate for these films is that, as the Warner Bros. cartoons became more obviously "designed," they frequently appear to be almost formally structured around spatial concepts—concepts that question the issue of animation, of giving life to empty space. Though the later 1940s and 1950s would see cartoons at many studios following the trend toward this more graphic or designed style—the cartoon modern, as we have referred to it—many of the Warner Bros. efforts had already codified new approaches to space both by stylizing their imagery and by framing their narratives around what we might think of as spatial conceits, such as the rabbit hole in the case of Bugs Bunny or the yawning canyons of the Road Runner and Wile E. Coyote series.

Even in his first screen appearance in the Ben Hardaway–Cal Dalton film *Porky's Hare Hunt* (1938), Bugs Bunny is consistently connected to an almost magical ability to appear and disappear—into a tree stump, into a hollow tree, into a hole in some rocks, and, perhaps most tellingly, into an upturned top hat that is treated like a magician's prop. In fact, after popping out of the hat and then using it to make Porky's hunting dog disappear, the rabbit too disappears to the soundtrack tune of "Hooray for Hollywood," a clue that this character and the world he inhabits are cut from the same cloth as other Hollywood products—all from a world of illusions. And in subsequent films that locus of appearance-disappearance would increasingly become the conventional rabbit hole, a key development for these narratives. Typically, it indicates both the rabbit's unseen position—literally his home, but more important the place at which adventures seem to start—and his special, magical ability to move at will and unseen, as the hole becomes literally a sign of his tunneling capacity and thus metaphorically of his ability to suddenly appear, without reason or excuse, almost anywhere.

Describing his work as an animation director, Chuck Jones helps explain the importance of this sort of spatial development. He notes that "the purpose of a great designer is to design an area where the actor can perform. Or the animator can perform. And where the action shows itself to its best advantage" (Furniss, *Chuck Jones* 60). That approach to spatial design shows especially clearly in his *Homeless Hare* (1950), a cartoon that is effectively built around the locus of Bugs's rabbit hole, a bit of nature incongruously situated in the heart of a metropolis and about to be bulldozed to make room for yet another skyscraper. When what Bugs refers to as "the sanctity of the American home" is violated by Hercules, a burly construction worker, a typical "war" begins, one in which the rabbit and the worker fight amid the skyscraper's bare girders, its skeletal structure providing an abstract battleground that starkly contrasts to Bugs's solid, earthy home. Of course, the conclusion to this sort of battle is foregone, long before Bugs offers his ultimatum, "Do I get my home back or do I have to get tough?" And the film ends with a track down the side of the newly completed skyscraper to depict a compromise in space: an indentation in the building's facade, a quite literal warping around a patch of ground holding Bugs's hole that is marked, as is so often the case in these cartoons, by his mailbox, which serves both as a proprietary notice and as a kind of warning sign for any who might threaten that spot or underestimate the power in that hole.

In fact, what makes this admittedly slim narrative noteworthy is not its simple story of violation and reprisal, or even its interesting evocation of the threatened American home. Rather, it is the warping power of that hole: its challenge to the seemingly substantial modern world that we see being constructed, and its—and Bugs's—ability to deconstruct that conventional space. Bugs, as the magical and assuredly pugnacious inhabitant of that underground realm, not only reminds us of the shaky foundation on which our reality is constructed, but also cautions against taking that base too lightly. His hole, in short, is always much more than a hole or home; it marks the uncanny dimension of our world, under assault by all manner of forces that take themselves and their reality too seriously: construction workers like those in *Homeless Hare*, the prying eye of a mad scientist in *Hair Raising Hare* (1946), Wile E. Coyote in *Operation: Rabbit* (1952), a hungry Tazmanian Devil in *Devil May Hare* (1953), and especially the guns of numerous rabbit hunters, as in *Rabbit Seasoning* (1951) and many other cartoons.

A far more complex film conceptually, *Rabbit Seasoning* adds a further design dimension to this effort at narratizing space. One of what is referred to as Chuck Jones's "hunting trilogy" of films (the others being *Rabbit Fire*, 1951, and *Duck, Rabbit, Duck*, 1953), it introduces Bugs's hole not as some minor space, but as precisely what it is for any Bugs Bunny cartoon—a central point of attraction, the real jumping-off point for the narrative. The cartoon opens on a variety of signs, posters, banners, and even fake footprints all directing our attention—and that of the prospective rabbit hunter Elmer Fudd—to Bugs's home (complete with its identifying mailbox), deep in the forest. All these signposts are, on the one hand, a trick played by Daffy who, in an aside, notes that he just wants "to have some fun," while trying to hide the fact that it is actually *duck* hunting season. Yet on the other hand, they represent a trick played on us as well, for in this highly "designed" film—a design that seems to flatten out this world—the opening suggests an illusion of depth, only then to bring us up short. Following the various signs, fake tracks, and a pointedly winding path, the camera offers an extended tracking shot that, as in conventional film narratives, seems to draw us deeper and deeper into this world, although the backgrounds and spatial markers are hardly realistically conceived; in typical cartoon modern fashion, they are just vague splotches of color to indicate greenery, tree trunks, and background hills; shadows and modeling are practically absent. The layout for this cartoon was designed by Maurice Noble, one of the key stylists at Warner Bros. in this era and an artist given to what has been described as "playful design work" that is typically marked by exaggerated perspectives, large silhouettes, and abstract line patterns (Amidi 175). The resulting clash here between the conventional perspective constructed by the signs, pathway, and tracking camera and the otherwise flat, highly stylized space forecasts the narrative conflict that follows, one that develops from Daffy's efforts to get Elmer to "shoot the rabbit" and Bugs's constant twisting of the duck's language that results instead in Daffy's being shot—repeatedly—and thereby ironically producing precisely the result Daffy had sought to avoid: duck season.

Prompting much of this constant mistaking—and the mis-shootings that follow—is Bugs's demonstrated mastery over language, his easy ability to warp language as well as space, producing what the repeatedly victimized Daffy can only describe as "pronoun trouble." Bugs seems to recognize what none of these other characters does—namely, that here language has no real depth and is just as slippery and misleading as that constructed perspective and those signs of a fake rabbit season that have allowed Daffy to take Elmer along a winding path to Bugs's hole, even to lead him to stick his gun into the hole and to demand that the rabbit come out. Of course, the ability to turn language into this sort of pointless playground is precisely the sort of thing for which Jones's chief writer, Michael Maltese, was especially noted. Yet, as we have previously suggested, such ironic play works mainly because Jones has here crafted a most appropriate performance space—a complementary visual design—where contradiction and reversed expectations are both appropriate and practically expected. Slippery language and slippery spaces

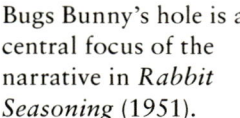

Bugs Bunny's hole is a central focus of the narrative in *Rabbit Seasoning* (1951).

conspire to produce a fully comic environment. In this world that the primary characters are constantly reconstructing to suit their needs—or the season—the only real depth or depth of understanding seems to be down that rabbit hole.

It is a hole, we should note, that also opens onto other holes, as we see when, in response to Elmer's intrusive shotgun, Bugs emerges from another, connecting hole to offer his usual, seemingly innocent bystander's inquiry, "What's up, Doc?" The ease with which the rabbit slips out of danger, both physically and verbally, and even out of character—as when in *Rabbit Seasoning* he suddenly emerges in drag and easily enthralls Elmer—points to another spatial construct that surfaces in numerous films. In a further development of the Bugs design scheme the hole becomes a rabbit tunnel, a kind of subversive space that seems to run, invisibly, practically everywhere, an underground construct that can transform any place that he surfaces into a set for comic action. For example, though Jones's film *Bully for Bugs* (1952) opens on what might be described as a kind of stylized rabbit hole—a bullfighting ring—the action only really begins when we see a meandering mound of dirt coming into the ring and Bugs Bunny eventually surfacing in its center to note, "This don't look like the Coachella Valley to me." On his way to the Big Carrot Festival he has apparently taken a wrong turn and crossed the border, reminding us in the process not only of how the rabbit's ability to tunnel might be used to create a stage entrance into any potentially comic context, but also of Bugs's potential for—literally—undermining this world, as we see here when he pops up to disrupt the stylized performance of reality that is the bullfight at the center of *Bully for Bugs*.

Following the initial encounter with a clearly vicious bull, the majority of this cartoon quickly becomes the fulfillment of Bugs's often-heard promise to his new antagonist, "Of course, you realize this means war." The subsequent battles in this war—in which the rabbit, while taking an unusual number of lumps, repeatedly bests the bull—all transpire, as we might expect, within the performance space that is the bullring; its formal entrances and exits are used to structure the action. In fact, Bugs's tunneling into the arena and emerging in the midst of a bullfight herald an interesting shift from tourist to performer, as his tunnel opens the door to an assault on the flat, conventionalized space of performance, much as we see in numerous other Bugs Bunny cartoons and most notably in *What's Opera, Doc?* Here the war begins with Bugs reentering the bullring from its formal entrance, dressed as a matador and holding the customary cape—which the bull quickly and painfully learns hides an anvil, which he crashes into. Bugs subsequently repeats this gag by luring the bull to chase him into one of the ring's "splits" (or *burladero*), which allows the rabbit to exit but leaves the bull's horns embedded in the flat wooden panel. Later, as Bugs seems caught against a barred and locked doorway while the bull is rushing toward him, he makes out a will and says his prayers—before suddenly lifting the gate, as if it were a garage door, sending the bull rushing out of the stadium in a cloud of dust. Finally, he opens the same door to admit the charging bull but forces him to ram into another split, over which Bugs then, with a matador's formal swirl, unfurls his cape bearing the message "The End." These repeated movements around, through, and outside the ring obviously send up the formal action of bullfighting, but at the same time the constant play of entry and escape pokes holes in the very space of the performance, emphasizing the nature of the "set," the artifice of this reality. And Bugs, before heading back into his tunnel, underscores his mastery over this conventionalized world by offering the only real exit in this carefully constructed world, that "The End" sign *he* has created and with which he dismisses us.

Jones is just one of several filmmakers who well understood and successfully mined the potential of the rabbit, but his development of the

Wile E. Coyote and Roadrunner pairing may best justify Amidi's description of him as "the most design conscious of the Warner Bros. directors" (173). In these efforts he was working with far more pointedly *designed* characters than ever before and was able to manipulate them in an equally designed space, one of stylized deserts, abstract cacti, and gaping canyons distilled from the vast spaces of the American Southwest. In fact, Jones explains that he approached the Road Runner and Coyote cartoons not from the perspective of narrative, but rather as a chance for "experimenting" with objects in space, and he notes with some pride that these cartoons have subsequently been "used in many art schools to show objects working in space. Pure space," since "one of the goals in drawing is to achieve an object working in pure space" (Furniss, *Chuck Jones* 31). It is that sense of a pure or abstract space that makes these efforts such an important contribution in the development of animating space that we have been tracing.

Michael Barrier has suggested that much of Jones's work, at least his cartoons of the early 1940s, is marked by a stylistic conflict. The cartoons seem, he says, almost "at war with themselves," since his characters were "insistently three-dimensional . . . and they did not belong in the same universe with aggressively artificial backgrounds" (448) of the sort that he was increasingly deploying. That assessment is open to some question, but it does point to a key line of development in his work, an increasing tendency in later efforts to develop a stronger stylistic relationship between the figural and the spatial, to see them as "designed" all of a piece. As we note in the discussion of *Rabbit Seasoning*, Bugs Bunny seems to be the only character in that film who understands just how pliable and illusory the world can be—an understanding that certainly depends on his own trickster nature, but also on the "aggressively artificial" nature of the world he inhabits. And in the Roadrunner and Coyote cartoons, beginning with 1949's *Fast and Furry-ous*, we see perhaps the culmination of this line of development, as the sparse and artificial spaces of the films cast in relief the single-minded compulsions of the characters who move through that stylized world, marking both as similarly constructed or designed.

In one of the most often cited discussions of the Road Runner cartoons, Richard Thompson suggests a way to think about this unusual characteristic when he describes how "*Road Runner* films rank among

Wile E. Coyote tries to conquer the vast spaces of the American Southwest with the help of the Acme Company in *Fast and Furry-ous* (1949).

the most austerely pared-down works of modern art" (38). And Jones acknowledges that this paring or distilling was both intentional and central to his approach; it is what he terms a "discipline," a self-imposed limitation—a set of blueprints—out of which he tried to make both gags and style naturally flow. Part of that discipline, as he explains, was an element of characterization, such as the Coyote's fundamental "ineptitude" or Bugs Bunny's almost unfailing sense of control over his situation (Furniss, *Chuck Jones* 54). But another shape that discipline took was one of presentation, as we see in the absence of real dialogue in the Road Runner–Coyote cartoons; without speech, action is all—at least until the point at which the Coyote's actions lead to disaster, which prompts him to break the proscenium and produce a sign directed to the audience, reading perhaps "Egad!" "Yikes!" or, in one supremely reflexive touch, "How about ending this cartoon before I hit [the ground]?" Yet another is the unwavering plot trajectory, as all the Coyote's schemes, usually abetted by the products of the Acme Corporation, meet with escalating frustrations and disastrously lengthy falls. Such discipline obviously resulted in a highly conventionalized sort of narrative, allowing for easier planning, budgeting, and execution, but also draining away an element of reality and casting the cartoons' structure into relief.[6]

When we look at space in the Roadrunner films in the context of this discipline approach, that artifice becomes especially apparent. For the setting of choice is nature reduced almost to abstract principles: the vast open spaces of the southwestern deserts, where roads become lines stretching seemingly to infinity, where great, irregular—and irregularly colored—buttes suddenly jut up, and where canyons unexpectedly yawn, readily inviting the Coyote's fall, as if the baseline of the cel frame had suddenly disappeared, allowing him to plummet into emptiness. In fact, though it is the Roadrunner's speed that gives reason to much of the action in these cartoons—as the Coyote is never able to match his pace and so must resort to all manner of schemes and devices to catch his prey—it is the Coyote's repeated falls from one cliff, peak, or mountain road after another that provide the most common comic payoff in these films. It is as if conventional movement in space were there only to precipitate an encounter with a very different sense of space, the negative space of the frame that suddenly becomes, to recall Kern's description, "positive negative space," a measure of the Coyote's failure.

Lickety Splat (1961) typifies the sort of discipline-driven formula and the result we are noting. It begins with the Coyote walking along a desert road when the Roadrunner suddenly rushes past him, as if begging to be pursued. The Coyote gives chase, but the bird's velocity is such that the road itself rolls up behind him, a tunnel stretches as he goes through it, and a bridge is pulled along after him—effects that leave the Coyote pointedly contemplating ideas for overcoming such absurd speed. Roller skis lead to his rolling off a cliff, impaling another butte with his skis, and, when the skis eventually break, plummeting to the ground far below and producing a small cloud of dust and a vague thud—both measures of the great distance he has fallen. Using a giant bow, he attempts to shoot himself across a chasm at the bird, but the bow goes awry and shoots him down into the canyon. Using a balloon, he tries to launch explosive darts at the Roadrunner, only to have one of the darts burst his balloon and then another the parachute he has donned, sending him plummeting down to the canyon floor, which we again see—and hear—from far above. That long shot is held for several seconds as another explosive dart drifts into view, spiraling down to the same distant spot where the Coyote landed, providing us with yet another small cloud and a distantly heard explosion. Later, trying to drop an anvil on the Roadrunner from a cliff, a section of rock breaks off, and even though the Coyote jumps to seemingly more solid ground, that part too breaks away and he once again falls into the canyon. Certainly, the constant shift from chase to fall, from horizontal to vertical movement, dramatizes the Coyote's Sisyphean persistence, while also mocking his supposed intellectual prowess. But that pattern also provides us with a distinctive stylistic marker; as Chuck Jones admits, "As we went along, the Coyote's primary enemy became . . . gravity" (Furniss, *Chuck Jones* 34), not the Roadrunner or the Coyote's own fascination with elaborately plotted schemes. As the series advanced, conventional space, the space of horizontal movement and chase, increasingly proved unstable, broke away (like so many cliff ledges), disappeared, and was replaced by the abstract space of space itself—the air through which the Coyote falls—as measured by his diminishing size, the very small puffs of smoke or dust that indicate his landing, and the distant sounds of impact.

These effects underscore another element of design that Jones discovered in his work with such open spaces. He notes that in animating action within "deep space, the depth is identified by the movement, not by perspective lines. The fact that the character diminishes off into the distance is what determines how deep the background is" (Furniss, *Chuck Jones* 60). Though conventional horizontal movement did not effectively exploit the desert spaces wherein these characters are locked in constant chase, the Coyote's repeated falls do, and they provide an effective measure of the vast distances on which the entire drama is being played out. But the tendency of the ground in these cartoons to suddenly disappear, repeatedly leaving the Coyote falling through space, is probably less important than the principle that is at work here. For the Roadrunner films constantly remind us, in a way that Bugs's rabbit hole increasingly hinted at, of the way space is constructed, designed for effect, and even understood as designed by the audience. A recurring gag in these films is the Coyote's painting of a landscape as part of a trap to catch the Roadrunner, as in the case of the tunnel opening that he sketches on a cliff face in *Fast and Furry-ous* (1949) or the road scene he paints on a flat to disguise a yawning canyon and collapsed bridge in *Gee Whiz-z-z-z* (1956). In these scenes and elsewhere, the Roadrunner simply races into the painted effect, in the process constructing a new geography for the scene, whereas the Coyote, as he attempts to emulate and follow his prey, smashes into a suddenly solid rock or runs through a painting and into the open canyon beyond—the victim of his own designs, the genus/genius whose calculations always fail.

Of course, such events only remind us of a point we initially noted, of the "noticeably nonnaturalistic" nature of this seemingly natural environment. It is a point emphasized every time the Roadrunner or Coyote is introduced with a freeze-frame and a subtitle, providing a comic Latinate genus name for each, such as *Accelerati incredibilus* (the Roadrunner) and *Carnivorous vulgaris* (the Coyote). These titles, along with the pause in the action that they herald, satirize our taxonomic tendencies, underscoring how nature here functions under the aegis of human categories—as well as under the direction of the cartoonist. And when *Lickety Splat* begins with the characters themselves stopping, turning to the audience, and holding up such comic category signs, the sense of artifice is only further emphasized; the chase is reframed as a performance, spatially constructed, bound by the rules of Jones's disciplines, and enjoyed especially for the precise workings of this construct.

As a final note on this linkage of space and artifice, we might briefly consider a late Roadrunner cartoon, *War and Pieces* (1964). Its concluding sequence begins with the Coyote astride a rocket aimed at the Roadrunner, and when it hits a curved outcropping, it arcs and plummets—as we would only expect—back to Earth. Yet instead of showing us the falling rocket from above as it gradually disappears in the distance, or offering the customary thud and cloud-of-dust payoff, the scene continues as the rocket penetrates the ground, as if it weren't even there, as if it had no substance. The rocket continues into and then through the center of the Earth, rendered in various abstract patterns, and it eventually emerges upside down, apparently on the opposite side of the world. There the Coyote immediately comes face to face with a Chinese Roadrunner who taunts him with an extended tongue and the usual "Beep! Beep!" With that confrontation the chase simply begins again, complete with its immediate frustrations—as the Coyote quickly runs into a Chinese gong, which sends him reeling, falling back into the hole from which he just emerged and through the Earth to the other side, again encountering his American nemesis-prey, and so the chase goes on. Space, it seems, does not really matter. It is just the stage on which these stylized actions are played out, the constructed set that constructs their actions as a game we can all enjoy.

These cartoons were almost a swansong for Warner Bros. animation—the studio would shut down its animation unit in 1964—but they are a fitting measure of how far the studio had come in its development of a late-modernist sensibility. Its venerable Looney Tunes series had been launched in 1930 by two former Disney animators, Hugh Harman and Rudolf Ising, and their initial creation, Bosco, was very much in the tradition of Mickey Mouse.[7] The cartoons that followed throughout the 1930s were, stylistically, largely in the Disney mold, if also typically a bit more anarchic. But as a talented group of animators gradually came together at Warner Bros.—figures such as Tex Avery, Bob Clampett, Friz Freleng, Robert McKimson, Chuck Jones—and began to exploit the freedom that the producer Leon Schlesinger, through his general lack of oversight, permitted them, the studio became linked to a line of iconic cartoon characters who acted out their adventures in increasingly abstract environments. Those cartoons, as Timothy White has shown, struck a chord not only with audiences but with a critical establishment that, in the late 1950s and 1960s, embraced the auteurist and self-reflexive art cinema of Antonioni, Buñuel, Godard, and Resnais. Yet that critical resonance followed not so much from the Warner Bros. popular stable of characters as from the animation unit's continuing exploration and development of animating space. In them we find not a Disney-like illusion of life, or a rediscovery of flatland, but an abstract, constructed world in which space itself—as we see especially in the Roadrunner films—practically becomes a character, or at any rate, a trickster in the best "wascally wabbit" manner.

8

TOONTOWN SPACES AND THE NEW HYBRID WORLD

The postmodern world, as we have previously noted, seems to confront us with a bewildering array of appearances, of false fronts, of illusive dimensions. As Paul Virilio and others describe this situation, we often feel that we have reached a state where a "reality effect" has replaced "immediate reality," and consequently we increasingly feel "cinematized" or "mediatized," as if we all inhabited a world of movies (*Lost* 24). We have seen how elements of that effect almost inevitably seem to surface in instances of hybrid animation, that is, in those narratives that combine traditional, usually flat animation with live-action figures. In such films—as if they were trying to figure this very situation for their audience's closer examination—real and cartoon figures share the same spaces, and the reality of each invariably reflects on that of the other. In fact, as the Disney animators Frank Thomas and Ollie Johnston note, because the characters in such narratives "come from different worlds," the Disney artists typically found that they had to give "special consideration to make them compatible," make special efforts at disguise, at shifting "the audience's attention . . . into other areas" (527), such as backgrounds and overall mise-en-scène, so that audiences would not notice an inevitable draining away of the real. Yet in spite of all considerations, including ever more sophisticated image technologies, the very constructedness of such dualistic worlds quickly becomes apparent; the fact that we are literally facing a "reality effect" is simply unavoidable, although its larger implications often go unexplored.

Yet despite such problems, hybrid animation has a long history in the American cinema; many of the major studios turned to it at one time or another, either as the central focus of their work, as in the Fleischers' Out of the Inkwell cartoons, or as a special feature in otherwise conventional, live-action film, as in MGM's *Anchors Aweigh* (1945). Disney, of course, started out in this mode with its Alice comedies of 1923–1927, returned to it in a more ambitious manner with a string of postwar features, and then revisited it periodically with such efforts as *Mary Poppins* (1964), *Bedknobs and Broomsticks* (1971), *Pete's Dragon* (1977), and others. Thus, its participation with Steven Spielberg's Amblin Entertainment to produce *Who Framed Roger Rabbit* (1988) must have seemed quite logical, a state-of-the-art multiply hybrid project: a partnership with another company to create a stylistic combination that would bring together various cartoon characters (especially those of Disney and Warner Bros.) in a kind of "buddy story" about a "Toon" and a real private detective—a comic film noir. This partnership and project, however, would open a door onto more than just new company and character relationships. For in revisiting this old approach to animated films, in its retro styling, and in its resurrection of numerous classic cartoon characters, *Roger Rabbit* had to deal with the implications of hybridity in a way that the animated film had never done before, in fact, in a way that pointedly reflects on the postmodern character that was becoming endemic to film animation and to animating space.

To help gauge both the difficulty and the implications of that negotiation with postmodernism's reality effect, I consider *Roger Rabbit* alongside another work that also sought to capitalize on this return to hybrid animation and that similarly invites audiences to examine that same new spatial territory, Ralph Bakshi's *Cool World* (1992). It is a film that is remarkably similar to *Roger Rabbit*: also offering parallel realms of humans (or "noids") and cartoon characters ("doodles"); involving a male human protagonist, the cartoonist Jack Deebs, who, like *Roger Rabbit*'s Eddie Valiant, is sorely in need of redemption; introducing a highly sexualized female doodle, Holli Would, who is clearly kin to the earlier film's Jessica Rabbit; and even involving a human detective character, Frank Harris, who works in the Cool World of the doodles. More important, it focuses much of its narrative, just as *Roger Rabbit* does, on the tensions between those two worlds, although in this case the Cool World that the narrative depicts is every bit as dreary and noirish as the human realm, and the possibility of mingling those worlds, of joining real and animated space, of hybridizing, is presented as an act rife with potential calamity.

Of course, both films had reason behind the anxieties over animating space that they reflect in different ways. It was not that their styles were in some way at fault, but that this period had already seen a great many challenges to the world of traditional animation and would soon be confronting many others that would invariably influence animating space and add resonance to the films' reality effects. Foremost among those earlier challenges, of course, was the world of television cartooning that was characterized largely by limited animation, repetitive actions, and generally flat worlds. Admittedly, the advent of television had created enormous possibilities for new programming, while providing jobs for skilled veteran animators who had been released by studios like Warner Bros. and MGM as they abandoned the production of cartoon shorts in the 1950s and 1960s. The television cartoons that flowed from studios like Hanna-Barbera Productions and Jay Ward Productions, however, were for the most part the products of restricted budgets and breakneck schedules; their flatness and visual simplicity reflected the harsh and hurried conditions of production, not the sort of designed aesthetic we earlier observed, that which Michael Barrier, speaking of the UPA cartoons, describes as a stylistic desire to suggest "drawings that moved—not . . . characters who happened to be drawn" (527).

And even beyond this industrial push for "quantity and predictability" (Barrier 561), American animation was confronting a number of other forces, influences that could well come to dominate the form. Japanese anime was at this point becoming very popular in the American media environment, bringing with it a different and quite distinctive style. Working with both machines and software developed by Pixar, the Walt Disney Company had begun a slow but deliberate move toward digital animation by shifting the inking and painting processes for its animated films onto computers and exploiting the multiplane effect built into the new software to add a greater sense of depth. Employing its proprietary RenderMan software, Pixar Animation had already released to much praise several fully digital short cartoons—*The Adventures of André and Wally B.* (1984), *Luxo Jr.* (1986), *Red's Dream* (1987), and *Tin Toy* (1988)—that demonstrated a new dimensionality in animated film. And feature films like *Tron* (1982) and *Young Sherlock Holmes* (1985) had established the possibility for placing live-action characters in three-dimensional, computer-generated settings (*Tron*), or conversely, for introducing three-dimensional, computer-generated characters—essentially a new kind of animated figure—into the world of live-action film (*Young Sherlock Holmes*), thereby blurring the boundaries between animated and live-action cinema in ever more complex ways, while also creating new possibilities for hybrid narratives. It was thus becoming obvious that animation, at least as it had been traditionally conceived and practiced, was facing major changes, even a challenge to its distinct identity. And such elaborate hybrid efforts as *Roger Rabbit* and *Cool World,* by their very nature as liminal or border-straddling texts, both of which used conventional technology, would naturally underscore some of these challenges, in fact, would almost inevitably invoke and involve them at the narrative level.

Jane Goodall partially points in this direction as she describes the vogue for such narratives in the 1990s as symptomatic of and reflecting a general postmodern cultural sensibility.[1] She suggests that hybrid animation had "begun to admit its resonances as one of the most insistent thematics of an era obsessed with difference, cloning, grafting and taxonomic slippage" (Goodall 156). And certainly there is much of that concern to be glimpsed at every level in *Who Framed Roger Rabbit,* as it uses its human-Toon interactions to create multiple "resonances," and especially to evoke a variety of the era's key cultural anxieties. Most obviously, by casting its Toon characters in the role of a racial underclass, the film underscores racial difference and serves to indict racist attitudes, after a fashion found in many live-action films of the period. Here the segregated Ink and Paint Club clearly recalls the famous Cotton Club of Harlem, where black entertainers performed for an exclusively white clientele—or in this case, "humans only." The "law" that Judge Doom dispenses to the Toons of Toontown—without benefit of trial or rights—readily mirrors the experiences of America's racial underclass. And Toontown itself, set off as a separate, chaotic, and even frightening area, pointedly suggests the cultural mythos that justified an earlier era's geographical segregation. These are all conditions that not only suggest the film's general cultural sensibilities, but are also linked to the film's foregrounding of spatial concerns, thus reminding us of Henri Lefebvre's argument that "social space is a social product" (26).

Almost as often as they evoke that element of ghettoization, the same hybrid elements cast into relief an endemic sexism and the sexual power struggles that were also coming into focus in contemporary society. It is a focus that the highly sexualized Jessica Rabbit particularly points up when she explains, "I'm not bad; I'm just drawn that way." And just as frequently the live-action–animation combinations frame for our inspection surprising cross-species and less surprising cross-age relationships, such as those of Roger and Jessica Rabbit, Jessica and Marvin Acme, and Baby Herman and his "babysitter," all of which suggest, in different ways, the sort of hybrid cultural world that audiences increasingly found themselves inhabiting. These and other resonances, however, result largely because the film's concern with difference extends over such a broad landscape, part of which is the very field of animation, which similarly becomes a point of commentary throughout the narrative.

In fact, as we should begin to see, *Who Framed Roger Rabbit* may be most interesting because of the ways in which it links its comments about human life and contemporary culture with the story it also tells about the changing realm of animation. The film appeared at precisely the time when the new digital technologies were starting to have an influence—on both live-action and animated film—and when that new sense of "social space" and its meanings was also beginning to impinge on what we have termed animating space. Though not specifically addressing a graphic art like animation, Paul Virilio has already staked out these cultural, spatial, and aesthetic intersections, as he describes how a "crisis in the conceptualization of dimension"—that is, the dimensions of everyday life—was beginning to have an unexpected fallout, "a crisis in the conceptualization of narrative" (*Lost* 24–25) in the cinema and elsewhere. He argues that we increasingly face a world that seems to have "lost dimension," to be flattened out, to be transformed by the pervasive media network that surrounds us. As our world becomes ever more mediatized, its "depth of space . . . vanishes" (*Lost* 34), and with it our experience of reality gives way to that reality effect he describes. As a result, he likens life in the postmodern world to living in a movie set with its simple, two-dimensional facades and suggests that we can all too easily become "victims of the set" (*Art* 79). One consequence to this new sensibility is a challenge felt in the world of traditional film narrative, which depends on the construction of a realistic space occupied by characters driven by realistic or goal-oriented motivations.[2] In the case of *Who Framed Roger Rabbit*, which uses realistic space for most of its action, that challenge translates into an internal dialogue throughout the film about its interweaving of the real and the animated, about the different valences of the real produced by the narrative's hybrid characteristics.

Adam Eisenberg recounts how, before beginning production on *Roger Rabbit*, the director Robert Zemeckis, his animation team, and other technicians directly addressed this issue by discussing the sort of reality effect they hoped to craft. They wanted to determine whether it would be possible to make the combination of live action and animation more believable than in any earlier hybrid films. Significantly, they determined that the key to combining these elements successfully would be the film's spatial experience, particularly the possibilities for creating convincing character interaction across the different sorts of spaces the characters would occupy and effectively using camera movement to join those spaces, to suture the live and animated worlds as seamlessly as possible. Zemeckis, for example, was adamant about "having the Toons not only move physical props, but also interact with the real environment around them" (qtd. in Eisenberg 9), thereby underscoring the fact that they inhabited the same three-dimensional world as their human counterparts and were not simply imagined presences to which the live actors reacted. Working from the same impulse, Richard Williams, the lead animator, decided that to achieve those effects, they would have to violate a customary rule of hybrid animation by moving the "camera"— that is, changing the audience's viewing position—as much as possible, even when the animated characters were themselves in motion. That scheme was important because, as it moved, the camera would produce a sense that *it* was measuring real space, a space that was occupied or that *could* conceivably be occupied. Williams also "broke another rule that said you couldn't draw hard-edged cartoons and have them interact with blurred live-action" in real space, even as he worked out a lighting scheme that would keep the animated elements from looking "flat and pasted on" (Eisenberg 8). To ensure this effect, the optical supervisor,

Ed Jones, developed a new technique that helped bond the animated figures to the real world, one that he terms "interactive light." In this lighting scheme, Jones explains, "if there was a real source of light in the scene, we would bounce that light source off" the cartoon figure and then onto other elements of the scene (Eisenberg 28), thereby binding characters and objects throughout the scene in a web of light and a space that was multiply sculpted by highlights.

Yet in spite of these and other stylistic efforts at generating a new sort of animating space—or perhaps because of their very success—we cannot help noting and even being impressed by the "trick" of combination that resulted. In fact, one of the dangers that *Roger Rabbit* had to negotiate is that the audience can easily become so caught up in appreciating the wonders of its combinatory vision that the narrative itself can slip out of focus. To counter this effect, the film also adopts a number of strategies designed to keep viewers from focusing primarily on the tricks of its hybridity. One of these is a consistent foregrounding of the movies as a form themselves—an approach that interrogates their very artifice rather than trying to disguise it. The film's opening nicely frames this approach in the way it not only immediately presents us with the latest Maroon Cartoon, *Somethin's Cookin'*, but reveals that this film is still in a difficult production stage. When the cartoon's action is suddenly interrupted by an angry shout of "Cut!" and the camera in a single long take tracks out from its close-up of Roger within the cartoon world, we not only see the cartoon's live-action director coming forward into the animated world with script in hand and interacting with Baby Herman and Roger—treating them just like live-action actors—but also the dynamics of the shooting process—the camera, lights, set dressers, sound people, additional three-dimensional props (implying that what we have been watching, despite its seeming flatness, is actually a three-dimensional world), as well as the finite boundaries of the "set" in which the animated scene is supposedly being shot. This long tracking shot attests to the reality of the cartoon's *space*, but at the same time the various mechanics of apparition underscore the artifice of the movies, immediately submerging any wonder viewers might have about this hybrid creation into a larger fascination with the "real" trickery that is fundamental to the movies, with the way that all that we see in the movies is always already constructed, and with the sense that we

The live-action director intrudes into the cartoon world in *Who Framed Roger Rabbit* (1988).

are always on some level "victims of the set," as Virilio puts it. With that submersion, the narrative both establishes a realistic ground for what follows and indicates that the very process of construction is central to the story that is unfolding here.

To carry that strategy beyond the opening sequence—and indeed throughout the narrative—the film provides us with a protagonist, the private detective Eddie Valiant, who must constantly interact with both Toons like Roger and the world of the film industry, thereby modeling a certain type of response for the audience. On the set, watching the shooting of this cartoon, Eddie seems both familiar with yet constantly amazed by the antics of the animated but also manifestly alive figures he sees. In the opening sequence, the same tracking camera that sutures Roger into the three-dimensional space of the film studio introduces Eddie as he enters the frame from the opposite side, takes a drink from a pint bottle, and dismissively shakes his head at Roger's antics, muttering, "Toons!" Later in the sequence, as he stands in R. K. Maroon's office and then as he wanders through the lot, Eddie encounters a variety of other Toons, including Disney's Dumbo the elephant, "half the cast from *Fantasia*," and an array of other animated figures that variously draw from him expressions of surprise and bemusement. Here and throughout the film Eddie becomes more than just a character in the narrative; his physical reactions and comments serve to model the sort of response the audience might have, and

Despite appearances, Jessica Rabbit is not bad, just "drawn that way."

in naturalizing that wonderment and building it into the narrative, he helps release us from it.

Those reactions can be easily naturalized, though, because of yet another, subtler strategy at work here. Zemeckis has created a pointedly stylized, nostalgic, noirish world, that of Los Angeles in 1947, when Hollywood cartoons were near the peak of their popularity. More to the point, it is a world that has already sorted out for itself this other stylized realm, specifically the curious breach of reality that the mingling of humans and Toons represents, which is always one of the astonishments of every hybrid narrative. The film clearly avoids talking about the creation of the Toons—how they came to be in this world and to have a life of their own—although it does imply a kind of answer, as Jessica Rabbit's comment suggests: that they have all been intentionally "drawn" in certain ways to satisfy human designs or desires and thus have been imaginatively willed into being. Yet even as humans seem to control those constructed characters, even keeping them largely exiled to Toontown, they also clearly have minds—and desires—of their own, as we see when Roger spontaneously writes a love poem for his "honey bunny," or when Eddie tells Jessica that he cannot understand what she sees in Roger, and she suggestively answers, "He makes me laugh." Moreover, in a darker register, we learn that some thought has also gone into how to eliminate the Toons. As police lieutenant Santino explains, "we always thought there wasn't a way to kill a Toon" until Judge Doom developed his "dip," a mix of chemicals like those that would have been used to wash the paint from animation cels. Most important, the Toons—unlike many of the humans here—seem to have a sense of purpose to their lives, to *entertain,* and that sense of purpose constantly impels their actions. Thus, Roger explains to Eddie why he has to sing and dance for the patrons of the Terminal Station Bar instead of just hiding out as he has been instructed: "I'm a Toon. Toons are supposed to make people laugh." It is an attitude that this world readily understands—and that we come to as well—because the Toons are consistently presented as such a natural part of it and not an oddity or point of question.

And yet the terms by which this world has sorted out the Toon-human relationship, this hybrid coexistence, increasingly crowd into the narrative foreground, converging especially with issues of space. While they are generally understood and manifestly appreciated, and while they obviously share the same sorts of desires as humans—and, we are told, can just as easily have their flat hearts broken—the Toons are also identified as *different.* As I noted above, they are referred to in various derogatory, even racial terms, such as "water color," and are generally ostracized from the human world like a racial (or "colored") underclass. For such reasons, Eddie repeatedly notes that working for them is perceived as degrading. And in keeping with that cultural attitude, they are relegated to the ghettolike Toontown—literally, to their animating space—and can mingle with humans only within the artificial world of the movie industry or at special, controlled-access spots like the Ink and Paint Club. This context, moreover, develops another peculiar resonance, this one with Hollywood history, further underscoring how cultural and aesthetic concerns intersect here. It reminds us of how animation, even within the precincts of a studio like Warner Bros., was often looked down on, treated as a separate—and lesser—entity. Yet more important for the narrative is the larger attitude that results as *Roger Rabbit* consistently portrays such spatial separation, a kind of cultural proscription of hybridity, as rather "looney-tuney." It is for this reason that, at practically every turn, the film also emphasizes just how similar Toons are to humans and how unfounded the sort of "species" discrimination practiced here is, as it helps us take the measure of this rather paradoxical and inevitably mixed world.

The most important of those measures comes from Eddie Valiant himself, a down-on-his-luck private detective who seems no longer to care about sorting out the truth and who, because a Toon killed his brother, has come to embrace his culture's—as well as the film industry's—prejudices. Yet as the narrative proceeds, we increasingly glimpse how very Toon-like Eddie himself is. The framed picture of him, his brother, and their circus clown father, the images of Eddie and his brother in clown makeup, and especially his ability in the film's final sequence to distract Judge Doom's weasels by singing and dancing to "Merry-Go-Round Broke Down," just as Roger earlier had, all attest to his own clownishness, to his own latent ability to tap into that Toon sense of purpose, "to make people laugh." If not "drawn that way," as Jessica explains, he certainly seems a natural enough clown or Toon, and in rediscovering his own Toonishness over the course of the narrative, in animating that space within the self that both he and his world seem ready to deny, repress, or even eliminate, Eddie demonstrates an alternative to that paradoxical character of his culture, even a path back to that "lost space" of the contemporary world.

That lost space is, very simply, the space of difference—a space literally represented in *Who Framed Roger Rabbit* by the world of Toontown. In fact, despite the film's constant paralleling of Roger and Eddie Valiant and its emphasis on the latter's ability to find or redeem himself, its most compelling commentary finally centers on the space of Toontown: the space of difference or supplement, the space that we want to control, repress, or, in postmodern fashion, compress, and that Judge Doom wants to eradicate and replace with a world of simple flat surfaces—of paved roads and indiscernible differences. This new world that Paul Virilio has so evocatively described as "speed-space" would allow people to move rapidly across the contemporary American landscape but also discourage them from ever stopping, seeing, or sampling the variety of the culture—from ever actually inhabiting a space, much less noticing how much of their world has been lost or irrevocably changed. Thus, Judge Doom gleefully describes the effects of his plan: "Who's got time to wonder what happened to some ridiculous talking mice when you're driving by at seventy-five miles an hour?"

That question too reflexively resonates, since it cannot help evoking the whole world of animation and our own historical relation to that form. From within our cultural position in the new world of "speed-space," it asks: Do we really care if the animated characters who have had such an influence on our culture—an influence commensurate with that of many living beings—were simply to disappear, or perhaps be replaced by the sort of flat, limited animation and almost lifeless figures that did indeed take over much of the animation market with the rise of cheap television cartoon programs in the 1950s? If life—or animation—were to be drained from that formerly very rich cultural space constructed for us by the Fleischers, Disney, and Warner Bros. animators, among many others, would we even know or really care?

Yet Toontown stands as a potent answer to that question and a challenge to the vision Doom offers. From the point at which the curtain literally goes up as Eddie, despite his fears, enters the seemingly foreboding world of Toontown, it is manifestly—and despite its strange sense of difference (thanks to its quilted landscape, talking buildings, and dancing trees)—a very welcoming world. Far from threatening, it encourages the new arrival to "smile, darn ya, smile." Here even the roadways are flexible, as Eddie demonstrates when he picks up a piece of road striping and diverts it into the side of a building; here every structure seems alive, smiling, and able to change shape; and here there is all the variety of life that one could ever imagine—or at least draw. Most important, it is, as the film reminds us, a very real space and an essential part of our world, if also a part at risk, in danger of being "dipped" and becoming one more "lost dimension" of the postmodern human environment (Virilio, *Lost* 101) if Judge Doom and his ilk have their way.

For this reason the film's conclusion is especially evocative, as it juxtaposes the disappearance of the Toons—Doom's threatened "dipping" of Roger and Jessica, along with the erasure of all of Toontown and its replacement by superhighways—with a parallel possibility for saving and recouping that animating space, and in the process making the human story a more hybrid narrative after all. It does so not only by the defeat of Judge Doom when Eddie manages to tap into his own Toonish nature, but also by literally breaking through the wall that divides spaces here, Toontown from Los Angeles. The destruction of that wall allows the heterogeneous family of Toons—black and white and Technicolored, old and new, Disney types and Warner products—to come into the human world, there to mingle with the humans and reanimate

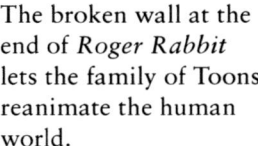

The broken wall at the end of *Roger Rabbit* lets the family of Toons reanimate the human world.

the space of the Acme warehouse by opening up a new dimension; and it permits the Toon sun that always seems to shine—and sing—in Toontown to light up that noirish human world. With the breaking down of that dividing wall and letting the sun shine in, with the historical addition of this other space, there comes at least the possibility that we might begin to see our own cultural craziness, begin to recognize that perhaps *ours* is the real insanity that needs to be reined in—as unfortunately it was not back in 1947, before our now familiar world of superhighways, fast food, and cheaply made television cartoons.

Still, opening up that wall and letting the Toons practically pour into the human world are narratively quite satisfying actions in themselves, and they form a most fitting coda for the film. With this development, difference is embraced, vitality trumps Doom, and a potentially lost dimension is recouped. Yet it is on this last point that we need to linger and further consider. For in what is perhaps the most astute analysis of the film, Alan Cholodenko argues that *Who Framed Roger Rabbit* is more than just a surprisingly serious tale about contemporary American culture, told through the mechanism of hybrid animation; it is also a work, as its title hints, "about framing," in fact, one that "frames the frame" (*"Who Framed"* 210) of film. Cholodenko explains that the film asks us to consider the relationship between its live-action and animated elements by looking through a double lens, seeing how "film frames animation" and how "animation frames film" (*"Who Framed"* 213). Part of this double question points directly at the live-action world, the *real* space into which a character like Roger simply walks at the end of the first scene, as he follows the director off the set of *Somethin's Cookin'* and as the various Toons do as they curiously crowd into the Acme warehouse in the final scene, reinvigorating that dark space. Both are most pointed signs of how intimately related these two realms are, as well as a forecast of the extent to which the space of the live-action or human circumscribes and controls—whether through scripts or dips—the animated, even lends it a kind of three-dimensionality through the live-action space the Toons traverse. Seen in this context, the narrative's trajectory becomes one of liberation, of breaking not just through but free of that frame, as that brick wall is opened up, the Toons enter, and they are deeded (by both the character Marvin Acme and the director Robert Zemeckis) a piece of this world. That liberation essentially rewrites animation history, suggesting an alternative history wherein animation itself might have similarly broken free, might have located a space in which the constraints of the major controlling studios—Maroon or Disney or Warner Bros.—might be countered and various styles and characters might function together, freely interacting, just as we see Daffy and Donald Duck do in their act at the Ink and Paint Club. And providing some support for that notion, we might suppose, is the very existence of a film like *Roger Rabbit,* with its stylistic echoes of a cross section of animation history—as Roger seems to be a mix of Warners' Bugs Bunny and Disney's Brer Rabbit, and Jessica channels Tex Avery's various Red Riding Hood cartoons for MGM.

The other direction of framing here, that provided by the animation, brings us back to earth, however, to the postmodern world wherein, the film reminds us, we are always, much like Toons, constructed by forces and circumstances beyond our full control or understanding, and where that other dimension the Toons represent remains "lost." For the Toons ultimately point up the fantasy here, interrogate *our* three-dimensionality, and in the way they frame the action and suggest what might have been, they underscore what has occurred in the real world to help us see some of the noirish coloring that it indeed sports. In fact, though fantasy figures, they remind us that a Doom-ing judgment of sorts has already been passed on our world, a judgment measured both by our freeway-bounded, fast-food culture and by the trajectory of animation itself: the disappearance of most classic animation, the dissolution of most of the major Hollywood cartoon units, the empty triumph of the flat, limited animation that came to dominate the industry as cartoons became the province of television. The world of the Toons and of Toontown, as Porky Pig's closing "That's all, folks" reminds us, is finally a nostalgic one, an appealing frame but finally no more than a frame that leaves us longing for that lost dimension, for that always surprising "warped" space, as Vidler terms it, that our animation once opened up for our entertainment—and possibly even our instruction.

Perhaps it is because of this dual framing that Paul Wells has found *Who Framed Roger Rabbit* such an unsatisfying film. He describes it as a conflicted work, one that is finally "unable to reconcile the differing premises of the Disney, Warner Bros., and Fleischer cartoons brought together in the film, and the preoccupation with a convoluted narrative which remained ambivalent about the radical conditions which under-pin cartoonal forms and their effects" (126). The result, he argues, is that it by turns seems to celebrate the "redemptive . . . influence of the cartoon characters" and "to question the meaning of cartoons" (126–27). I suggest, though, that the questioning ultimately seems directed more at our culture than at the cartoons, which are, after all, both the product and a reflection of that culture. Certainly *Who Framed Roger Rabbit* seems an undiluted celebration of traditional animation, as well as a deliberate effort—as the resulting, if short-lived, series of Roger Rabbit short cartoons would attest—at trying to reinvigorate the form.[3] Yet it is also inevitably a haunted effort—or "framed," to adopt Cholo-denko's term—haunted by cultural and cinematic history, and by a new sense of animating space that requires us to see the cartoon world as fundamentally disconnected from the real world, the traditional Toon space simply not available to be tapped for its potential vitality.

That disconnect is precisely the focus of Ralph Bakshi's effort in this same vein, *Cool World,* a work whose hybrid style similarly reflects on the relation between the real and the animated, between modern and postmodern notions of space—and indeed, between two different atti-tudes toward the animated image. Whereas *Who Framed Roger Rabbit* immediately immerses us in the context of an animated cartoon, only to gradually reveal the nature of its Toons and the surprising dimensional-ity of their world, even how that other world complements our own,

Frank Harris threads his way through the exaggerated, nightmarish sets of *Cool World* (1992).

Cool World is more intent on emphasizing a sordid human realm: that of Frank Harris, a returning World War II veteran who, as the narrative opens, prods his mother into riding on his new motorcycle, only to see her killed in a crash with a drunken automobile driver; that of Jack Deebs, just released from prison for murdering his wife's lover and now unable to find any sort of satisfaction in the human realm, haunted as he is by dreams of the Cool World that he believes is a product of his own desperate imagination; and that of the gaudy gambling mecca Las Vegas, which holds the Golden Spike of Power—apparently all that keeps the human and cartoon dimensions separated. Here the Cool World of the doodles is no potential supplement to the real, but a kind of hallucinatory other realm, independent of our world and populated by figures who long to be real, while its constantly dark and chaotic atmosphere seems testimony to Bakshi's comment that he had originally designed the film to be "the first animated horror film" ("Interview").

As this description might begin to suggest, although *Cool World* combines live action and animation after the fashion of *Who Framed Roger Rabbit,* it never seems concerned with the sort of careful, nearly seamless integration of animated and live-action images we find in the earlier film, and its overall, pointedly contemporary look differs markedly from *Roger Rabbit*'s studied retro styling—effects that are generally consistent with Bakshi's other work. He began his animating career with Terrytoons and Paramount cartoon studios in the 1960s, a background that, Michael Barrier rather harshly judges, was "not suitable training grounds for work on any kind of animated features" (572), thanks to those studios' emphasis on highly conventionalized characters and a restricted animation styling most suitable for television. Yet Bakshi clearly developed a distinctive style of his own, one that often recalls the wildly inventive look of underground comics of the 1960s and 1970s. And his early features, most notably efforts like *Fritz the Cat* (1972) and *The Lord of the Rings* (1978), were efforts at pushing the boundaries of the art of animation, the former by introducing that unconventional, underground comics look and incorporating the sort of X-rated material that had never before appeared in mainstream cartooning, and the latter by rotoscoping an epic, live-action narrative to give a highly realistic appearance to Tolkien's fantasy material. In fact, referring to his possible influence on the form, Bakshi proudly asserts, "If I have made one major change in animation, it's that I'm directing as a live-action filmmaker would" (McGilligan 273).

That approach, however, does not serve Bakshi as well in *Cool World* as he tries to meld a variety of image elements: live-action images of the human world, exaggerated but static animation of the Cool World, the often grotesque characters populating that realm who, with their rubber-hose arms and legs and cycled movements, often recall the early days of animation, the realistically conceived and rotoscoped character of Holli Would, and various combinations of these disparate elements. The result is an often ill-fitting conglomeration of images that consistently proves both fascinating and puzzling, attractive and even repulsive. Though the various buildings of the Cool World have faces, teeth, and eyes, like some of those in *Roger Rabbit*'s Toontown, they never really come alive—and thankfully so, since they all seem menacing rather than welcoming. In fact, they are not really animated, just presented as static background tableaux. When Frank walks through that world, it changes and becomes a strange hybrid itself, as animated backgrounds segue into pointedly solid, three-dimensional, yet still exaggerated sets, somewhat in the fashion we saw in Disney's *Song of the South*. But as Frank or the camera moves around the various stylized props and sets, we recognize that they are essentially flat, as if cut out of plywood. The effect is to suggest a world that defies normal logic, since it is, stylistically, both flat and three-dimensional, both fake and real. Though Holli herself is a doodle, the rotoscoping (of actress Kim Bassinger) pointedly distinguishes her from the other grotesque and sometimes crudely drawn cartoon figures here. Her movements seem totally natural, her proportions are precise, and her intense desire "to be real" seems quite appropriate. At any rate, her proud assertion that "I'm not your ordinary doodle" is clearly supported by her rotoscoped figure, which seems an almost natural outgrowth of Bakshi's efforts at sexualizing animation and framing that work in a live-action style. Yet the narrative never explains her manifest difference from the other doodles or how she is able to reach into the human world and, as if at will, simply pull Jack into the Cool World's other dimension. The overall effect here is of a chaotic and unrationalized mix of styles that never quite satisfies, as it pointedly develops a sense of space that stands in opposition to what we find in *Who Framed Roger Rabbit*, yet also seems to recoil from its own hybrid vision.

Admittedly, that rather disjointed sensibility is in some ways appropriate to the disjointed world that *Cool World* sketches. For its world is obviously a dualistic one, its animated and live-action realms existing independently, even if Jack mistakenly believes his comic book drawings have created the Cool World. And that separation is important since, we learn, interaction between the two dimensions could result in calamitous destruction—as if they represented positive and negative matter. Here walls or barriers need to be reinforced, not broken down. Still, doodles like Holli long to be a part of the real world, to be able to feel just like real people do, and humans who have seen images of the Cool World in Jack's comic books equally long to be part of that world—as the Real World Comics cashier confesses to Jack, she believes his "stuff is like crucial spiritual nourishment for people," and she has friends "who want to be Holli Would when they grow up." The dual worlds Bakshi has created are thus similarly ones of longing and frustration, as those in each realm sense the poverty of their world and vainly assume that the other offers something that will make them complete, will add a necessary dimension to their lives.

Yet the film presents neither the tawdry human world of Las Vegas nor the dark, nightmarish Cool World as particularly attractive. Both, as I have noted, are places from which most of their denizens simply want to escape. Their similarity, however, allows Holli to pose a logical and telling question as she challenges Jack's impression that she and her fellow doodles are just products of his imagination. Her teasing query, "Am I dreaming you, or are you dreaming me?" not only, in the best modernist tradition, puts the assumed stability and certainty of the

The doodles invade Las Vegas in the conclusion of *Cool World*.

viewing subject into question, but also opens onto the essential postmodern issue of our own constructedness, of how much the human is itself a kind of imagined—or drawn—product. But posing that question or opening that intellectual door—like the opening of the rift between the Cool World and the human—never brings a satisfying response on any level. It certainly never opens onto what Paul Wells terms the "redemptive . . . influence of the cartoon characters," never helps us interrogate "the meaning of cartoons," never provides any sort of special insight into a human realm of Vegas-dwellers, save for when the doodle invasion that follows Holli's efforts to open a pathway between the two worlds results in humans being transformed into cartoon characters that roughly correspond to their real natures, as slot-playing matrons become grotesque caricatures of themselves and a predatory male literally is transformed into a lounge lizard. Unlike the puncturing of *Who Framed Roger Rabbit*'s wall, removing the barrier between the real and the animated realms produces no hopeful supplement, no satisfying hybrid reality, only a rampant and disturbing reality *effect*. Thus, the film presents the Cool World as a kind of infection that must be countered, a threat to the real, as we see when both Jack and Holli (transformed into a human by having sex with Jack) find themselves changing, beginning to take on the look of cartoon clowns, of flat, grotesque figures. These transformations prove unpredictable and uncontrollable, and they become more frequent as the two dimensions interact, so that the real begins to be replaced by what might most accurately be described as a reality effect, albeit one of an almost hallucinatory and even frightening nature.

Appropriately, these transformations at first go almost unnoticed since the breach occurs in Las Vegas, itself an ersatz world, a place that is all show and entertainment, whose populace already exhibits what might charitably be described as clownish behavior. And perhaps that is the film's real point, that our world has already taken on such grotesque dimensions, has increasingly replaced reality with the effect, that we are becoming, through our own foolish distractions, little more than doodles, cartoon caricatures of the human. But Bakshi's film offers no better alternative in its Cool World inhabitants. Though Jane Goodall in her discussion of the film argues that "mutation . . . is innocent and inconsequential within the confines of the Cool World," and that the various "lunatic Toon mutants are powerless" (162) there, those grotesque creatures tellingly take on a monstrous aspect once they are in the real world, not only by attacking the humans, but, as more and more of them cross over into the real, by threatening to destroy the human dimension completely. Indeed, as more monstrous doodles flood across the portal opened up by the Golden Spike, the very look of the film changes; two-dimensional images crowd out the three-dimensional and effectively literalize the central problem that the film diagnoses: the notion that the real world has become a very fragile place, its spaces ready to flatten out, its inhabitants easily seduced by simple, cartoonish thrills: a speedy motorcycle, a beautifully drawn woman who wants to "do it" with you, the rush of gambling, the thrill of bright lights, garish colors, and loud sounds.

Of course, such a commentary hardly speaks well for the world of animation either. Even if we might "love" our cartoon creations—and in Jack's case, even want to explore that desire's physical consequences—the doodle is certainly a poor substitute for the human. Holli, for example, despite all her attractions, remains just a desperate distraction from Jack's sordid real-world circumstances and a reminder of his inability to form real-world relationships, as his wife's infidelity and his own rejection of romantic overtures by both his neighbor and the comic book store clerk point up. The doodles, the narrative emphasizes, must remain exiled to their world, the breach in the dimensions has to be closed, the two-dimensional cannot be mixed with the three-dimensional lest we all follow Jack's sociopathic path. In light of its potentially catastrophic effect, the flatland of animated images has to remain a kind of "undiscovered country from whose bourn no traveler returns" (*Hamlet* 3.1.778–79), as the death of Frank, the detective who has explored this territory, underscores.

If reaffirming such boundaries seems a strange posture for a postmodern narrative, it is one on which we need to linger because it is precisely here that *Cool World* so pointedly contrasts with *Roger Rabbit* —and here too that both films offer their key glosses on the trajectory of animation. If *Roger Rabbit* finds a note of hope in that animated space of Toontown—and ultimately in the human ability to animate—*Cool World* pulls back from that possibility, almost as if animation itself—or creativity of any sort—were open to suspicion. Thus, taking Jack's pen from his pocket, Frank offers a warning that resonates for both his sexual desires and his cartooning: "One should be careful how they wave this thing." And the film's narrative resolution underscores that caution about how freely we animate space. In fact, it seems to suggest that only by renouncing that "cool" space, the warped space found in the modernist landscape, can we hope to counter what Virilio describes as postmodernism's resulting *"de-realization* of the world" (*Lost* 42). And yet, confusingly enough, the Cool World has the last say here, as the narrative closes on the only successful relationship in the film, that between the doodle "hostess" Lonette and the dead but resurrected-as-a-doodle Frank. According to this conflicted vision, the only satisfying relationship is to be found in that dark and chaotic other realm, in a world whose very unpredictability and chaotic nature seem to make almost anything—even resurrection—possible. In this context that comment we earlier noted, that Jack's "stuff is like crucial spiritual nourishment for people," loses its ironic bite and begins to seem almost an accurate diagnosis of the postmodern situation and its attendant absence of meaning.

Yet the problem, as I have suggested, is that *Cool World* offers little beyond this retreat into animation, really just an acknowledgment of the problem with which Holli confronts Jack when she wonders who is dreaming whom, who is actually the creator here. Bakshi seems content with merely posing that arch question, since despite all the pleasure he apparently takes in giving his imagination free reign, in playfully crossing the boundaries of custom and censorship, his film remains equally skeptical of both the animated world (which, Jack notes, served him as a kind of buffer from the dark reality of prison life) and the real world, whose only embodiment here is the gaudy artifice of Las Vegas. If Bakshi's career as an animator has become stalled, lost the direction suggested by earlier efforts such as *Fritz the Cat* and *The Lord of the Rings*, it may well be because he has, in postmodern fashion, lost some of his own faith in the possibilities of animating space.

Yet historically, *Who Framed Roger Rabbit* and *Cool World* help us gauge what has happened to both the space of animation and our ability to give life to that world. Both detect—and respond to—a kind of crisis in animating space that, they equally suggest, runs parallel to a crisis in the real world: a loss of direction, of dimension, of meaning—in effect, a loss of our own sense of reality.[4] Though *Cool World* uses its hybrid vision to evoke the allure of animation, to point up how our creations might help us cope with an inescapably dreary world, it also pulls back from that point, as if recognizing the implications of its essential equation of doodles and noids, of the sort of leveling out, flattening, and derealization that *its* hybrid style seems to champion. In contrast, *Roger Rabbit*, with its more archeological approach, digs into both our cultural and cartoon past to open up another possibility for the future, seeing in its hybrid figures not a threat to our own dimension—and dimensionality—but a valuable supplement to its dimensionality, even a way of reanimating our own world, bringing it back to life. Perhaps that hopeful vision helps explain the great success of this film, even as the world of animation was on the verge of a revolution in both style and technology, as the possibilities for digital animation were beginning to become apparent. But just as important was its sense of the very value of animation—how it could appeal across generations, speak to our larger cultural concerns, further open up our experience of the cinema. In fact, as we break through the wall of the Acme warehouse at film's end, we literally open up a new dimension, as *Roger Rabbit* draws out of the past a vision of animation's new three-dimensional promise that would soon be fulfilled in the cartoons that have come flooding forth from Pixar, Dreamworks, Blue Sky, and the various other animation houses that the new digital regime has called into being.

And in this respect *Cool World* too deserves some credit as a kind of model for this historical development. That two-way desire to "cross over," to become an inhabitant of another world, is a driving impetus behind our technological replacements for rotoscoping: the motion-capture and computer-generated imagery (CGI) effects that would allow live characters to become animated figures (as in the case of Golum in Peter Jackson's *Lord of the Rings* films) and animated figures to seem almost tangibly real (as in the *Pirates of the Caribbean* films' Kraaken). Holli and her ilk did not call these works into existence, draw them across a real or aesthetic divide, but the interrogation that this film, along with *Who Framed Roger Rabbit,* undertook certainly helped prepare the way, signaled the great possibilities. For both effectively frame the question of animation, of what happens when one opens up cinematic space and gives it life. Through their respective hybrid visions, each suggests how crucial Virilio's caution about the reality effect that has become pervasive in postmodern culture might be to both animated film and life itself.

9

THE PIXAR REALITY

Digital Space and Beyond

The groundbreaking Pixar animated film *Toy Story* (1995) opens on a curious note of what I have elsewhere termed "surface play" (*Mouse* 168). As the narrative begins we see a pattern of very white clouds set against a bright blue background, the clouds all evenly spaced and stylized, the blue "sky" far too consistent and bright to be real, and the overall image, lacking in any depth cues, unnaturally flat. It is, we soon realize, a fake sky, actually the wallpaper in the child Andy's room, as the tracking camera reveals by showing us the various toys with which Andy is playing, buildings he has artlessly constructed of old boxes, a baseboard horizon, and, a bit later, a sharply contrasting view through an open window of "real" clouds and a hazy, "real" blue sky. The trick here is a wonderfully resonant one, not only because of the way it evokes the workings of a child's imagination—showing how easily he can construct worlds within worlds for his own amusement—but also because of the manner in which this surface play directly addresses the work of animation and especially the perceived power of the new digital regime to offer a different level of realistic reproduction, a major leap beyond traditional 2-D animation.

In opening with this trompe l'oeil effect, *Toy Story* quickly signals its own attitude toward that reality effect I discussed earlier. On the one hand, it is somewhat disarming in the way it seems so forthrightly to address what digital animation might do, how nearly it might, even in this first fully computer-animated feature, be expected to approach the

The artlessly constructed narrative world of the child at the start of *Toy Story* (1995).

real and catch us up in its simulacrum effect. In fact, we might even see the flat, evenly spaced, and stylized images, along with the clumsily constructed world of old boxes and cardboard pieces that Andy has put together as "sets" for his game playing, as a kind of joke about those expectations—one in keeping with the various other self-referential or inside jokes that we find scattered through our first glimpses of Andy's room, such as the lamp from Pixar's Academy Award–nominated short *Luxo Jr.* and the various books on Andy's shelves that bear the titles of previous Pixar films, such as *The Adventures of André and Wally B.*, *Red's Dream*, and *Knick Knack* (1989), or the later reflexive effects in the film, including references to other Disney movies, such as *The Lion King* (1994). Yet, on the other hand, that self-conscious imagery also pointedly contrasts with the world we eventually see through Andy's window and that the narrative later explores in greater detail when Woody, one of Andy's toys, is forced to leave the safe space of Andy's house to rescue another toy, Buzz Lightyear, from the neighboring child Sid. That reality is indeed impressive, a striking indication of what Pixar was already able to achieve with its RenderMan software, which was quickly becoming an industry standard.[1] A convincing sense of depth because of its built-in multiplane effect; varied image textures; complex figure and structure modeling, thanks to its lighting effects—these are all hallmarks of that "outside" space that the narrative increasingly puts on display as it takes us deeper into its world, and as it unfolds its more complex vision of what lies behind those naive and childish images on which the film opens.

Perhaps more important, in laying out two very different sorts of constructed imagery, and in playing on both the lowest and highest expectations that its audience—or at least its adult audience—might have entertained for this landmark animated film, *Toy Story* quickly establishes a level of dialogue between these different expectations, between different possibilities for the new digital art it was heralding. Certainly the makers of *Toy Story* ultimately did not want to play down what they were up to, what they hoped to achieve, and what a decade of creating experimental animated shorts had tantalizingly suggested they *could* achieve. But they also recognized that the text they produced, one that is, as we have already suggested, highly self-conscious on a number of levels, needed to stay aware of both the different sort of world they were creating and the possibility that their audience might respond to it differently from the way they would to traditional two-dimensional, hand-drawn animation of the sort that Pixar's partner in this effort, Walt Disney Pictures, had built an entertainment empire on. In effect, what they sought to do was to clear out a space for their own approach to animation, one that, as the art director Ralph Eggleston notes, was intentionally "highly stylized—a cross between live-action reality and a typical squash-and-stretch cartoon world" (Street 85). In fact, that negotiated style would eventually come to be known at Pixar as "hyper-reality," a term that means, as David A. Price explains, "a stylized realism that had a lifelike feel without actually being photorealistic" (213).

Michael Barrier notes something of this difference in approach in his brief assessment of *Toy Story*. He suggests that the film was fundamentally—and even "cannily," as he puts it—informed by a sense of both its limits and its potential. With its cast composed mostly of toys, it could build its narrative around "highly artificial characters . . . whose reality is more charming than disturbing" (572)—and whose "reality" would provide the animators with some important stylistic leeway. By emphasizing toys, the filmmakers would not be so troubled by the difficulties of capturing skin and hair textures, and the plastic sheen that typically marked early digital images would even seem natural. And another level of the natural could also prove less disconcerting for audiences unaccustomed to the surprisingly realistic effects that Pixar was already able to accomplish. As we initially noted, the film manages an almost uncanny sense of visual space, achieves a three-dimensionality that evokes the world of live-action cinema without actually threatening our sense of the real. For Barrier that effect follows from its generally "charming" character, lodged in its almost nostalgic tone, its endearing characters, and the comforts of its narrative about the values of friendship. Yet I suggest that this effect owed as much to that carefully considered style as it did to a nostalgic tone or set of simple values.

Before proceeding to sketch that style, we should consider the context from which *Toy Story* and its digital brethren emerged. For example, we might note that even before Pixar and Disney launched into the coproduction agreement that would beget *Toy Story* and a string of other successful features, and before Disney had fully committed its own animation program to the new digital form, there had been other efforts at negotiating a kind of compromise with digital technology. In fact, Disney for a number of years had been trying to develop ways of bringing together traditional hand-drawn and computer animation on its own, of integrating their aesthetics and possibilities. Following its groundbreaking work on the science fiction film *Tron,* which used then-state-of-the-art CGI effects to visualize the virtual world inside a computer, the company had combined conventional hand-drawn animation with computer imagery for the climactic fight inside London's Big Ben tower in *The Great Mouse Detective* (1986), to produce the remarkably three-dimensional ballroom dance scene of *Beauty and the Beast* (1989), to depict the Cave of Wonders in *Aladdin* (1991), and to create the wildebeest stampede scene in *The Lion King.* So by the time *Toy Story* had entered production, the combination of differently sourced visuals—what we might well think of as another, if almost invisible, sort of hybridity—was becoming just as common in the world of Disney animation as the combination of live-action or miniatures with CGI effects was in big-budget, nonanimated fantasy productions during this same period, as films like *Terminator 2: Judgment Day* (1991) and *Jurassic Park* (1993) illustrate. As Charles Solomon suggests, it was becoming a case of the animating artists realizing that they had "another arrow in their quiver and another tool in their kit" (Lyons 62), at least as long as the animators did not succumb to one of the primary lures that CGI also offered, the ability—and the temptation—to dazzle audiences with impossible camera movements and angles, with a vision totally divorced from the world of live-action cinema to which they were accustomed.[2]

Yet in notching that digital arrow, the Pixar animators were also "cannily" evolving a theory for their digital animation, one that drew

on those earlier efforts at marrying traditional and computer animation. *Toy Story*'s director, Jon Lasseter, notes that, with their cutting-
edge technology, particularly the new RenderMan software, he "knew
that we could produce settings that looked absolutely real"; but at the
same time he "didn't want the audience to think it was a real world. I
want the audience to say, 'I know this isn't real, but my gosh, it looks
real.' It was very important that this be a caricature of reality" (French
32). Following this lead, the art director Ralph Eggleston explains the
sort of guidelines that he and the Pixar animators then established to
further promote that internal dialogue Lasseter describes, how, even
with living toys as characters, they did not want them "doing things
they weren't physically capable of doing. Their eyes don't pop out, like
Roger Rabbit, because it's physically impossible—they're made of plastic. We were very careful about how far we pushed things" (French 33).
Consequently, they consistently sought "to tread a fine line between
making the settings too realistic and too cartoony" (French 33), to follow what we might describe as a compromise aesthetic.

It was a compromise that became especially pointed in efforts at
dealing with the space that was to be animated. As Lasseter explains,
the animating team created a guiding philosophy for "the look of the
film," for their animating space: "We went beyond reality, caricaturing
to make it more believable" (Street 83). And Eggleston explains how, in
designing the houses in which much of the action takes place, "we did
things like making the doorknobs bigger, the baseboards higher, and
the doorways narrower, but nothing too obvious. It was taking elements
from reality and making them into a heightened reality, because I didn't
want to make it photo-realistic" (French 33). In fact, in some instances
size and volume become curiously fluid, such as when Sid's porch light
can in the same scene both fit through a hole in the ceiling and sit
securely over the hole, as if had suddenly gained in circumference. And
for the various scenes in Sid's room, the decision was made to fashion a
stylized, almost expressionistic look by using a wide-angle lens effect
that warped straight lines to make the audience sense that things were
not quite right, thereby helping foster what Eggleston terms "a creepy
feeling" (French 33) for that environment, which was, in turn, enhanced
by a very unnatural lighting scheme.

Contributing to this philosophy is an effect that early digital artists

The distorted, caricatured reality of Sid's room in *Toy Story*.

often noted and that Pixar's founder and former president, Dr. Edwin Catmull, has analyzed. He explains that the group decided specifically "to make humans that are stylized, not real," because "the closer you get to reality, that's when the brain starts to kick in with its auto-recognizers, and thinks something is a little weird. If you back off, and make the humans more abstract, audiences will accept it more readily" (French 20). What he is referring to is a principle commonly cited in robotics studies that is called "the valley of the uncanny." As Dennis Muren, a visual effects artist, explains, "As something gets closer to reality, it's more enjoyable; and then it drops off immediately, just before it hits absolute reality. . . . As soon as the stuff becomes really close to reality, it starts to look bad" (Duncan et al., "State" 77). Or to be more precise, it becomes unsettling to the audience in the way that uncanny occurrences typically do; viewers get, as the computer effects artist Andy Jones proposes, "weirded out by it" (Duncan et al., "State" 77). So only flirting with the effect, or just trying to avoid that "valley" alto-gether, became a guiding policy for *Toy Story,* as well as for Pixar's sub-sequent productions.

What is important to emphasize, though, is the way in which this stylistic approach would also affect the very narratives of the Pixar films, as they consistently seem to reflect the difficult dynamics of this underlying aesthetic, as a new approach to animating space inflects the animated story. As we look at the range of Pixar productions that fol-lowed *Toy Story,* we see a kind of internalizing of this principle, as the "valley of the uncanny" became not only a stylistic marker, but also a kind of story guideline. To further contextualize this development, we might recall Hal Foster's description of the shift from modernist to postmodernist notions of space, as typically demonstrated in architectural design. He notes how "the modern paradigm . . . in which the form expresses the building almost sculpturally, sometimes with its space, structure, and program distorted in the interest of monumental effect," gives way to a "decorated" paradigm, a model in which—and here he cites two iconic figures of pop-postmodern design, Robert Venturi and his wife, Denise Scott Brown—there is "a rhetorical front and conventional behind," a flat, decorated facade and a more functional depth (H. Foster 167). The result is a spatial construct that presents a level of flatness but also reveals a necessary if surprising depth. It thus always seems to speak of an internal tension between the functional and the decorative, the hidden and the displayed, the full space of modernism and the "lost" or "compressed" space of the postmodern world.

To explore this pattern of internal tensions further, I will trace their workings in several later Pixar films, most notably *Monsters, Inc.* (2001), *The Incredibles* (2004), and *Cars* (2006). I choose these films particularly because each of them pointedly addresses some of the new stylistic challenges facing digital animators: *Monsters, Inc.,* the great variety of surface textures, and especially fur, found in its monstrous stars; *The Incredibles,* issues of skin texture, hair, fabric, and the effects of water; and *Cars,* concerns with motion and space. And each embeds its increasingly sophisticated imagery within a narrative that seems designed to carry on its own dialogue about how nearly the film might approach the real, about the relation between its "rhetorical front and conventional behind" that is, as we have seen, so neatly visualized in the opening scene of *Toy Story.*

In fact, the introductory scene of *Monsters, Inc.* clearly echoes that of *Toy Story,* as it plays a similar visual joke on the audience, and in the process lays out the terms for its own commentary on the space of animation. Here we begin with a far more common and naturalistically conceived scene, an image of a child sleeping in his bed, and a variety of effects—the soft lighting of dusk, a view of trees swaying just outside a window, and curtains being gently moved by a breeze—all reinforce the scene's realistic nature. That scene quickly changes valence, though, as we hear ominous sounds, a looming shadow rises over the child's bed, and gleaming eyes appear in the darkness. The seemingly innocent scene has suddenly taken on all the coloring of a generic narrative, of a slasher horror film in the tradition of *Halloween* (1978) and *Nightmare on Elm Street* (1980). Yet here too the joke quickly follows, when a snarling monster, confronted by the screaming child, is himself scared witless, even though he knows that this is all simply "a simulation," a training set to teach young monsters how to scare. The lighting, breezes, swaying trees, even the child are all just created and manipulated effects, although like most of the effects in conventional film narrative, they are convincing enough to capture in the narrative's coils those who are willing to play by its rules. And it is a reminder, right from the start of *Monsters, Inc.*, of how easily the real might become lost in that play of surfaces, of conventionally conceived and read icons and effects.

If *Monsters, Inc.* initially underscores the fact that the three-dimensional world is often simply "a simulation" or series of coded effects, it also seems far more conscious of and more intent on evoking a sense of depth than this opening might suggest. Movement into or from the center of the frame is a constant, as we see when the monster heroes Mike and Sully exit their apartment building and walk to work down a tree-lined avenue (along with a back-tracking camera that leads them into the foreground), when they enter the monumentally designed Monsters, Inc., building, and as a group of monsters enters the cavernous "scare floor" from the background in slow motion, evoking a live-action telephoto shot. Centered, balanced, with a clear vanishing point, and using movement directly into the foreground or background, such shots suggest the conventionally constructed depth that we find throughout classical film narrative and in what we might also term classical animation.[3] And the film trades on that effect at every turn, since much of the action becomes a series of chases, primarily through the corridors and back passages of the Monsters, Inc., facility. Thus, we see Mike running down a series of three corridors while being chased by his nemesis Randall; Sully running through corridors and bursting through a door in search of Boo; Mike, Sully, and Boo running through another corridor as they try to get back to Boo's special door; and Sully and Boo searching through a dark passageway in the recesses of the factory for Mike. All these scenes are centered on lengthy and repeated movement directly into the foreground or background, and with the aid of constantly tracking (virtual) cameras all effectively convey the sense of real space that is one of the advertised strengths of digital animation—in fact, one of the rationales for describing it as 3-D as opposed to 2-D animation.

And yet the film's central design scheme, as the abstract, limited animation credit sequence points up, is based on a flat surface: a multitude of doors that must constantly be opened and reopened to produce screams from scared children—and thus power. This repeated two-dimensional image effectively stands for a practical three-dimensional space, the "rhetorical front," commanding and controlling the "conventional behind" of children's bedrooms, and thus suggesting the sort of spatial dialogue we have already described.[4] In fact, I would argue that the narrative's key sequence grows directly from this relationship. Just off the "Scare Floor," the area where the monsters enter those doors, is a vast warehouse, wherein millions of doors are stored and almost constantly pushed along conveyors at dizzying speeds. To complete the logic of the scare "industry," the film has to visualize this process, which it does through a combination of subjective shots—from the vantage of the monster heroes Mike and Sully—and extreme long shots. Looking down a single conveyor into the center of the storage facility produces a sense of imposing, even foreboding depth, and racing along the conveyors repeats the chase pattern we have already noted, but the great many shots showing the enormous number of doors and the crisscrossing conveyors, all done from a variety of angles, produce a dizzying Escher-like vision, where depth disappears, where opening a door on a vertical plane can inexplicably land one in a room arranged on a horizontal axis, and where breaking a door can effectively make its reality disappear. It is, as Virilio describes the often confounding nature of the postmodern world, "an environment where the appearances are against us" (*Lost* 24), where the experience of depth again seems a kind of trick produced by a flat surface.[5] Yet it is also one wherein the connections between those appearances and the depths they variously signal seem to be in constant negotiation.

Intriguingly, the film's final scene shifts from this spatial dialogue to suggest a different sense of depth and of reality. It ends with Mike presenting Sully with a reconstructed version of the child Boo's door; Sully opens it, and with a look of outward regard he stares—and then smiles—into the camera. That lingering look of recognition satisfyingly suggests what has been regained here: that Sully and Boo will get to see each other again and their warm, almost familial relationship might be reaffirmed. But it also seems an effort to regain something more, a sense of the conventional spatial depth that marks so many of the scenes of casual movement and the chases that occur throughout the narrative. In classical narratives that depth is often built up from such characters' looks, sutured together through eyeline matches, glance-object relationships, subjective shot–reaction shot editing, and so on. But here we are left with only one side of that relationship, as if pointing to a more extensive space that continues to lie, elusively, just offscreen. We might take it as another sort of acknowledgment of what this animation might achieve, another mark of the compromise approach we observed in *Toy Story*. The real space—and the true depth of relationship—*Monsters, Inc.* suggests, always remains just beyond the "rhetorical front" of the film itself, in the world of the audience, which is also implicated in and firmly fixed by Sully's final gaze. In the best postmodern manner, his look implies that real space is always partly constructed by our own point of view.

With *The Incredibles* Pixar at least on one level sought to fill in that look of outward regard. It was the studio's first feature effort to focus its own gaze entirely on the human realm, and thus to deal in greater detail than ever before with the problems posed by creating digital human figures—with issues of skin texture, hair, clothing fabrics, the expressions involved in *human* interactivity—while also addressing the complex issues presented by fire and *wet* skin, hair, and clothing.[6] Adding to the challenge was the fact that such technical issues were largely outside the director Brad Bird's experience. He, along with several collaborators he brought onto the project, all veterans of his previous feature, *The Iron Giant* (1999), had worked mainly in traditional cel animation. In light of these various challenges, as well as the expectations of audiences who had experienced an unbroken string of successes from Pixar, we might well wonder if we should read Mr. Incredible's opening remark in the film in the same reflexive, self-deprecating, and even disarming vein as the openings of both *Toy Story* and *Monsters, Inc.*, as he tells a television interviewer, "Who wants the pressure of being *super* all the time?"

And indeed, some reviewers concentrated precisely on how well Bird and the Pixar team managed to meet these technical challenges and ultimately live up to the animation studio's reputation for being "super." Jessica Winter of the *Village Voice,* for example, while recognizing a newly sophisticated tone for *The Incredibles,* remarks that "everything here, from foliage to human skin, appears crafted from the same chunk of cold, gleaming titanium." And the *Observer*'s Mark Kermode effectively dismissed the film as little more than a technical showcase, suggesting that its main appeal was "for those geeks who 'ooh' and 'aah' at the hyperspace mathematics involved in digitally animating hair and water." Of course, the film would prove far more successful than these minority grumblings would have predicted, as it was nominated for multiple Academy Awards, won for Best Animated Feature, and finished in the top five for domestic film grosses for 2004, truly a super performance.

In this case the narrative does not begin with a visual trick to demonstrate how easily the illusion of depth and dimensionality might be constructed, although there is a kind of self-conscious narrative prologue. *The Incredibles* opens on a set of markedly grainy and flat images, offered in Academy aspect ratio (the standard screen shape of television and of film into the 1950s), rather than the sort of highly polished, wide-screen ones audiences had come to expect, as a television program offers interviews with the superheroes Mr. Incredible, Frozone, and Elastigirl, all in the prime of their careers, sometime in the 1950s. In each case, the interviews are done as direct addresses to the audience, all as extended looks of outward regard, after the fashion of the final shot of *Monsters, Inc.* On the one hand, they serve to establish from the start of the narrative the personalities of these three key figures—Mr. Incredible's smug, self-confident manner, Frozone's cool, humorous detachment, Elastigirl's protofeminist insistence on playing "up there with the big dogs." Yet, on the other, they invoke the offscreen space of the audience, that depth that is always elided from the film narrative but that becomes especially important here, as *The Incredibles* establishes that its key concern is what is going on in that "real" space: our rising cultural tendency to suspect and even attack the extraordinary, to embrace the simplistic, or as Mr. Incredible, after the government assigns him the new identity of Bob Parr, will later sum up, "to celebrate mediocrity."

In fact, the narrative develops largely around the contrast between the everyday, mainly domestic world that has become the home of the various "supers" in hiding, including Mr. and Mrs. Incredible and their children, Violet, Dash, and Jack-Jack, and the fantastic world of super-heroes and supervillains, represented by the hidden lair of Syndrome—Nomanisan Island, a place clearly modeled on the various fanciful retreats created for the villains of such James Bond films as *Dr. No* (1962) and *You Only Live Twice* (1967). The everyday world in which Bob, Helen, and their family live is quite conventional, as the film focuses on their suburban tract home, the city, and the Insuricare offices where Bob works. That world is depicted in highly conventional cine-matic techniques: layering of subjects, parallel actions in foreground and background, movement into the background or foreground, focal shifts between foreground and background elements, and so on. In a montage of the "happy" Parr household, for example, we see Bob in the foreground sneak up on Helen in mid-frame and kiss her; Bob chase Helen across the background while Violet, in the foreground, listens to music on her headphones, oblivious to what is going on; Bob back his car into the street from the garage in the foreground and, following a dissolve, drive a new car back into the garage and toward the camera; and Bob and Helen pass between foreground and background and, alternately, each turn to pinch the other. In these scenes and elsewhere the narrative seems intent on building up a solid and conventionally cin-ematic three-dimensional world, a reality familiar to filmgoers and one to which these superheroes (like the Pixar animators, we might add) are trying to conform as they work hard at becoming a conventional cine-matic family.

Yet at the same time the narrative also deploys that conventional sense of space it constructs as a key metaphor, specifically as a way for measuring the problems that Bob and the other supers have had in accommodating to this conventional world. While Bob's friend Lucius, aka Frozone, recalls how their mutual acquaintance Gazerbeam "had trouble adjusting to civilian life" and so became an activist for "super-hero rights," the narrative repeatedly provides us with a more immedi-ate visual measure for Mr. Incredible's own difficulty in this regard. In Bob's fifteen years as a "civilian," his already exaggerated physique has greatly expanded, and so in scene after scene he tries with great diffi-culty to squeeze into too-tight spaces—his minicar, his work cubicle, small chairs, his "super suit," even an airplane escape pod—and often with some embarrassment. That conventionally three-dimensional world, we are constantly reminded, simply does not fit his larger-than-life—and now fatter than most—physique, while it also effectively externalizes his psychological difficulties in trying to conform to the patterns and restrictions of an everyday, nonheroic life.

In contrast to this everyday world, the narrative offers the more fantastic space of Syndrome's island—a world conceived not two-dimensionally but after the fashion of *Monsters, Inc.*'s "rhetorical front and conventional behind." Nomanisan Island is a pointedly mysterious and tricky setting, its jungle disguising the sinister activities going on there, its volcano cone a hidden launch site for ballistic missiles, the island interior honeycombed with caves and constructed tunnels and passageways. When Mr. Incredible is taken to the island by plane, the plane does not land on a conventional runway; rather, it suddenly dives into the water and surfaces like a submarine somewhere inside the island. The entrance to his host's headquarters lies behind a giant waterfall, which must be parted by a device that suggests a massive windshield wiper. The wall of a conference room suddenly rises like a garage door to reveal the jungle, and a robot that then tries to kill Mr. Incredible. And Syndrome's secret computer control room lies behind a sheer wall of lava, which can also be mysteriously parted for access. It seems that the island is marked by a great variety of such surprising facades, trick entries, and disguised passages, suggesting not only Syndrome's own mysterious nature and secret plans, but also the complex nature of this world—a complexity that cannot be repressed or hidden by the government, as that of the

An instance of the fantastic space found on Syndrome's island in *The Incredibles* (2004).

supers has been, and one that cannot be represented in the customary dimensional manner of conventional cinema.

The pattern that we might note in *The Incredibles,* then, is one wherein the space of narration forms a parallel to and indeed *becomes* the stuff of narration, as our conventional sense of space is shown to be inadequate for suggesting the complex, dangerous, and indeed incredible nature of this world's reality. As a further example, we might consider two similar scenes that the narrative arranges in parallel: a dinner scene in which Bob, Helen, and their kids gather around the family table, and a later scene in which Mr. Incredible dines with Syndrome's assistant Mirage on Nomanisan Island. The former scene emphasizes the conventional space of the home: Bob reaches across the table to cut Dash's meat, Dash and Violet chase around the table and need to be restrained by a stretched-to-the-limit Helen, and Bob comes into the image to "engage," as Helen urges him, by picking up the table while characters seemingly dangle from every angle. The scene thus nicely conveys its three-dimensionality but also produces a visual chaos to match the verbal cacophony of their arguing, which testifies to the dysfunctional nature of the family and thereby hints at a threat to the nuclear family that is bound up in (or hidden behind) this "normal" reality. The latter scene, in contrast, depicts Mr. Incredible's meal with Mirage as quiet, understated, and filled with witty, sexually charged repartee, after the fashion of many James Bond films. More significantly, it occurs with the principals at opposite ends of an impossibly long table, arranged horizontally in the frame and lit to reduce the image's sense of depth. Yet that exaggerated flat tableau gives way to a series of shot/reverse-shot images showing each character at an end of the table, but with both in the frame, and condensing space as if with a telephoto effect to suggest an intimacy to their discussion and a mutual pleasure in each other's company. It is a scene that pointedly *constructs* space, does so in a fantastic manner, and thereby reinscribes the different nature of this world. But its very sense of difference also underscores a lack in that earlier image of the modern American family meal, while pointing toward what the culture of modern America, as depicted here, has consistently sought to repress—the importance of difference and even the pleasure in being oneself, in this instance in being super.

In fact, it is in this context that we might see *The Incredibles'* style best serving the film's key thematic structure. In an interesting model of formal and spatial complexity, it stages its primary concerns with repression and expression, conformity and individuality, the mediocre and the incredible, precisely in terms of space—the space of what we would think of as normal, everyday life, and the space we would consign to the realm of fantasy. What the film suggests is that our efforts to limit how we think of the real or even to visualize it solely in a conventionalized three-dimensional way are no more appropriate for dealing with its complexity than are government strategies for transforming the supers into insurance adjusters and the like. Those efforts all constitute another sort of "rhetorical front," one that is destined to be blasted apart when this world's complexity once again asserts itself. And this is precisely the point emphasized by the film's final scene when a mundane event—a middle school track meet—is suddenly disrupted by the appearance of a new supervillain, the Underminer, a cartoonish-looking character whose massive tunneling device bursts through one of those "fronts," a normal downtown city street, and he announces to the panicked populace his plans to rule the world. There are, quite simply, depths that escape us, that are repressed, that fall outside our conventional representations, and *The Incredibles*, for all its accomplishments at creating a simulacrum of live-action cinema, acknowledges that fact, even makes it part of its design scheme.

It is a pattern of what we might term technical self-consciousness that we can easily note in other Pixar films, but most notably in *Cars*, which heavily foregrounds one of the key breakthroughs of the company's RenderMan software, motion blur. In representing a character or thing in motion, computer animation, before RenderMan's introduction, typically produced multiple perfect images of the subject, which resulted in a motion sequence that could seem, for all its crispness, unnaturally pixilated. RenderMan, however, introduced three-dimensional motion blur to produce a more naturalistic illusion of motion—or rather, to imitate how we typically *perceive* objects in motion. With its focus on racing, *Cars* naturally makes elaborate use of that capability with both its extreme long shots that transform the speeding race cars into brightly colored but almost indistinct shapes, and its track-level shots in which small details such as tire lettering, lug nuts, and small sponsor decals blur, whereas larger images such as car numbers and the "facial" details

Selective spatial blurring in Pixar's *Cars* (2006).

that have been created for the personified autos—visual elements that we need to see clearly for narrative reasons—remain distinct. The result, even in mobile shots, is an intense spectatorial sense, as if we were witnessing real movement through real space. In fact, *Cars* almost seems like a narrative designed to foreground and capitalize precisely on issues of movement and vision.

Thus, the director John Lasseter mines that convincing illusion of motion for narrative effect by fundamentally integrating a concern with speed and its implications into his story. *Cars* is at every level concerned with reminding us about how exciting and involving the world of racing is, but also how much we miss—both personally and culturally—as we commit to the excitement of constant motion, how much of our world becomes little more than a blur if we always speed through life, as is the case with the new racing star Lightning McQueen. Bypassed by the new interstate expressway, thrust into the background of contemporary life, the town of Radiator Springs, once a picturesque stop along the famous Route 66, now struggles to survive, while its car inhabitants nostalgically recall its once vibrant times. But when McQueen becomes stranded there and is forced to slow down, to spend some time with its inhabitants and consider their needs, he becomes more fully dimensioned, even a better racer, as we see when he employs Doc Hudson's advice to avoid crashing in the Piston Cup Race and later stops just shy of winning the race to help his competitor the King cross the finish line and so end his career on an affirmative note.

That slowing down by McQueen, moreover, heralds a shift in this world. His subsequent decision to base his racing team in Radiator Springs prompts others to slow down as well, to visit the town and effectively put it, as McQueen notes, "back on the map." In fact, the film concludes with a montage of shots that emphasize this new spatial status, as a map of the Southwest fills the screen, prominently showing Radiator Springs near the expressway; cars take the Radiator Springs off-ramp; billboards point the way; and another prominent sign reads, "Here It Is," as an aerial shot then provides an overview of the now-bustling small town. With that shift in speed, it seems, space itself has been rediscovered and reconfigured, as the blur of modern life (Virilio's "speed-space") finds its complement in the lost dimensions of the past.

That same emphasis on reclaiming a lost space, we might note, is also at the core of a more recent Pixar release, the Academy Award–winning *WALL-E* (2008), wherein the Earth itself—much like Radiator Springs—has been abandoned and left in the hands of robots who are tasked with cleaning up the planet, rendering it beautiful and habitable once more. That narrative foundation offers a compelling fable for a postmodern culture, one awash in its own physical and intellectual discards, and all too ready to abandon its past rather than examine and learn from it. At the same time that narrative conception is also wonderfully resonant, easily mapped onto the situation facing the digital animator who sees him- or herself tasked with a version of the titular WALL-E's work: recovering that lost space, cleaning up and revealing the forgotten beauties of reality for a humanity that has distanced itself from this world, in this instance abandoning it to sail through space on speedy rocket cruise liners. But the consistent project of the Pixar films is to suggest ways to get back, to map out alternatives to a postmodern retreat from the real and from the world. They have done so by creating a "complexity in both composition and construction," by folding the work of the digital animator and the problems of animating space into the work of the narratives,[7] in the process effectively marking the studio's films off from those of their competitors in the suddenly crowded territory of the contemporary digital animated feature.

On that note, though, we should acknowledge that Pixar's efforts represent only a small portion of what has recently become a very competitive field of digital animated features. Of course, since its full acquisition by Disney in 2006 and John Lasseter's repositioning as chief creative officer and head of Imagineering at Disney, both Pixar and the Walt Disney Animation Studios, which has already released such accomplished digital animated features as *Chicken Little* (2005), *Meet the Robinsons* (2007), and *Bolt* (2008), promise to pursue an even more ambitious production policy, one that also includes another sort of spatial initiative, the use of the latest 3-D image technology (specifically, Disney's Real-D technology). But Pixar's consistent ability to produce major box-office successes and its demonstration that computer animation can appeal to a large cross section of the movie audience have inspired a number of other studios to enter the business of digital animation—some of them already rivaling Pixar's success, at least at the box office. In fact, a record twenty films were nominated for the 2010 Academy Awards in the Best Animated Feature category, the majority of them computer animated.

The most notable of the competitors to Pixar is Dreamworks Animation, which has produced some of the highest-grossing films in the field with its *Shrek* features (2001, 2004, 2007), and indeed the first of these films won the initial Academy Award given for Best Animated Feature. And Dreamworks' successful challenge to Pixar's dominance, accompanied by the ready availability of software and massive computing power, has prompted a number of other companies to begin producing animated features. Among them we might especially point to the Paramount/Nickelodeon collaborations *Jimmy Neutron, Boy Genius* (2001) and *Barnyard* (2006); Warner Bros.' *The Ant Bully* (2006) and *Happy Feet* (2006); Blue Sky Studios/Twentieth Century–Fox Animation's *Ice Age* films (2002, 2006, 2009), *Robots* (2005), and *Dr. Seuss's Horton Hears a Who* (2008); and Sony Pictures/Imageworks' *Open Season* (2006), *Monster House* (2006), and *Surf's Up* (2007). These and a variety of other recent features suggest that 3-D computer animation is a vibrant field that provides opportunities for new talent and demonstrates that there is a strong audience for such family-oriented efforts.

And yet, at this stage few of these efforts have been able to match the combination of box-office and critical success that has marked the Pixar Animation Group's work. Dreamworks' most successful films, the *Shrek* stories, though clever in their efforts at inverting the conventions of the traditional fairy tale, are also a bit mean-spirited and predictable—highly self-conscious efforts at being hip and anti-Disney. As one commentator notes, they seem to operate under a "compulsion to check off categories (up-to-the-minute hipsterism, fart jokes for the kids, blueish double-entendres for the teenagers and adults, a barrage of visual and aural cues that keep the action cynically grounded in hip-hop/mall/Internet culture)" (Jones 24). The company's *Madagascar* (2005) and *Madagascar: Escape 2 Africa* (2008), while also weakly constructed, have been more adept at matching highly stylized characters to a designed world, while also linking their stylized vision to narratives about escaping from conventional spaces. Blue Sky's *Ice Age* and *Robots* movies have captured some of the same kinetic attractions that marked Warner Bros.' Bugs Bunny and Road Runner cartoons of the 1940s and 1950s, but they are also invariably weighed down by weak plots and characters. Although they are at times visually impressive, most of these films seem to stumble on the postmodern moment, as Kent Jones suggests when he describes how they "continually ricochet between verisimilitude and playacting, . . . erect visions only to reveal their flimsy undersides" (24).

Pixar, however, has consistently managed to address new challenges in digital animation, to develop tools for coping with those challenges, and even to fold the problems of digitally animating space into the space of its animated stories. It has, as a result, consistently led the animation field into the digital era, while maintaining an important continuity, even a dialogue, with the traditions of conventional 2-D animation. That success follows largely from the sophisticated conceptualization of computer animation that was practically forced on the artists and technicians at Pixar. They have had to figure out, essentially from the start, what could be done in and with this new approach to the art form, how they might negotiate with reality to blend together what we earlier describe as a "rhetorical front and conventional behind," or what we might think of as the simultaneously realistic and fantastic possibilities that both challenge and mark all digital animation.

10

DIGITAL EFFECTS ANIMATION AND
THE NEW HYBRID CINEMA

The film industry will enter into crisis when it ends production of the false day, when it pretends to verisimilitude.
—Paul Virilio, *The Aesthetics of Disappearance*, 63

In reacting to the sudden flowering of another sort of heavily designed film, the German expressionist cinema of the post–World War I era, the art critic Herman G. Scheffauer praised its potential influence on cinematic representation. As we note in our discussion of Mickey Mouse, he felt that it heralded the dawn of a new "stereoscopic universe" in film. Despite expressionist cinema's frequent reliance on painted backdrops, on stylized studio sets, on forced perspective, indeed, on a highly artificial mise-en-scène, he was struck by the extent to which it seemed to suggest that "a fourth dimension" had "begun to evolve out of this photographic cosmos" that was the conventional silent cinema (77). Certainly no one would suggest that the unnaturally flat and vertiginously angled sets of a film such as *Cabinet of Dr. Caligari* (1919) actually mirror the world of everyday human experience, but the very difference of its look from what he termed the "crude phantasmagoria" of most films of that day was an important signal: that the cinema was discovering new possibilities, new spaces, a new visual regime that promised to change how film worked and how we experienced its narratives. The striking combination of a kind of graphic or artificially dramatized space with a conventional photographic space, that hybrid of fantastic and realistic worlds, did more than simply add a three-dimensional aspect; it resulted in something different, what Scheffauer could not easily describe but only allusively refer to as a "fourth dimension," as film seemed to open itself up for reinvention.

That notion of a fourth dimension, or at least of the openness of cinema to more than simple photographic effects, might well be more accurately observed in the new generation of digital effects films, works that provide us with another kind of hybrid vision by merging computer-generated graphics with a conventional photographic vision, usually through the use of what are known as "digital intermediates."[1] The result of this combination is an entirely new visual regime and ultimately a new type of animating space. Films like *Pirates of the Caribbean: The Curse of the Black Pearl* (2003), *Sky Captain and the World of Tomorrow* (2004), and *Beowulf* (2007) are essentially creating virtual worlds and characters through the use of CGI and motion-capture technologies, and in the process staking out the new territory of animation, and perhaps—as some might either hope or fear—of all cinema. I choose these films as exemplars not just because they are works whose appearance put on display some of the latest developments in digital animation, but because they suggest a series of steps in this ongoing development. The first convincingly mixes digitally animated characters, such as its cursed, skeletal pirates, with live actors, much in the way that Peter Jackson's *Lord of the Rings* trilogy (2001, 2002, 2003) does on a far more massive scale—or that we have seen in a number of earlier works previously discussed. The second sets its live actors down in a fully digitally animated realm, almost as if they had fallen into a cartoon—or had been sucked into one, as we saw in *Cool World*. And the third combines the promise—or premise—of the other two, as its digital motion capture combines with sets constructed entirely within the computer to produce an animated narrative that completely replaces the live action and live world of traditional cinema, providing us with a new sort of film experience, a new version of what Virilio might refer to as film's "false day," although one that might just as well be seen as heralding the end of that false day, even the end of traditional cinema.

In 2005 *Cinefex* magazine published a "State of the Art" roundtable discussion on the latest developments in visual effects that invariably focused on the increasingly pervasive place of the computer in film, and in turn the computer's effect on animation and the potential ramifications of CGI and motion capture for the future of that art. Andy Jones, who has served as animation director on a number of prestigious effects-driven films, including *Godzilla* (1998), *Final Fantasy: The Spirits Within* (2001), and *I, Robot* (2004)—all works that are at least partly animated—attempted to reassure traditional animators that, in spite of the advances he was seeing in such technologies, and of the increasing merger of live-action and animated elements, traditional animators would never be "out of the picture" (Duncan et al., "State" 75). In this new industrial and aesthetic situation, he counseled, there was no real crisis such as that which Virilio alludes to, and animators should be no more worried about being replaced "than actors should be scared of digital replacements. The technology is never going to fully replace us. There's always going to be a need to animate, to adjust things. Even if the mocap [motion capture] looks great, you're still going to need somebody to maneuver and tweak it" (Duncan et al., "State" 76). Of course, rather than offering reassurance, Jones's comments, perhaps unwittingly, actually articulated the real fears of those involved in traditional animation—that they would be relegated to the periphery of production, exiled from animating space, turned into functionaries whose job would simply be "to maneuver and tweak" what had been ordered up by others from a massive memory bank of stored images, electronic sets, and virtual actors (or "vactors," as some refer to them). No longer able to find work as creative artists, no longer able to breathe life into their own visions—to animate space—animators in this brave new technological world could well become little more than necessary mechanics, there "to adjust things" as needed.

It is a point only slightly qualified by the media theorist Lev Manovich when he, too, far more positively, recently set out to describe the promise, the "image future" of the "post-digital visual landscape" ("Image" 26), particularly as it would affect the coming generation of animators. While suggesting that a similar destiny awaits live-action film—"the subordination of live action cinematography to the graphic code" through the process of "universal capture" ("Image" 27)—he describes not so much a new age for animators as a future reliant on a process of menu selection. Manovich explains that the method of universal capture, which he sees as opening onto the ultimate trajectory of film and other media, typically works by photographing an actor's performance (or, we might also assume, a set on which a performance might be digitally "staged") using five synchronized high-resolution digital video cameras; the resulting information is then mapped onto a "neutral" or base image of the subject that, when combined with other detailed information of the subject, can be "played" from an arbitrary angle ("Image" 33). But the notion that such a process, that the result of five synchronized points of view (or even many more, as the technology advances), could possibly capture what he terms "all the possible information from an object or scene" ("Image" 34), seems both to overclaim for the process and to underestimate the work and contribution of the animator, who is ultimately more than a sampler, more than someone who selects from a purportedly infinite menu.[2]

Just as significantly, there is implicit in this exchange another sort of threat, one that seems aimed at the very field of animation. As boundaries blur, as we increasingly collapse the distinctions between live-action and animated film, there is the danger that animation itself might well lose its identity or simply go out of style. It is a worry that briefly surfaced in the 1920s and 1930s as the Fleischer brothers put their rotoscoping invention to work, producing startlingly natural character movement but also generating figures that simply looked out of place in an animated environment. Michael Barrier has well captured that reaction in his more recent description of their rotoscoped work: "Its animation was not really animation at all. It was instead a tracing from live-action film" (22). And given the new regime of CGI and motion capture—which is, for all practical purposes, really a modern form of rotoscoping—we might expect that same attitude to be voiced in response to films such as *300* (2006) and *Beowulf,* in which motion capture allows all the characters to be digitized and then variously enhanced or exaggerated—rendered more muscular, more perfect, more desirable, or in some cases more grotesque. In following the digital path, such films essentially approach full animation; yet they do so by capturing a living reality, by doing what traditional, live-action cinema has always sought to do.

These fears, then, certainly have some foundation in fact, in what is already working with some success in the contemporary cinema, as evidenced by the popular response to works like *Sin City* (2005), *300,* and *Beowulf.* Yet exactly what is it that seems to be "working"? Is it the transformation of imagination into menu manipulation, the substitution of a select group of points of view for the potentially infinite number on which (and of which) an animator might draw, the "perfecting" of an image that has been effectively captured through ever more complex mapping processes—or is something more involved? Whether describing the work of "mocap" (as Jones does) or the effect of "universal capture" (as Manovich does), the tendency in all these discussions and predictions is to focus attention on what we have referred to as the figural, on that which has been animated or brought to life. The very world of animation, the animating space in which such a momentous event occurs, however, tends to slip away from discussion, as if its own "false day" would simply dissolve in the technological turn to character verisimilitude, or to what Jean Baudrillard refers to as the "simulacrum" that he sees as the inevitable focus of an "age of simulation" (167).

Although hardly what most people readily recognize as an animated film, *Pirates of the Caribbean* might give us a bit more insight into what is involved—and at stake—in these latest developments. A live-action work in the long tradition of the pirate genre, it marshals a wide array of additional effects—scale models, full-sized mock-ups, matte paintings—to achieve what Michele Pierson describes as the "experience of wonder" that is fundamental to the appeal of all such effects-driven cinema (52). And as we might expect from the contemporary cinema, a digitally animated world and characters also regularly—and at times disconcertingly—intrude into the live-action space: as actors repeatedly give way to their digital analogues, as both the live and the digitized figures move within various computer-generated spaces, and as the boundaries between these different realms are examined, blurred, and even significantly configured into the narrative. In this film—and no less in its similarly popular sequels, *Pirates of the Caribbean: Dead Man's Chest* (2005) and *Pirates of the Caribbean: At World's End* (2007)—we can begin to see the extent to which live-action filming is merging with the animated and perhaps better examine some of those claims being made for, or against, the new digital regime.

As the film's title suggests, *Pirates of the Caribbean* is fundamentally concerned with what we might term border characters and situations, with pirates and their predatory actions in and around the Caribbean, as well as with a kind of piratical or rebellious spirit that, the film implies, lurks in us all. And the sudden appearances and disappearances of the narrative's pirates, such as when a young Elizabeth Swann turns her head and, for a moment, thinks she glimpses a pirate ship only to have it just as swiftly disappear into a fog bank, leaving her doubting her eyes, or when the crew of the *Black Pearl* suddenly attacks the town of Port Royal and almost as quickly slips away into the night mists, underscore this context, reminding viewers that what we think of as the normal, the everyday, the *real* is simply one side of this boundary position and vulnerable to challenge by a different order of things—including a technology that can seamlessly insert or delete objects and characters in the narrative, or have them disappear into a digital fog bank. It is a point that, we gradually come to understand, lies at the very heart of the narrative—and perhaps implicitly of the narrative's use of digital animation—as we learn that driving these pirates, *animating* their bodies, as it were, is an ancient curse, one that motivates almost all the action here and that holds a special transformative power over the characters, as if they were all nothing more than digital constructions.

Stranded in the Port Royal jail, just as he had once before been stranded on a desert island by his mutinous crew, Captain Jack Sparrow suddenly finds several of those former shipmates, crewmembers of the *Black Pearl,* standing outside his cell. When one threateningly reaches from the dark corridor into Jack's moonlit cell, his arm, framed in the moonlight, turns skeletal, prompting Jack to recoil in horror, but also to observe: "So there is a curse . . . that's interesting . . . that's very interesting." That reaching across a boundary—from dark to light, from corridor into cell—and the transformation that results are indeed "interesting," for they effectively describe the trajectory of digital animation in this film. Besides updating the power of transformation that, as we have several times noted, has from animation's earliest days typically formed one of its key appeals, that movement suggests how easily the supernatural can intrude on the real, even take it quite menacingly by the throat, as the skeletal arm and hand do to Jack, and metaphorically, within the current cinematic environment, how easily a digital animation might also wield its own, similar power over the real. Hardly expected and only recognized in the right circumstance—or lighting— the animated image, as this film suggests, could well be a constant presence—or a curse—for all that audiences can know. Here it is, at any

Captain Jack of *Pirates of the Caribbean: Curse of the Black Pearl* (2003) encounters an "interesting" amalgam of the real and the animated.

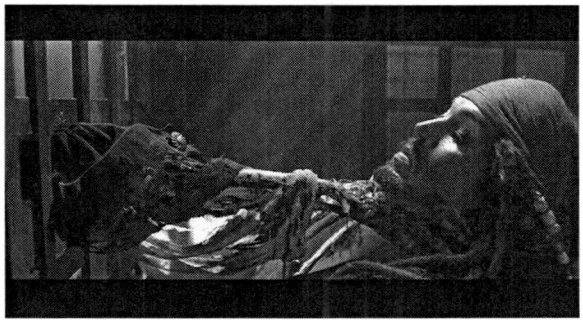

rate, an "interesting" phenomenon, something that allows us to cross borders, to effectively "pirate" the real, and ultimately to consider its consequences.

Later in the narrative, when Elizabeth has been kidnapped by those same pirates and taken aboard their ship, that curse comes to suggest a more extensive threat. As she refuses to be intimidated by her captors and tells Captain Barbossa, "I hardly believe in ghost stories anymore," he responds, "You'd best start believing in ghost stories, Miss Turner [as he mistakenly calls her]. You're in one." And his comment is punctuated by another one of those reaching arms, as he extends his hand into the light, notes that "the moonlight shows us for what we really are," and reveals his own cursed, decaying body. Yet in this instance that gesture marks more than just a case of arresting character animation, for as Elizabeth reels from that frightening vision, she sees all about her on the ship's deck the rest of the cursed pirates, now shown by the moonlight as skeletal, fantastic figures engaged in their mundane tasks of scrubbing the deck, trimming the sails, and setting the rigging. As she bumps into one after another of these horrific figures and as the camera's point of view careens wildly around the ship, it is as if she has been suddenly swallowed up in a totally animated world, one that produces the nightmarish sense that Elizabeth is indeed *within* a ghost story, as the solid space of her world, that of the Age of Reason, which supposedly no longer believes in such tales, suddenly dissolves and is replaced by a spectral space populated by ghoulish figures and a ghost ship. In the process, I suggest, the moonlight becomes a kind of cognate for digital animation, or at least for what digital animation can accomplish. It reminds us of another—and perhaps more reassuring—observation Manovich

Elizabeth Swann "inside" a CGI horror story in *Pirates of the Caribbean*.

has offered, that "the computer makes it possible for us to literally see in a new way" (*Language* 329), much as Elizabeth does, although the promise inherent in that new seeing certainly seems little appreciated by the frightened young woman.

The full extent of that "new way" of seeing shows especially in one of the spectacular concluding scenes of *Pirates of the Caribbean*. Sent off by Captain Barbossa to attack the British warship *Dauntless,* the cursed pirates, told simply to "take a walk," suddenly appear in a most unexpected context. An underwater scene of a school of fish—all animated—is interrupted by a line of those skeletal figures now incongruously walking on the sea bottom, where just enough of the full moon's light penetrates the water to reveal again their decayed bodies. It is a surprising and effective, if almost surreal, moment in the film, one that binds together sheer curiosity—as we inspect the unexplored details of the ocean floor, the ship's anchor and cables, the ship's barnacled hull— with a sense of stark horror—as tattered bits of skin and clothing alike drift in the undulating water, moonbeams reflect off the pirates' menacing weapons, and the water creates even eerier shadows on these already ghastly figures. That combination of curiosity and recoil is itself curious—or "interesting," as Jack Sparrow offers—for it not only suggests that strange dynamic of "wonder" that is endemic to such fantasy, but also points toward our own wonder at the promise of such digital animation. What we marvel at, ultimately, is what Virilio terms a reality effect that has replaced our "immediate reality" (*Lost* 24), a constructed dimension that stands in for a lost space, producing in the process a mixed response that closely tracks those different "appreciations" of the digital regime that we earlier note.

That mixed response, though, is one that *Pirates of the Caribbean* must eventually reject. It is, after all, a live-action film that is only flirting with animation and its digital possibilities; its narrative pursues a trajectory of life and love, not death and curses. So even when Jack knowingly consigns himself to the realm of cursed pirates by taking a piece of damned gold, it is only for a moment, a brief trick of the narrative as he spars for time with Barbossa. When he too steps into a space of moonlight and is similarly revealed to have taken on a ghostly, skeletal aspect, he pauses to admire the effect—providing the audience the lead to do the same—and once again observes, "That's interesting," before surrendering his gold piece to Will Turner, who can return it and, in the process, render all the pirates mortal, vulnerable, and *real* once again. It is a transformation that signals the end of the curse and, along with it, the end of the spell of animation, by recommitting the narrative to a world of reason, reality, and the all-too-solid realm of live-action film.

But what *Pirates of the Caribbean* offers us is more than an exciting narrative, and more too than a demonstration of how state-of-the-art computer animation might be effectively integrated into and even subordinated to the world of live-action cinema. In an almost step-by-step progression throughout its narrative, it suggests the deeper issues behind those dissatisfactions or suspicions of the growing influence of computer animation. Like those pirates, the digital seems almost to be stalking the real, revealing its presence and power only in certain circumstances, and suggesting ultimately an apparently common postmodern fear that the real itself might simply disappear, collapse, or prove an illusion, that what Virilio terms the "lost dimension" might never be regained because of the "curse" of our times and our technologies. And yet it offers us another vantage as well, an unavoidable admission that what is happening here is also—and despite those fears—"interesting," revealing, even appealing, something in which we cannot help finding some attraction, even some use. Like Jack Sparrow, both audiences and animators find the possibilities intriguing and exciting, the new animating space a world of potential, including the potential for, as Benjamin once suggested of film itself, helping us see our world with fresh eyes, and the new ability to animate space a worthwhile challenge—if only those possibilities do not also disrupt the animatic status quo. Even in its limited use here, digital animation thus speaks to a range of possible effects, as it embodies both the threats that many sense in this new regime and the visual—even visionary—potential that has led many to eagerly embrace it.

We have already cited Paul Virilio's belief that our highly mediated—or "mediatized"—environment has radically altered our senses of space and of dimension. In fact, he describes this contemporary situation as nothing less than "a crisis of whole dimensions," as "our habitual notions of surface, of limit and separation, have decayed, and given way to those of interface, commutation, intermittence and interruption" (*Lost* 110), leaving us feeling lost, even victimized by the cinematic "set" that has, for many, become reality (*Art* 79). This diagnosis of the human situation resonates tellingly with the increasing mixture of animated elements in our live-action features, which add a further dimension to that problematic attitude toward digital animation that we have been observing. To explore this attitude further, I turn to Kerry Conran's landmark effort, *Sky Captain and the World of Tomorrow*, the first feature film to combine live-action figures with an almost entirely computer-generated—and thus pointedly mediatized or cinematized—world. In its narrative we can see starkly laid out the basic terms of this "crisis," of the threat that many see implicit in the future of digital animation. Yet at the same time the film articulates in a far clearer fashion than *Pirates of the Caribbean* an interesting alternative vision, as it tries to stake out grounds on which we might not be so easily victimized by "the set" of this new world and might even see our technology as offering us a kind of mastery over it.

It is worth noting from the start that Conran approached his innovative film as an effort to break free from a variety of traditional constraints, in fact as an experiment at compromising with conventional ways of moviemaking and methods of animation. While a student at California Institute of the Arts, he had become fascinated by how his colleagues were beginning to use computers to do experimental work that straddled traditional boundaries between live action and animation, and he began to study how he might exploit the possibilities offered by the digital realm to, as he says, "cross the line." As part of his effort "to try to fuse those two worlds" (Fordham, "Brave" 16), Conran began

Real actors enter and respond to one of *Sky Captain*'s fully animated sets.

working on a film set in the watershed year of 1939—a year that itself marked a crucial transition between peace and world war, between a variety of hopes for the future bound up in the landmark New York World's Fair and the apocalyptic destruction that would soon be unleashed, between technologies of life and technologies of death. His film would have the look and feel of a science fiction serial from that era, incorporating much of that form's physical action and ambiance, while making maximum use of digitally animated sets, props, effects, and motion capture.[3] But as a consequence, according to the film's visual effects supervisor, Darin Hollings, practically "*every* shot in the movie [would be] a visual effect," as the filmmakers entered into "a brave new world of visual effects" cinema (Fordham, "Brave" 19) that fully capitalizes on the possibilities inherent in a digital space.

The result is a hybrid film in which live actors do almost all their acting in front of blue screens, often using blue props that were later replaced with more elaborate, digitally animated ones. In fact, Conran explains that when the production moved its shooting location to England's Elstree Studios, the effects people went a step further; they "constructed a virtual Elstree in the computer . . . then built our set inside the virtual studio and rotated it to fit" the digital graphics (or "animatics," as he terms them, by way of insisting on his film's links to the world of animation) that had already been created for specific scenes (Fordham, "Brave" 22). In sum, they substituted, wherever possible, animated spaces for the real space of live-action sets, as they previsualized each element of the narrative through CGI storyboards, constructed each scene within virtual space, and then had their actors work as if in a real environment—within what Virilio would term a "lost dimension." And the advantages of this approach were many, since it allowed the film to be shot for a fraction of the cost of a similar live-action work, the virtual "sets" could be speedily redressed to allow for a tighter shooting schedule than any live-action film could have managed,[4] models and archival photographs could be readily integrated into the action, and a stylized look could more easily be created for the entire production. So though real space virtually disappeared here, the trade-off was a fundamental appeal to our sense of wonder, the fashioning of a world—and an atmosphere—that is strikingly authentic looking and yet finds its central attraction in our curiosity about what fantastic images we, like the live-action characters who are immersed in this world, might see next.

Yet more than simply gaining a distinctly "period" look, Conran's approach opens a door onto a different world, even a sort of hybrid of live-action and animation that is different from what we have been accustomed to seeing. What his approach produced is not just a series of unexpectedly authentic images or even instances of live actors reacting to effects, as is most often the case in traditional stop-motion animation films. Rather, it is a three-dimensional creation that effectively embraces the characters, as we see when the animated dirigible *Hindenburg III* appears in the New York skyline at the film's opening. Evoking a traditional approach to producing a depth illusion, it moves from the deep background directly toward the camera, and even as it turns, it flies through a convincingly realized snowstorm and a web of crisscrossing searchlights that together create texture, refract light, and lend a further sense of depth to the frame—effects only enhanced by a subsequent cut to an interior shot of the dirigible's gondola, where real actors crowd the windows to look out at the same spectacular vision just offered to the audience. That cut not only links the movie audience with the characters in the film—suggesting that we should be just as awestruck by this view of 1939 New York as these characters seem to be—but also immediately cues us to Conran's larger strategy, that is, the tendency to treat reality as a kind of onion whose layers might be peeled away and replaced with others that have been digitally fashioned, and ultimately to sandwich his players between the layers so that their embedded presence can further build the reality illusion. And that constructed illusion is, in many ways, a very appealing one, since it is not necessarily bound

The computer-animated 1939 New York City in *Sky Captain and the World of Tomorrow* (2004).

by the same laws of nature or probability that burden us. In fact, as we subsequently see, it allows planes to dive, full-speed, into and under the ocean, giant robots to fly, and the dirigible to actually dock with the Empire State Building and disembark its passengers, just as the building's designers had originally hoped, before reality got in the way and they recognized that upper-level wind currents, snowstorms like the one shown here, and the inherent instability of airships would render any such attempts disastrous.

Storms do affect our plans, however; dirigibles proved unstable, even prone to exploding, as the *III* appended to this *Hindenburg*'s title slyly suggests. And even an appealing vision of "tomorrow," a vision of great possibilities, like those proposed in the New York World's Fair, remains bound by history and the fallout of the technology used to conceive it— a link that prompted Roger Ebert to strike one cautionary note in his otherwise admiring description of *Sky Captain and the World of Tomorrow,* as he termed it, "like a film that escaped from the imagination directly onto the screen, without having to pass through reality along the way" (*"Sky"*). More to the point for this film's rethinking of hybrid animation, a reality effect retains a disconcerting surplus of meaning— that sense of the substance that has been replaced, of the space that has been peeled away and swapped for a sepia-toned, vintage image, of a visual design that at times seems almost overwrought in its period detail. In crafting a film—and a world—dependent on a virtually animated space, Conran produced a most attractive world, and he certainly did so in a cost-effective manner. Yet his all-too-real actors also seem practically haunted by what is missing, by the layers that have been peeled away, just as they are narratively by the "ghost" of Sir Laurence Olivier, who has been pressed into service as the virtual antagonist Dr. Toten-kopf, warning Joe and Polly that it is too late to stop his plans, to stand in the way of *his* "world of tomorrow" and its trajectory of worldwide destruction.

Though that warning comes in the film's conclusion, it is one that resonates throughout the narrative, which constantly seems pulled—and to pull us—in two different directions, almost as if it were address-ing different attitudes toward its manner of visualizing that "tomorrow." On the one hand, the film consistently impresses with its vision of the world of 1939 and the sense of possibility that informed the art, archi-tecture, films, and world's fairs of that time. In fact, it establishes a per-sistent motif about possibility, about a world of ever more amazing images. Yet, on the other, the film just as insistently mines the dark potential of that same year—the year the world would be plunged into another kind of possibility, a cataclysmic world war—to describe the destructive potential not only of the latest technology, but of the creative impulse that brings such technology into the world. The resulting tension speaks in a revealing way to the very technological "future" that has made Conran's film possible, even as it continues to haunt our efforts at trying to animate a digital space for the "world of tomorrow."

Part of a running gag in *Sky Captain and the World of Tomorrow* is ace reporter Polly Perkins's desire to take pictures of everything she encounters—a desire balanced by fumbling efforts with her camera and by the loss of her extra film. As she tags along with Joe Sullivan in pur-suit of the spectacular story of Totenkopf (a story that, she tells her edi-tor, "grows stranger at every turn"), Polly repeatedly hesitates to take a photograph, even when confronted with the most astounding images—flying robots, exotic ruins, the real Shangri-La, frightening genetic exper-iments, living dinosaurs. At one point when Joe questions her hesitation, she tells him, "I've only got two shots left. Who knows what's waiting for us out there?" Finally, at the film's conclusion, faced with what must surely be the topper to all of these visions, Joe asks, "You honestly think you're going to find anything more important than every single creature on Earth being led two by two inside a giant rocket ship?" and still she wavers, noting, "I might. . . . I'll know when I see it." That hesitation lends importance to her eventual use of her last shot to capture Joe's smiling face as he sits next to her after saving her—and effectively the world—from seemingly certain destruction. It also forms a constant reminder, however, as this motif plays out through the narrative, of what the film itself, through its elaborate use of computer animation, offers audiences, and thus what it is, effectively, *about:* a host of ever more elaborate and enticing images, each seemingly stranger and certainly more spectacular and enticing than what has gone before, yet none quite as appealing, it seems, as the real human face.

The film develops this pattern of visual anticipation in part by looking back, by cultivating a host of nostalgic images from the full range of 1930s American culture, and especially by evoking a world of earlier cinema. For the most part through effective visual quotes *Sky Captain* repeatedly places both its characters and the audience amid some of the most spectacular films of the period, offering us Shangri-La from *Lost Horizons* (1937), Oz from *The Wizard of Oz* (1939), both Skull Island and New York from *King Kong* (1933), massive aircraft that recall H. G. Wells's futuristic vision of *Things to Come* (1936), as well as flying robots directly lifted from the Superman cartoon *Mechanical Monsters* (1941). When combined with the seriallike narrative, we cannot help feeling that we are not in *a* movie, but in *the* movies, exploring, even celebrating one of the factors that has made them so striking and popular: their historical ability to offer us something new, entice us with a sense of wonder about "what's waiting for us out there," tap into the rich cultural vein of cinephilia. Appropriately, Polly arranges to meet a mysterious German scientist at Radio City Music Hall, and when her editor cautions against going there, she reassures him about her safety, noting that "it's only a movie." Of course, it is not "only a movie"; it is one of our most iconic and culturally resonant films. *The Wizard of Oz* forms the backdrop for their meeting, as Dorothy intones her well-known observation, "I have a feeling we're not in Kansas anymore"—a comment that invariably reminds us of the movies' power, of their ability to transport us to other worlds, if at times by making our own seem strange. The point is that this immersion in the movies strikes a promising note, evoking our cinematic dreams, seemingly giving them substance, and suggesting their inherent promise constantly to open up new spaces for our delectation, to show us something more—possibilities only furthered by the new digital regime in which Conran was working.

Yet at the same time the narrative balances that sense of possibility with a threatening alternative—the sort of world that Totenkopf represents, that Virilio describes, and that many feel is actually implicated in the digital. We might easily see the shadowy figure who haunts this film, Dr. Totenkopf, as an example of what Donald Crafton, in his commentary on early animation, terms an element of "self-figuration" (11): the filmmaker's own image injected into the narrative. Like Conran, Totenkopf is using the latest technology, in this instance a combination of robotic devices and genetic manipulations, to create a new order, to redream the world, even to create a perfect human simulacrum, as we see in his Asian henchwoman who, we eventually learn, is actually an android. Wherever Joe and Polly track the sinister Totenkopf, they encounter the traces of his disturbing creations: mutilated people, strange combinations of animal species, outsized skeletal remains, resurrected primitive creatures. Indeed, one of the scenes deleted from the film's release version was designed to underscore this activity, as Joe and Polly are shown a room in Nepal where the doctor conducts "unspeakable experiments" on native workers, suggesting the similar work of Dr. Josef Mengele on concentration camp inmates during World War II.[5] The final step in creating this monstrous "World of Tomorrow" is Totenkopf's reacquisition of two vials that have been spirited away by one of the scientists in his employ, vials that contain the genetic material he created for the next step in his plan, the seeds of a manipulated and perfected humanity, a "new Adam and Eve." With that material in hand, he can then send his rocket ark out into space, and from there incinerate the Earth and all its occupants, effecting a definitive break between past and future so that he can then begin life anew in what he terms his "technological utopia."

It is, of course, the dream of a madman, but one that evokes what some might see as the very spirit behind *Sky Captain and the World of Tomorrow* and the problem behind our digital technology, the urge—and even the seeming ability—to completely replace the real with a convincing reality effect. Yet whereas Totenkopf's manipulations and re-creations are marked at every turn by death and destruction—indeed, we learn that he has actually died long before the action of the narrative and exists only through his robots, genetic experiments, and holographic projection, all these things, in effect, the dreams of death—Conran's alternative is a different sort of reality effect, a creative possibility that supports life and offers a continuity between past and future. This is the possibility symbolized by the research that Joe and his chief engineer, Dex, are carrying on at their secret base, work that, we learn, has already helped "save the world" several times, work that produces such wonders as the flying aircraft carrier and submersible aircraft that help thwart Totenkopf's plans. They are, in fact, the sort of digitally realized wonders that the 1930s *did* dream about but could only envision on the covers of the pulps and *Popular Science* magazine, in films like those noted above, especially the utopian fantasy *Things to Come,* in the idealized cities and structures of figures such as Le Corbusier and Hugh Ferris, and, of course, in the various world's fairs of that time.

In fact, as the title should suggest, the New York World's Fair of 1939 is a touchstone for the film's dialogue on creativity and on the double potential of digital animation. "The World of Tomorrow" was that fair's official theme—one that here clearly points in two quite different directions. It literally refers to Totenkopf's plan for a world remade in his image, following his destruction of the existing "flawed" world. His holographic image says as much, uttering that title, claiming it for his scheme of a recast scientific utopia. And when Joe and Polly reach Totenkopf's secret Tibetan base, we briefly glimpse the fair's iconic structures, the Trylon and Perisphere, digitally matted in there to further underscore that linkage. With that tie to the fair, the film admits that the menace is at least implicit in this technological vision—a menace that would, historically, soon be visited on the world with the advent of World War II, and one that gains an even darker coloring here through Totenkopf's plans for a holocaust that would far surpass what the Nazis ultimately orchestrated.

Yet for the prewar era that title promised far more, as the 1939 World's Fair envisioned a near future—actually, the world of 1960—that would be marked by great advances in transportation, communication, food production, living standards, and especially world harmony. In fact, the fair's president, Grover Whalen, announced that the New York World's Fair would provide visitors a vision of "orderly progress in a world of peace" (5). And as a recent chronicler of the fair, David Gelernter, suggests, when the fair's designers "turned their minds to the future, what they saw was *good.* Technology in particular was good.

The future in general was good" (25). And to underscore that emphasis, we might note that this vision was offered in a space that modeled this transformative possibility, a space that had been turned from a garbage dump into a kind of model city through the efforts of the latest technology. The film's title, as a result, does more than just nostalgically direct our attention to an earlier era, one filled with great hope even as the world was beginning to veer terribly off course. It also points to a double potential in our technological vision, in the promise of what we might, as Grover Whalen put it, "build from the best of the tools available to us" (5): simultaneously frightening and hopeful potentials that would have to be negotiated, as we see here by heroic individuals like Joe Sullivan—and at a further remove perhaps by risk takers like Kerry Conran.

I return to the "self-figuration" of Conran here precisely because the film, through its vision of yesterday's "tomorrow," seems to speak so directly, so self-consciously, and ultimately affirmatively to another "tomorrow"—that of a digital cinema and its potential for animating the world and reshaping its spaces, even for raising the dead through a nearly infinite menu of electronic images. In fashioning such a convincing animated world for his live actors to "inhabit," Conran opens a door onto a different world, even a kind of "technological utopia." *Sky Captain and the World of Tomorrow* reminds us how much of the Totenkopf vision actually took hold through the agency of the Nazis, but the film also manages an effective affirmation by figuring Conran as Joe Sullivan. Just as Conran managed to replace the costly, studio-bound sets of live-action filming with digitally animated sets and props, perhaps altering the future trajectory of the movies, so too do his Sky Captain and the intrepid reporter Polly succeed in altering the path of Totenkopf's rocket and presenting us with a new world and new future—a history that, like Polly's planned story on these events, has yet to be written. And that is precisely the case for Conran's work and the work of others who have taken up the challenge of working in and with the new digital spaces, of animating in new ways. We might note that when Polly finally does use the last shot in her camera, when she turns the camera away from the spectacular events she has witnessed and tries to snap Joe's smiling face, she fails to capture anything because of a simple mechanical mistake—the lens cap is on. But it is a lapse that further resonates with the film's larger commentary on the new spaces of film and animation. In fact, its final scene leaves Joe and Polly practically surrounded by many of these animated wonders, while reminding us that it might take more than a camera (i.e., a photographic technology) to capture such wonders, that it might take, as Conran notes, a "digital filmmaking [that] is only bound by imagination" (Fordham, "Brave" 33).

Admittedly, that "imaginative" use of the new digital regime remains qualified with *Sky Captain and the World of Tomorrow*. Though attracting generally good reviews, it did not do spectacularly well at the box office—certainly not as well as a number of other films that have followed a slightly less radical hybrid program, such as Frank Miller and Robert Rodriguez's *Sin City* or Zack Snyder's *300*. While similarly fashioning highly stylized worlds—in both cases, worlds drawn from the exaggerated realms of Miller's graphic novels—these films step back from the spectacle of a digital world to emphasize the presence and the actions of their very real figures; they pointedly privilege what Lisa Purse describes as "the material physicality of the pro-filmic body" (22), while placing those bodies in almost minimalist digital sets. These films take this approach, Purse suggests, because of a specter that still haunts *Sky Captain and the World of Tomorrow* and other efforts at combining live action with digital animation—a free-floating fear of what those digital possibilities might portend. As Purse says, these films emphasize the real body in an effort to "allay or counteract underlying anxieties about the integrity of the human body that digitally animated (and thus digitally *mutable*) bodies might provoke" (22). In effect, they recognize and respond to something of the threat that attaches to the digital and that is narratively suggested through the figure of Totenkopf and his plans for a special "world of tomorrow"—a world wherein everything, even the human, can be reproduced and thus replaced, as his robotic assistant and the vials containing the designer genes of his new Adam and Eve suggest.

Purse's observation is important, for it points to the larger negotiation in which our hybrid films are presently engaged, as they try to work out a relationship between the real and the animated, the live action and the digitally fashioned, which inevitably has implications for our own natures. On the one hand, these films seem almost intent on confronting the uneasiness that lurks in the digital image, crossing that "valley of the uncanny" described in chapter 9. The increasing use of "performance capture," seen in a more recent work like *Beowulf,* points even more directly to that effort. On the other hand, those "underlying anxieties" Purse identifies persist at the cultural level and suggest why *Sky Captain and the World of Tomorrow* may have missed for so many people. Certainly the film provides much action, although not so much of the visceral sort—of the fistfights and chases that we find in its cinematic ancestors, the serials. For the most part its live-action characters seem spectators, inhabiting Conran's imagined and digitally born world, simply flying or swimming through it while encased in impossible technological—or digital—cocoons. As a result, the issue of real involvement remains as unresolved as Polly's dual interest in Joe and a big story. Those anxieties, in short, still trouble this and other digitally driven narratives, as the following discussion of *Beowulf* will show.

Sky Captain and the World of Tomorrow, however, at least suggests a strategy for addressing the larger cultural problems that Virilio and Purse both identify. If we are indeed today such a thoroughly "cinematized" culture, if we have all to some extent become, as he says, "victims of the set," might it be possible to dissolve that set, to reclaim the "lost dimension" of our world by making it the very site of the imagination's powers? This possibility seems implicit in one of the alternative tomorrows that this film describes—the liberating, profilmic one that allows us to visualize ourselves within other, perhaps better worlds by deploying the new cinematic possibilities of a digital cinema to animate a space that, as Conran puts it, is "only bound by imagination." It is this point, one at which the *space* of animation coincides with our ability to *animate* space, to control our own spaces, even to visualize our own futures, that *Sky Captain and the World of Tomorrow* tries to envision for us.

Lev Manovich has described the emergence of a "new hybrid aesthetics" that is rapidly becoming "the norm" in film production. The product of that new approach to film, termed "universal capture" (described earlier in this chapter) and sourced in the ubiquitous computerization of all moving image production, is a process that "systematically takes physical reality apart and then systematically reassembles the elements into a virtual computer-based representation," resulting in "a new kind of image" ("Image" 33) that effectively juxtaposes many different kinds of images—hand-drawn, cinemagraphic, video, computer-generated graphics—even combines those image types to produce a new hybrid language, one that, at least for the time being, we still describe under the blanket heading of the cinematic. In the context of universal capture, animation does not so much disappear, as some traditionalists might fear, as it becomes repurposed; it "functions not as a medium but as a set of general-purpose techniques—used together with other techniques in the common pool of options available to a filmmaker/designer" ("Image" 26).

That resulting identity, of "filmmaker/designer," seems an important, perhaps even reconciling notion for those who might find these sea changes disconcerting, who would see the blurring of distinctions between live-action cinema and animation as heralding just the sort of "crisis" Virilio forecasts. As both spatial and figural elements verge on a new kind of verisimilitude, and as it becomes increasingly difficult, if not impossible, to make out the trick of the "false day," we have to understand that the very way in which the artist describes what he or she does might have to be changed as well. And despite its own awkward hybridity, the designation "filmmaker/designer" seems an appealing one, a term that weaves together the work of photography and conventional art, even suggesting a more complex role for the animator—and I think that single term will suffice—of tomorrow.

Yet let me suggest that a figure such as the director Robert Zemeckis, more than a theorist like Manovich, seems to point the way for animation—and the animator—of tomorrow, even if it is a troubled way. Following *Who Framed Roger Rabbit,* Zemeckis explored several other possibilities for combining animated and live-action cinema, most notably directing the special effects–heavy *Back to the Future* sequels (1989, 1990) and *Contact* (1997), the 3-D motion-capture animated feature *The Polar Express* (2004), and the "performance-capture" film *Beowulf.* In all these works, as in *Roger Rabbit,* he has repeatedly pushed at the boundaries of conventional cinema, exploring how the latest technology, especially that involved in digital imaging, might be employed not only to enhance the possibilities of cinematic narrative, but also to transform it through an expanded sense of animation. Though much of his most recent work, including *A Christmas Carol* (2009), has turned on the evolution from simple motion capture to what is generally described as performance capture,[6] it is a move that also has had consequences for the entire image field, for all that is bound up in the notion of animating space, for what Manovich terms the "image future" ("Image" 25).

One might well argue that Zemeckis's first real step in this direction of image future was his critically praised and financially successful *Forrest Gump* (1994). In it he uses state-of-the-art CGI technology to insert the title character into important moments in recent American history in which Forrest encounters a variety of significant figures—among them Lyndon Johnson, Richard Nixon, Abbie Hoffman, John Lennon—either by digitally erasing a figure in historical footage and then painting Forrest into the previously occupied space or by reworking the film frame to create a new space where Forrest could be sutured in.[7] Though hardly a film that would normally be considered under the heading of animation, *Forrest Gump,* with its ability to erase figures from live-action footage, to alter characters—as in the chroma-key erasing of Gary Sinise's legs so that he could play the double amputee Lieutenant Dan—and the opening up of what is essentially a nonexistent space in the film frame, clearly points in directions that Zemeckis would further explore in his subsequent fully animated works, *The Polar Express* and *Beowulf.*

For *The Polar Express* Zemeckis undertook one of the most ambitious experiments in the use of motion-capture technology. To provide coverage of his virtual set, Zemeckis arranged a total of 72 special cameras to capture the infrared light reflected off markers that were affixed to various parts of the actors' faces and the spandex bodysuits they wore in place of costumes, and these receptors were supplemented by 12 digital video cameras placed to cover various aspects of each scene (Fordham, "Dream" 118). For *Beowulf* 16 digital video cameras were employed, each with four times the resolution of those used in the earlier film, and 228 motion-capture cameras worked to track the actors' face and body markers. The increase in recording cameras and their power also affected the way the actors could work—or "fit"—within the filmic world. On the earlier film the motion-capture setup could take in only ten square feet of volume at a time, which required Tom Hanks—who played multiple characters in *The Polar Express*—"to

Performance capture produces both an animated cast and an animated world in *Beowulf* (2007).

perform traveling scenes in ten-foot 'chunks,'" at which spatial point the action would break, the actor "backing up and continuing the performance as he covered another ten feet, and so on—all of the chunks tediously stitched together by technical animators using motion editing tools" (Duncan, "All the Way" 46–47). With *Beowulf* the "world" for each scene expanded to a twenty-five-square-foot volume, which allowed for "a larger scope of action," and cut down on the layers of action that would have to be stitched together by the animators (Duncan, "All the Way" 47). So the final result is not only a more effective figural animation (through more detailed motion capture), but also more spatial possibilities for each scene, a far more expansive world wherein characters can interact and respond to a wealth of details that are digitally placed in that world. And in both films, although especially in *Beowulf,* Zemeckis also inserted elaborate fully animated (i.e., non–motion-capture) scenes that seem pointedly designed to sketch the spatial scope of the narrative beyond those carefully designed "chunks."

What is especially striking about this approach to performance is the marshaling of resources to create a space for it, as well as the use of the actors to measure out and suture together those separate chunks of space, thereby constructing the larger world of the film's narrative. It is an approach that certainly underscores the relationship between the figural and the spatial; it is, in fact, one that emphasizes just how interdependent they actually are and how that interdependence influences the narrative. That linkage shows especially in *Beowulf*'s scenes in King Hrothgar's famed mead hall of Herot, the setting for much of the film's first half, which comes alive and takes dimension only as the king and his warriors walk, dance, carouse, and fornicate in its various corners; later, as the monster Grendel—played through performance-capture by the actor Crispin Glover—attacks, leaving carnage, including bits of bodies, in seemingly every part of the hall; and finally as Beowulf lures the creature back to the mead hall by further noisy celebrations, traps it there, and mortally wounds it, thanks to his constant and highly athletic movements—he vaults from tables, hangs from the rafters, and swings from ropes and lamps, drawing every element of the place into the action. In fact, if these scenes seem almost unnaturally acrobatic, even dizzying in their use of motion, it may well be because here—quite literally, because of the technology—motion produces space, as if it had been lost and could be found—or constructed—only by the actions of the animated figures.

Of course, that approach can also produce what we might term the wrong kind of space. As Patrick Tatopoulos, an artist and production designer, has observed, "The dangerous thing about creating environments in CG is that because you can do anything, you can lose track of that sense of reality" (Duncan et al., "State" 57). This approach can create impossible spaces, improbable movements (like Beowulf's acrobatics), and pointless trackings through "space" with the virtual camera. And certainly *Beowulf* has its share of such effects, as, for example, when Grendel is introduced into the story. That introduction follows the opening of Herot and the raucous celebration that attends it, as a tracking camera follows one of the celebrants across the hall until it encounters a rat scampering along the rafters; the camera then follows as the rat emerges on the roof, where it is suddenly snatched by a swooping hawk that lifts it skyward and then into the foreground, soaring over fields, a forest of thorn trees that reach skyward, and finally to the mountains and the cave where Grendel—and his mother—dwells. It is a complex and dizzying movement that, thanks to the initial scamperings of an animated rat, takes us out of the carefully established human spaces of the mead hall to a fully animated realm, to a dark countryside and ominous mountains that we see from a bird's-eye perspective and for which we have no human presence to provide a spatial measure. Indeed, while this camera swiftly (in an approximately one-minute take) moves across the land, over a chasm, and into Grendel's cave, we have no real measure of the monster's size; it is not until he later attacks Herot and we see him juxtaposed with—and dwarfing—Hrothgar's men there that we comprehend his bulk. Certainly that rat-and-hawk-impelled movement rapidly binds together two central story lines and foreshadows Grendel's own predatory attack in the following scene, while it also builds a larger sense of space—of the world as something other than those discrete chunks I earlier describe. It also draws us out of the narrative, however, out of our "sense of reality," because we recognize that we are seeing movement for movement's sake (particularly in the case of the rat) and because of the virtual camera's moving so swiftly and, indeed, improbably through the virtual landscape—just because it can. And it is an effect that the film repeats for its conclusion, when Beowulf flies along with his own monstrous creation, the dragon, as it reverses the path of the earlier hawk's flight to attack his splendid and far more substantial castle home. That concluding sequence, with its kind of free-floating (dragon-borne) perspective, hardly works more convincingly than Grendel's introduction, and it would lead to a number of critical reservations, such as Roger Ebert's: "To say the movie is over the top assumes you can see the top from here" ("*Beowulf*").

And yet we can fairly easily recognize what Zemeckis is trying to accomplish in these acrobatic shots and the extended tracking and soaring camera movements, how he is trying both to exploit and to accommodate his visual style to the technology. On the one hand, he wants swiftly and easily to bind together characters and settings, to achieve something of the dynamic visual and editing style found in the film's source, Neil Gaiman's graphic novel version of *Beowulf,* and the virtual camera easily allows him to do so, while that sweeping motion also works to construct space for the narrative. On the other, as Jerome Chen, Zemeckis's visual effects supervisor on both *Polar Express* and *Beowulf,* explains, the ever more elaborate efforts at motion and performance capture in these films reflect the director's fundamental desire for greater control over his medium. Frustrated by the imperfections and "realities of filmmaking," and having "an exact vision of what he wants his film to look like," Chen explains, Zemeckis has pursued technologies that allow him to realize that vision better. He recognized that through performance-capture technology he could "chunk" much of the film, splitting the filmmaking process into multiple, more controllable fragments: "Shoot the performance first, without worrying about anything else. And then, once he has the performance captured, . . . begin to create the film cinematically. With the performances all locked, he can determine the camera work and the look of the entire movie"

(Duncan, "All the Way" 46)—and, of course, every element of the set as well, every nuance of the characters' looks and expressions, every detail of the world of the movie, every possible movement of the virtual camera. A strategy that begins with the impetus of splitting performance from world, figure from space, eventuates in an ever more detailed breakdown of the narrative's components, allowing the director to exercise a more effective control over them—although at some price.

In fact, we might even begin to sense Zemeckis's awareness of that price, of what it means to be a "filmmaker/designer"—or even animator—in this new regime, as we look at his own figurations in the text, for *Beowulf* lodges that very same desire for control in the persons of Hrothgar and Beowulf, as if they were analogues for the filmmaker himself. Both seek to express themselves, to expand their kingdoms (or spaces), to gain control over the contingencies of their world, and in both cases, as the film repeatedly points up, narratives are essential vehicles for accomplishing these ends. Hrothgar and Beowulf recount tales of their own exploits, encourage others to relate their feats, and seem impelled by a need to produce further stories of themselves—all efforts that measure their desire to master their environments and control their own destinies. As the narrative opens, we learn that Hrothgar is already celebrated in story, as his thanes sing about his many conquests and his slaying of dragons. Indeed, it is the recounting of those exploits as entertainment that leads into the fully animated hawk-borne introduction of Grendel—a figure whose appearance then undercuts those stories of heroism and Hrothgar's control over this world when the monster suddenly appears and decimates his followers. Beowulf is introduced in the same fashion, albeit with what naturally seems, by this point in the narrative, an appropriate note of skepticism—Unferth's terming him "a boastful fool"—as he tells the story of his five-day swimming race against Brecca the Mighty and boasts that he will kill Grendel, just as he has, so the stories of him say, "killed a tribe of giants on the Orkneys" and "crushed the skulls of sea serpents." And following Beowulf's destruction of the creature and eventual ascent to Hrothgar's throne, he is further celebrated in song and story throughout the surrounding kingdoms; as his friend Wiglaf notes, now "your legend is known from the high seas and the snow barriers to the great island kingdom." Even the dragon's attack on Beowulf's kingdom is pointedly

set in parallel to Grendel's assault on the mead hall by way of a performance depicting Beowulf's heroic deeds, again offered as a kind of entertainment for the assembled thanes. It seems that creating a legend,
fashioning a celebratory narrative, and encouraging that mythologizing
were what heroes and kings really strove for, a measure of their own
godlike stature in a period when a new Christian god was beginning to
win followers and challenge their authority. It is through those stories
that a figure like Beowulf can stand outside this world and construct a
kind of controlling narrative for it, effectively writing his own future.[8]

Of course, that control, as we see in the cases of both men, is only
illusory, achieved at the cost of conspiring with those very forces over
which men finally have little real control. Both Hrothgar and Beowulf
prove to be easily seduced by Grendel's mother, who uses each man to
help her sire monsters. Yet her seductions are, we gather, not simply the
result of her golden beauty (suggesting the allure of both physical perfection and wealth); they also reflect her promise of fame, of a prosper-
ous future, of control over their fates. We never learn precisely what she
once promised Hrothgar, but we can only assume that it was like her
pointedly twofold pledge to Beowulf: that he would be "the greatest
king that ever lived" and that he would "own the greatest tale ever sung.
Your story would live on when everything now alive is dust." And clearly
the tale seems the more important boon, since it promises to transcend
space and time, to offer the ultimate victory over this world, the only
sort of immortality open to humans.

It is tempting to see in that promise the lure of digital effects too, as
they beckon powerfully to Zemeckis and other filmmakers. As these
filmmakers/animators embrace the potential of digital animation, they
also subscribe to what Michael O'Pray has theorized is one of the key
attractions of animation itself, its sense of control, or at least what he
terms the "fantasy of that control" bound up in the creation and manipulation of self-conceived figures and spaces (200). Zemeckis, like his
Danish heroes, longs to tell stories—stories that, like Beowulf's, will
live on. And to do so, to gain his own control over the constantly shifting and elusive ground of the cinema, he has struck a series of deals not
with the magic offered by Grendel's mother, but with the technology of
"reality effects"—motion capture and performance capture especially—
the postmodern magic of simulacra found in digital effects animation.

Wiglaf reacts to Grendel's beckoning mother at the conclusion of *Beowulf.*

That technology has allowed him to produce compelling images, to move farther across that "valley of the uncanny" than any previous filmmaker, perhaps even to pioneer the future of animation.

It is a seductive achievement, yet one that also seems inscribed in this narrative with a hint of doubt, figured in the sadness and disenchantment that marks both Hrothgar and Beowulf—as an aged Beowulf notes, "we men are the monsters now"—and especially woven into the film's concluding scene. There we watch the character of Wiglaf standing on the seashore, looking out to the horizon as Beowulf's funeral ship sinks, and then glimpsing Grendel's mother, rising from the sea and, sirenlike, beckoning to him. He moves nearly waist-deep into the sea toward her as she summons him again, perhaps considering whether he too, already old and facing an uncertain future, might want to make a deal for his own immortality-conferring narrative, one that would, at least until whatever monster he sires inevitably surfaces, provide him with some control over an unruly reality and fate. But at this point Wiglaf pauses and the film ends with a freeze-frame. We leave him contemplating his next move, much as Zemeckis and all those who are involved in the future of animation might in this era be doing as well.

Certainly Zemeckis must recognize his own kinship to these events, to this craving for a time-defying narrative, to the reliance on a kind of magic—much like the modern magic that allows him to write so freely on the digital screen, film frame, or animation cel. And we might recall Jerome Chen's comment about Zemeckis's fascination with controlling the contingencies of his art, an attitude that links him to the very lure of animation. In this case, with *Beowulf* he has created a story that speaks directly about the anxieties that are bound up in the deals we strike for those stories, and about the elusiveness of the control that the best animation has traditionally displayed and celebrated. Such an implicitly reflexive narrative seems a very fitting response to the rapidly expanding digital power that beckons, even an appropriate end to this chronicle of American animation's figural-spatial developments, as it suggests the sort of uncertainty that today attends most approaches to animating space.

Able to construct a convincing world and to populate it with nearly real people, Zemeckis and the other digital animators of today find themselves facing not simply the problem of the "valley of the uncanny"—a spatial conceit that might well disappear as we become more familiar with the digital figures that beckon to us from the valley's other side—but what Michele Pierson has effectively described as a "simulationist aesthetic horizon" (152). Simply put, it is the point at which special effects are no longer "special" because the entire film is effects-generated, the point at which stunning images that "draw the eye and solicit the imagination simply disappear when all about them is the same photorealistic wallpaper" (Pierson 153), and at which animation and live action collapse into each other and the special appeal of animation effectively dissolves. In the postmodern climate, wherein everything seems a construct and reality has disappeared or collapsed, perhaps that horizon is more easily approached and seems less troubling. We simply build a world and fill it with figures, much as the earliest animators did. But many of those early figures, and here we might especially recall the work of Winsor McCay, recognized that doing those "simple" things might also open a door onto all sorts of complexity: that constructed characters can readily remind us of our own constructedness; that the space they occupy might prove to be more complex than we anticipated, or as Vidler evocatively puts it, "warped"; that animation itself might well be a way of suggesting not the three-dimensionality of our world but something on the order of the "fourth dimension" that Scheffauer vaguely describes. Perhaps such possibilities, imaged in the open space of the frame rather than in the beckoning monster figure, are the reason for Wiglaf's pause, although they might also give reason to a certain dis-ease that currently lingers about the influence of digital imagery and its effects on the trajectory of animation.

CONCLUSION

One of the underlying assumptions driving this study, this history-that-is-not-quite-a-history, is that we have generally neglected to recognize the extent to which animation is a spatial art. It occurs in a special sort of space that is not quite the human world but that seems to aspire to that status—thus animation's historical efforts at adding depth and dimensionality, at crossing the borders of live-action cinema, even combining human and animated worlds. And it finds a key attraction in its capacity to enliven space, to give spirit to the things that have been created there—"things" that have often rivaled our live-action movie stars in popularity and that now, as rotoscoped or motion-captured "vactors" or "veractors," even threaten to supplant them. Because of that spatial orientation, animation also lends itself to spatial analysis, to thinking through much in the fashion that Vidler has done with late modernist art, architecture, and film, and that Virilio has undertaken with his extended diagnosis of the postmodern world as a realm noteworthy for its lack, for a "lost dimension." In fact, in drawing together those two vantages—vantages that effectively span the historical trajectory of animation—we might even read cinematic animation in part as a symptomatic measure of cultural change: as a tool for exploring and experimenting with the new spaces of the modern world, and for responding to and perhaps even countering the anxiety-producing dissolution of those spaces in more recent times.

Of course, taking this sort of spatial approach is hardly new. We might recall that Walter Benjamin linked mechanical reproduction, and especially that represented by the cinema in its various forms, to a pointedly modern impulse "to bring things 'closer' spatially" (223), and that he subsequently employed that spatial conceit as a way of explaining the ongoing shift from cult value to exhibition value in the arts. As we have several times noted, the art critic Herman Scheffauer saw film, particularly in its more stylized forms, as blazing a path into new dimensions, as providing a way of representing, and thus helping us to see, a "stereoscopic" cultural reality. More recently, David Harvey, in his study of the postmodern compression of time and space, has turned specifically to film to demonstrate what he terms "the conceptualization and meanings" that attach to this historical compression (308). And more directly related to our discussion of animation is the fact that Norman Klein concludes his study of the popular seven-minute cartoon, once a characteristic feature of the movie experience, with a similar focus. He describes the "peculiar kind of architecture" into which animation had begun to evolve in the 1930s, with its "cartoon layouts [that] look like sound stages" (248), traces how in the 1950s "a kind of architectural significance was applied increasingly to cartoon imagery" (250), and eventually suggests that American animation has today found its fulfillment in yet another kind of architectural thinking, in the structures of the Disney-style amusement parks and their carefully controlled points of view, forced perspectives, and collapsing of spaces. It thus seems that such spatial conceits have already served others well in thinking about the movies, modern culture, and, as a reflection of both, animation.

In this study that same conceit has also provided us with a way to help provide some balance to our thinking about animation. Much of the history of the form has previously been written from what I have termed—following Donald Crafton's lead—a figural perspective, from considerations of the artists who have found ways of inserting themselves into their work and of the signature characters that have captured our imaginations and, in the process, become such effective corporate logos. We might note that in 1954, on the first episode of his landmark *Disneyland* television series, Walt Disney, even as he was introducing plans for his new theme park and thus announcing a whole new corporate direction, what Klein might describe as the new frontier for animation, pointed out that his audience should "never lose sight of one thing, that it was all started by a mouse." It was hardly a necessary reminder, particularly since for many years critics had been trying to draw links between Disney and his early "star," a figure that, Klein notes, "is unquestionably the most broadly marketed film image of the twentieth century" (55). But Disney's comment was significant because it reaffirmed the value of such a corporate icon, while reminding us of how important such studio personifications have typically been: giving personality to what was essentially an industrial process and product, creating an aura of fun or good humor for a studio and its products, and even providing a source of additional revenue in the form of toys, comics, and other character endorsements. Thus, Warner Bros., even after shutting down its animation unit, would continue to treat Bugs Bunny as one of its preeminent icons, UPA would rise and fall with the waxing and waning of its Mr. Magoo character, and Dreamworks, always in the shadow of Disney, has carefully cultivated the appeal of its own iconic Shrek figure. It is hardly surprising, then, that critical commentary has generally followed this lead, treating the popular cartoon character as the animator's projection into his or her films, and as embodying the essential focus of animation.

But as I note in the introduction, looking at our animated cartoons and features not only from a figural vantage, as sites in which characters suddenly come alive and perform for our entertainment, but also from the sort of spatial context we have traced here, casts them into an interesting and revealing historical light. They begin to "figure" the cinema's own passage from modernist to postmodernist representation, revealing a track of that geometrical-narrative "crisis" to which Virilio and others have called attention and with which the visual arts have throughout the last century wrestled. The movies as a form, particularly our live-action narratives, have grappled with the same sort of dynamics as has animation, and they have done a kind of spatial dance with similar fantastic and realistic possibilities, at times strictly mining the photographic possibilities that were an essential appeal of the Lumière brothers' first films, and at others exploring the imaginative manipulations and constructions from which Georges Méliès repeatedly drew out, as if from his magician's hat, the surprising images of his *féerie* films. Thus, though those extensive photographic spaces of the Lumière films, marked by the deep focus of their camera, suggest a world coextensive with our own, Méliès's theatrical flats and compressed spaces speak just as effectively of an emerging new space-time, evoking the surprising warped spaces of modernism. And over the course of its history, we have seen the cinema—and its theorists—repeatedly struggle with those different spatial possibilities and their shifting implications, particularly as new technologies such as three-strip Technicolor and wide-screen processes, with their inherent challenges to conventional spatial representation, were introduced and eventually embraced by filmmakers and audiences alike. It is a struggle that we find further traced by and imprinted on a host of contemporary live-action yet effects-driven—and thus partially animated—films, works such as *Dark City* (1998), the *Matrix* trilogy (1999, 2003, 2003), and *The Thirteenth Floor* (1999), which present lived space as constructed, phantasmal, virtual, and part of a larger illusion that we must confront. It is an illusionism that ultimately implicates the very activity of film, as if it were a most apt metaphor for the postmodern world. As a two-dimensional form that has almost always pretended to three-dimensionality, live-action film has a history of its own that readily opens onto the same trajectory of spatial descriptions and interrogations that have been marked off by Vidler and Virilio.

But what is more significant for this study is that by considering the development, shifts in, and deployment of the sort of aesthetic geometry on which animation depends—of those spaces variously marked by displacement, warping, even a sense of loss, but also constantly opening themselves up to reconfiguration and revealing their constructedness—we also gain a new perspective on the history of the animated film, or at least on what are often considered some of the key events in that history. It becomes a history not only about our age-old drive to give life to our own creations—a drive that Aristotle in his *Poetics* describes as one of the most fundamental impulses in human nature[1]—but also about another elemental struggle that has increasingly marked our lives and our arts: to fill the emptiness or absence that, in modern times, we see or sense all around us. Seen in this context, the great achievements in animation—and the efforts of our animators—become celebrations of a larger set of human efforts: at grappling with unfamiliar spaces, staking out a stable place from which to examine the unknown, constructing a human realm in a world of uncertainty, disappearance, and "reality effects."

As part of the strategy for examining the key figures and events in this history, I have employed what I hope has proven to be a rich conflation, that curious phrase "animating space." With it I have tried to provide a lens through which we might better consider the relationship between what happens in animation and the conditions under which it occurs, between the form's ability to bring something to life and the space in which that magic occurs, and between the figures that have dominated much of our thinking about and critical commentary on animation and the worlds that frame and give meaning to—and a stage for—their lives. It suggests a dynamic (the simultaneously centripetal and centrifugal impulses the introduction notes) that has generally been neglected—perhaps because it is so fundamental—as commentaries have instead often focused on the ideological implications of the form, on its relative ability to challenge or simply to mirror cultural circumstance. And though following that fashion has allowed animators, critics, and audiences more easily to make a claim for the form's importance, it has at times led us farther away from what we earlier termed an "animatics," from a systematic consideration of the form's aesthetics.

Through that same phrase I have also hoped to animate our thinking about space a bit, to help us see its constantly changing nature in the animated film. For much of early animation, space was little more than a backdrop or stage on which objects and characters could be displayed and their life given free rein, but for the pioneer Winsor McCay it also became another actor in the play, the source of an uncanny dimension that fueled his films. In trying in various ways to give substance to that uncanny space, to render it technologically with their various multi-plane devices, key figures such as Disney, the Fleischer brothers, and Ub Iwerks also tended to tame that uncanny spirit, rendering it more conventional, after the fashion of classic live-action cinema. Yet even Disney's illusion-of-life aesthetic remained bound by a sense of caricature, of exaggeration and stylization that would, perhaps ironically, show to best effect in the studio's efforts at hybrid animation, at straddling the borders between the animated and live-action worlds, in crossing boundaries. In fact, even as they hint at being essentially shortcuts for fully animated features, works like *The Three Caballeros, Song of the South,* and *Fun and Fancy Free* also seem to challenge that house aesthetic,[2] as if forecasting the shift from modern to postmodern conditions described by Jean-François Lyotard, as he recounts how "the withdrawal of the real" in the waning modernist era was followed by an effort to "put forward the unpresentable in presentation itself" (79, 81).

This emphasis on—and fascination with—"presentation" may be what best marks the late development of Warner Bros. and UPA animation in the 1940s and 1950s. In often stripping their worlds bare, in making the conventions of dimensionality and movement obvious, and in frequently emphasizing narratives about performance or presentation, about the set or stage, they pointedly move the animated film away from the real and into the realm of the constructed. Those films are driven by what Lyotard aptly terms an "incredulity toward" (xxiv) the conventional narratives of our world, as well as those of traditional cartoon art. And that attitude would increasingly eventuate in an interrogation of spaces, of the construction of our world, as we see most strikingly in a complex work like *Who Framed Roger Rabbit*. For it— along with a host of more recent hybrid efforts, including Warner Bros.' *Space Jam*, the Farrelly brothers' *Osmosis Jones* (2001), and especially the Disney production *Enchanted* (2007)—foregrounds the sort of reality effect that, as Virilio observes, marks the postmodern experience and that is congruent with the larger sense of our world as a mediatized realm that frequently seems to resemble a movie set. Moreover, by foregrounding that effect, these films have made for an easier acceptance of the 3-D digital features of a studio such as Pixar, with its pointedly negotiated style, or what David A. Price, commenting on that "house style," has described as "stylized realism" (213). Pixar's films, as we have seen, always seem to hesitate a bit, to stand back from the real, to use space not so much to suggest three-dimensionality—as often seems the case in Disney's traditional illusionism—but to indicate how much always remains repressed, "unpresentable," or, as the recent *Up* (2009) suggests, simply lost in time or the distractions of life.

The new fascination with films that effectively animate the real, with works like *300*, *A Scanner Darkly* (2006), and *Beowulf*, seems a most appropriate end point for this survey, particularly because of the challenge these works pose to our notions of both live-action and animated cinema. And here we might recall that evocative scene with which *Beowulf* ends, as Wiglaf stares out at the horizon, tempted by the technology of magic and the possibility of narrative. It not only presents us with a specter of open space, of a frame (or cel) that still waits to be filled and brought to life, but also reminds us of a potential danger in that process, of the potential for constructing something bad, even inimical to our world. With Wiglaf as a figuration of the artist-animator-director considering both the possibilities and the consequences of his work, of animating space, *Beowulf* leaves us at a kind of crossroads, a space of decisions that are fundamentally important to the world of animation—and, to some extent, all of cinema today. Of course, we have no evidence that Robert Zemeckis and any of the other filmmakers who are now engaged in merging live action and animation through digital-effects animation have actually paused in this way to ask the appropriate questions and to consider what might lie further down the road of such technologies as motion and performance capture. In typical postmodern fashion, however, the very narrative spaces they construct seem to embody and raise these questions, as if they were symptomatic of what Virilio terms a "crisis in the conceptualization of dimension" (*Lost* 25).

The fact that we are seeing such scenes, and indeed, entire films that can be read as interrogations of animating space, is important in itself. Those recurrent scenes suggest an inevitable reflexive tendency today as our filmmakers-animators approach the liminal situations that are implicit in digital film's valley of the uncanny or in the meeting ground of contemporary animation and live-action cinema. In talking about the contemporary intersection of technology and the arts, Virilio has suggested that those working in such liminal areas very commonly project a sense of wonder or question about the nature of what they are doing, whether in their productions they "represent the construction, or construct the representation" (*Lost* 103). That intriguing question is one that seems unavoidable for both animators and digital filmmakers. We might recall how in several of the Disney-Pixar films the animators drew on their software to inject lens flare or wide-angle distortions into specific shots. At such moments they were indeed representing "the construction" of a certain type of live-action narrative with which movie audiences have grown familiar, even comfortable, and which they have come to expect. More recently, Disney and Dreamworks have both announced that they will be adopting the latest 3-D optical technology to further enhance their animated films. As Dreamworks' president, Jeffrey Katzenberg, observes, the new technology provides "a new storytelling opportunity. We can immerse the audience" ("Katzenberg"). That move in part reflects the increased competition in the American animation industry today—competition that necessitates further technological efforts at innovation and product differentiation—but it also clearly commits these studios to constructing "the representation" of a conventionalized reality,[3] one in which audiences are invited to "immerse" themselves as if it were their own world—at least so long as they are able to ignore the cumbersome 3-D glasses that, like audiences of the 1950s, they still must don to participate in that construction. Such moves, it seems, are very much a commonplace for the contemporary animated film.

That these developments show most clearly in the spatial dimension of our films—and that the sort of questions Virilio notes seem fundamentally implicated in that dimension—should underscore the usefulness of the focus we have taken throughout this discussion on animating space. That focus helps us recognize not only the extent to which the various spaces of our lives have been thoroughly informed by media, shaped and in some cases even flattened by their seeming transformation into "sets," but also how those same spaces, when configured in our animated films, can also serve a most useful purpose, in helping us address these concerns by resisting, subverting, or working through them. Building on Chuck Jones's observation that in the best cartoons "people really believe these characters live" (Furniss, *Chuck Jones* 166), Alan Cholodenko has intriguingly suggested that we might think of animation as "that which indetermines and suspends the distinction between representation and simulation, what makes it impossible to say which is which" ("Introduction" 21). As we examine the space of animation, both the world in which our animators work and the one that they bring to life for us, we might be tempted to expand on this evocative description. For in animating space we can see, above all else, a location in which we can sketch our own world *and* its varied possibilities, including the future of film.

NOTES

Introduction

1. Maureen Furniss begins her study of animation aesthetics, *Art in Motion,* with a similar acknowledgment that, for much of its history, the work of animation has been conceptualized along the model of the "dominant form" of the American animation industry (13).

2. This response is one to which Tom Gunning also points in his discussion of early film audiences, as he notes that "the first spectators' experience" of cinema involved "an undisguised awareness of (and delight in) film's illusionistic capabilities," and he describes that response as "an encounter with modernity" ("Aesthetic" 876).

3. For an account of the various forms of early presentation of proto-animation forms such as the "lightning sketch" and primitive cartoons, see Crafton's historical study, *Before Mickey,* especially 48–57.

4. Gregory Waller surveys the early commentary on Disney animation and cites a number of Ferguson's reviews in his "Mickey, Walt, and Film Criticism from *Steamboat Willie* to *Bambi.*" Ferguson, like many other commentators in the 1930s, considered that realism "was always one of Disney's greatest virtues" (Waller 57).

5. It could certainly be claimed that such animators as Robert McKimson, Bob Clampett, Friz Freleng, Tex Avery, and Chuck Jones all had distinctive styles, although their generally unfettered approach to action and narrative, as well as their similar fondness for both evoking and exploding convention, also constitutes something of a Warner Bros. house style.

6. For a description of the stylistic changes that marked much of early television animation, and particularly the emphasis on restricted animation, see Furniss, *Art in Motion,* 142–46.

1. Early Animation

1. Blackton has recounted how, as a young cartoonist and reporter for the *New York Evening World,* he did a series of impromptu sketches at the Edison studio that were filmed and subsequently distributed. Though he makes no mention of trying to imitate other lightning sketch entertainers on this occasion,

we might surmise that when, shortly after, he began making films himself, he would have quickly adopted some of the conventions of this form. See Blackton, "Early History."

2. Maureen Furniss discusses the foundations of animation studio practice in her *Art in Motion*, 20–25.

3. For details on Hurd's patents and his partnership with Bray, see Barrier, 14–15, and Crafton, 150–54.

4. Reiniger provides a detailed history of the shadow and silhouette traditions from which she developed her animation technique in her book *Shadow Puppets, Shadow Theatres, and Shadow Films*. She specifically traces the origins of the shadow play to three distinct "groups of shadow-playing centres: China; India and Java; and the Middle East, Turkey and Greece" (15).

5. Kanfer, we should note, devotes a few sentences to the stop-motion tradition, mentioning in passing Gumby, George Pal, and the Wallace and Gromit films and remarking that they "never quite won the hearts of the audience" (183). Early efforts in this field escape his account too, however.

6. The *Official Guide Book* to the World's Fair emphasizes this 3-D effect, describing how "magically, parts seem to move almost to your side, to take their place in the 'car that can take it'" (200).

2. Winsor McCay's Warped Spaces

1. In his history of the cinema, Robert Sklar repeats this common account, noting that "legend has it that some spectators panicked as the engine appeared to come closer." See Sklar, *Film: An International History of the Medium*, 30. David A. Cook, albeit with a rather more pronounced skepticism, similarly reports that "audiences are said to have dodged aside at the sight of the locomotive hurtling toward them into the foreground of the screen." See Cook, *A History of Narrative Film*, 11.

2. McCay reproduced this well-chronicled vaudeville act as a complete film, one in which we see him standing beside the screen on which his animated dinosaur performs and addressing her through conventional title cards. The film version frames this performance with scenes in which he bets some friends at a gentlemen's club that he can reproduce a dinosaur and then shows elements of the animation process.

3. The famed animator Chuck Jones has repeatedly stressed the significance of this confrontation with space, noting that one of the most fundamental "goals in drawing is to achieve an object working in pure space." See Maureen Furniss, *Chuck Jones*, 31.

4. Vidler describes this new sense of space as resulting from a kind of cultural "crisis of identity," as "the landscapes of fear and the topographies of despair [were] created as a result of modern technological and capitalist development" (2–3).

5. As Crafton explains, the lightning sketch was "a hybrid of graphic and performing art," involving an illustrator-monologuist who would sketch a subject and then, in response to his commentary, quickly alter it into a series of changing representations. The aim was to amaze the audience by both the speed of the artist's alterations and the seeming ability of his subjects "to move, spontaneously change their shape, or become 'real'" (50).

6. See in this context Scott Bukatman's analysis of McCay's comic art, wherein he identifies a "parodic tendency," as McCay examined and, particularly in the case of *Little Sammy Sneeze,* then exploded the conventions of temporal-spatial representation ("Comics and the Critique of Chronophotography," 96).

3. The Stereoscopic Mickey

1. The ad appeared in the Dec. 1, 1930, issue of *Film Daily* and is cited by Neal Gabler in *Walt Disney: The Triumph of the American Imagination,* 150.

2. In the course of this opening show Disney also introduced his plans for the Disneyland theme park. To emphasize the links between his landmark television show, the then under-construction theme park, and his cartoon origins, Disney ended this initial episode with a series of Mickey Mouse cartoons, thereby underscoring his point that "it all started with a mouse."

3. In his essay "Disney and Others," Gilbert Seldes, writing in the period of Mickey's rise to stardom, offered a less extreme version of this same criticism, noting that "because Mickey Mouse is a character, Disney finds himself forced occasionally to endow him with a verbal wit and to give him too much to say, which is against the spirit of the animated cartoon" (170).

4. For background on what has been termed the illusion-of-life style, see its elaborate treatment by two of Disney's most famous animators, Frank Thomas and Ollie Johnston, in *The Illusion of Life: Disney Animation.*

5. Describing his days working in the cartoon industry in New York, first with Raoul Barré's studio and then with the Fleischer brothers, the animator Dick Huemer notes the extent to which others began to study the Disney products, particularly to learn how he "gave his characters weight and life and breath and naturalness" (Adamson 33).

6. The link to Benjamin lies precisely in his emphasis on the "exhibition value" of the artifact, on stripping away its "cult value" in order to open it—and our world—up for inspection and analysis. See Benjamin, "The Work of Art in the Age of Mechanical Reproduction," 224–25. It is worth noting that Benjamin addressed the significance of Mickey Mouse, not only emphasizing the mouse's anarchic energy and satiric spirit, but also applauding the realistic component of Disney's new character. See Leslie, 81–85.

7. This imitative element might also suggest a kind of metanarrative implicit in *Plane Crazy:* a reflection of Disney's own ambitions for his studio and new cartoon figure. With this film and his new character of Mickey, Disney was

certainly trying to imitate such previously successful cartoon characters as Felix and his own Oswald the Rabbit, which had effectively been stolen from him by his distributor. But at the same time, Mickey represented much more, a kind of emblem of Walt Disney's vaulting ambition, as Gabler interprets, "to make himself animation's indispensable man" (132). Mickey's desire to soar above the barnyard, even after a failed attempt, easily maps onto his creator's story of pioneering efforts, dashed hopes, and dogged persistence.

8. For background on the various efforts to imitate Lindbergh throughout American culture in this period, see Telotte, "Lindbergh, Film, and Machine Age Dreams."

9. Barrier notes that Felix had only "the rudiments of a personality," and we might add that this personality, in marked contrast to Mickey's, was practically characterized by a level of stillness, a notion at least hinted at in Barrier's reference to his "curious and rather hard-boiled" approach to everything (31).

10. Of course, Disney had earlier innovated three-strip Technicolor for cartoons in the Silly Symphony series with *Flowers and Trees* (1932). In part because of cost but also to further differentiate the Mickey Mouse series from the Silly Symphonies, Disney would delay adding color to the Mickey films until *The Band Concert*.

4. The Double Space of the Fleischer Films

1. Rotoscoping, as Michael Barrier notes, was essentially "a tracing from live-action film that was projected from below, frame by frame, onto a glass surface the size of the animation paper" (22–23), a process for which Max Fleischer received a patent on Oct. 9, 1917. The rotograph allowed the combination of those animated frames with live action by positioning the cels over rear-projected live-action scenes, which resulted in an early form of hybrid animation (see Barrier 28 and Maltin, *Of Mice* 88).

2. For the Fleischers the rotoscope was indeed a "figural" device in the sense used by Crafton, since its early use was to photograph Dave Fleischer in a clown suit, allowing him to *become* KoKo the Clown and thus insert himself into his own cartoons.

3. See Richard Fleischer's account of this technology in his biography of his father, *Out of the Inkwell: Max Fleischer and the Animation Revolution*, 84–85.

4. The Disney multiplane camera made its first appearance in 1937 with the Silly Symphony cartoon *The Old Mill*, a work that would win the studio an Academy Award for Best Short Subject, and it would be effectively employed in the groundbreaking feature *Snow White and the Seven Dwarfs*, released later that same year.

5. Since Disney had an exclusive agreement with Technicolor at this point, Fleischer was using the less expensive—and far less satisfactory—Cinecolor

process, a two-strip technique. Richard Fleischer claims that, because of his initial dissatisfaction with Cinecolor's results, his father, Max, developed "a secret method of using special filters" (84) to enhance the color effects.

6. See Kern's discussion of positive and negative space in *The Culture of Time and Space*, 153. The treatment of background space as "negative" here and in many other of the Stereoptical Fleischer films runs counter to the trend Kern notes in art of the period, as well as to Disney's narratizing of background space in the contemporary film *The Band Concert* (1935).

7. Perhaps it would be more accurate to term this shot a pan, since the camera in the Fleischer device did not move, and the set simply turned on its axis to produce the impression of camera movement and to suggest parallax.

8. See the discussion of Iwerks's development and application of this technology in chapter 5.

9. Michael Barrier notes that financial data on *Gulliver's Travels* "are scarce" but that it "was at least modestly profitable"—at any rate enough to prompt the Fleischers to proceed with plans for *Mr. Bug Goes to Town* (296). That second feature, however, could not even claim a "modest" success. Drawing on a Paramount financial document, Barrier cites advances of more than $713,000 to cover production and a final gross of just $241,000 (305).

10. In addition to the obvious aesthetic consequences, there were also economic and production difficulties that attended the Stereoptical Process. Creating the three-dimensional props and sets certainly required much time and money, but even shooting the Stereoptical shots involved additional delays; as Mark Langer has noted, it "was very time-consuming due to the remarkably long camera exposures required" to produce such hybrid images (344).

11. In its 1941 agreement with Paramount, the Fleischer Studio agreed to produce the Superman series with a budget of $50,000 for each film, a figure far in excess of the $16,500 that was allowed for each Popeye cartoon at that time (Barrier 604–5). Though the first episode did indeed cost $50,000, the subsequent cartoons were budgeted at approximately $30,000 each. Still, as Bruce Scivally has chronicled, the total cost for the series was $530,000, making it "one of the most expensive cartoon series ever produced" (25).

12. Those creatures are pointedly fantastic hybrids, bird-men whose ability to fly serves no real function in the narrative and who seem ill-suited to their underground world. Though the peculiar illogic of their character has a kind of nightmarish effectiveness, it clearly strikes at narrative realism, suggesting another level of compromise or negotiation at work here.

13. Skerry and Lambert offer this assertion, noting that the animating of Superman "was based on model sheets provided by Joe Schuster" (64).

14. The primary account of the various techniques bound up in the Disney illusion-of-life style is that offered by two of Disney's "nine old men," the animators Frank Thomas and Ollie Johnston, in *The Illusion of Life: Disney Animation*.

15. This and other comments on the use of both the Stereoptical Process and

rotoscoping are drawn from e-mail correspondence, particularly one note of Nov. 17, 2007, from Ginny Mahoney to the author. It might also be worth noting that the "Overview" section of the *Superman: The Lost Episodes* DVD (Fox Lorber Associates, 1999) describes how Fleischer and then Famous Studios "furthered" the "development and technique" of rotoscoping with its use throughout the Superman series.

16. The exception is the final film in the series, *The Secret Agent* (1943), for here there is no Lois Lane to remark on the disparity in character, or even a return to the disguise of Clark Kent.

5. Ub Iwerks's (Multi)Plain Cinema

1. For background on these and other technical developments and patents created by Iwerks, see Iwerks and Kenworthy, *The Hand behind the Mouse*, esp. 193–98.

2. We should note that Barrier's description of Iwerks's increasing tendency to distance himself from the day-to-day animation process is echoed in many other accounts as well, including that of Leslie Iwerks, his granddaughter, and John Kenworthy, who describe how, as Grim Natwick's "importance within the Studio grew and with Dorothy Webster and Emile Offermann handling the business matters in the mid-1930s, Ub retired to the refuge of the basement" to work on various technical projects (129).

3. The best account of the development of this aesthetic can be found in the study of Disney animation produced by two of the studio's famous "Nine Old Men," Frank Thomas and Ollie Johnston's *The Illusion of Life: Disney Animation*. These veteran animators worked on the classic Disney animated features that developed the basic principles of the Disney style.

4. Steven Watts in his critical biography of Walt Disney details the mutual admiration that Disney and Eisenstein shared. The Russian, he argues, believed that Disney's "protean animism" represented both "a revolt against capitalist rationalization" and a key contribution to "modernist aesthetics" (128). It was an assessment apparently shared by many in the 1930s.

5. That "strange" sensibility might also help explain why Iwerks was able to adapt to other studio styles after closing his own operation in 1936. He would, for example, go on to do several Porky Pig cartoons at Warner Bros. and then move to Columbia shortly before returning to Disney as a technical consultant in 1940.

6. Perhaps hinting at his dismissal of its importance, Barrier's history of Hollywood animation offers no mention of this device.

7. Some contemporary release versions of the Iwerks cartoons contain editing and cropping that diminish or largely eliminate the depth effects, as in the case of the silhouetted audience at the bottom of the frame in *Mary's Little Lamb*, an effect that disappears in some reissues of the cartoon.

6. Looking in on Life

1. For useful discussions of the shifting critical attitude toward Disney, see Gregory Waller, "Mickey, Walt, and Film Criticism from *Steamboat Willie* to *Bambi*," and Timothy R. White, "From Disney to Warner Bros.: The Critical Shift."

2. See Michael Barrier's discussion of the "casting by sequence" approach in his *Hollywood Cartoons,* esp. 314–16. As he suggests, one effect of this method was to turn supervising animators into directors for their specific sequences (315).

3. For an extensive discussion of the Alice cartoons, see Merritt and Kaufman, *Walt in Wonderland,* 53–85.

4. Numerous commentaries have chronicled the story behind Disney's South American projects, undertaken at the behest of the Office of Inter-American Affairs. Among the most informative of those accounts are those provided by Eric Smoodin in *Animating Culture* (see esp. 138–46), and by J. B. Kaufman in "Norm Ferguson and the Latin American Films of Walt Disney." Smoodin particularly pinpoints the problem on which most discussions of both *The Three Caballeros* and the earlier *Saludos Amigos* (1943) have principally focused, the implicit notion that "Walt Disney, a representative of the United States, could tour a foreign culture, come to understand it in just a short time, film it, and then bring it back home with him, all with the blessing and thanks of the culture he had visited" (141). That seems a rather harsh judgment, though, particularly since the film's focus on Donald as *spectator* pointedly emphasizes his consistently naive perspective, his general lack of actual understanding. The real focus, finally, is on celebrating the variety of different cultures, which is commensurate with the narrative's development of and focus on different kinds of *space.*

5. Steven Watts perhaps best captures the tenor of this criticism when he describes Donald Duck's actions throughout the film as "libidinous shenanigans" that suggested Disney might be losing touch with his core family audience (248).

6. Actually, this action was filmed in a parking lot at the Disney studio, sand having been trucked in to suggest an Acapulco beach, and secretaries and extras serving as the Mexican bathing beauties. For an account of this filming, see Kaufman's "Norm Ferguson and the Latin American Films of Walt Disney."

7. For a discussion of the assault on Disney's illusion-of-life aesthetic and a sampling of the various critical comments on the studio's changing style, see Gregory A. Waller, "Mickey, Walt, and Film Criticism from *Steamboat Willie* to *Bambi*."

8. As Steven Watts notes, though, Disney was well aware of the potential for controversy with the Uncle Remus tales, long before any decision had been made to do this project as a hybrid effort. He notes that, as far back as 1938,

Disney researchers had been put to work, "examining not only the Joel Chandler Harris stories themselves but a great deal of supplementary material" in an effort at achieving authenticity while trying to sidestep any possible racial fallout (278).

9. Harvey notes that postmodernist characters "often seem confused as to which world they are in, and how they should act with respect to it" (41), and to some extent that comment well describes the plight of Donald in *The Three Caballeros,* Johnny in *Song of the South,* and Willie the Giant in *Fun and Fancy Free.* In every case, though, these films also offer us other characters—Uncle Remus is the most obvious case—who seem to function precisely as a means of grounding the other figures, of showing them their way in a world of confusing spaces.

7. What's Up—and Down—Doc?

1. For background on this development with a particular emphasis on the 1950s, see Amidi, *Cartoon Modern: Style and Design in Fifties Animation.* One of his primary emphases is on the shift in the cartoon world from conventional backgrounds to highly stylized, "designed" worlds (10).

2. See Walz's "Charlie Thorson and the Temporary Disneyfication of Warner Bros. Cartoons," 50. In this article Walz describes the particular effect of Thorson, a former Disney character designer whom Warner Bros. hired in 1939 to help refine and design characters and who was, as his study of character model sheets shows, particularly influential in the early development of such figures as Bugs Bunny, Elmer Fudd, and Sniffles the Mouse. Walz's emphasis on the "temporary" nature of this emulation is most significant, though, for it points toward the stylistic shift that I describe here, a shift that can most easily be seen not just in the various Warners' characters, such as those that Thorson greatly influenced, but in the mise-en-scène, and especially in the ways in which these cartoons treat space itself.

3. Chuck Jones described this film as "the most difficult film I ever did," largely because of its effort at encapsulating an entire opera cycle in a traditional cartoon length. As he notes, "we took the entire *Ring of the Nibelung,* which runs, I believe, sixteen hours . . . and condensed it into a six-minute picture, a chestnut stew" (Furniss, *Chuck Jones* 82).

4. This pairing was all the more unlikely given that Garbo, unlike Bette Davis, was under contract to MGM, not Warners. Because of her status as a legendary beauty, however, Garbo provides an even more absurd potential pairing with the pig.

5. Warner Bros. in a few other instances mixed live action and animation, most notably *Two Guys from Texas* (1948) and *My Dream Is Yours* (1949), but the efforts represent brief moments—dream sequences—in these films, rather than the sort of ambitious narrative combinations found in the Disney package films and other hybrid features done in this period.

6. Leonard Maltin notes that this highly formulaic approach proved a

"definite advantage" in terms of production flexibility, as he cites Jones's explanation: "'If I got an idea like *What's Opera, Doc?*, which actually ran more than 540 feet and took maybe seven weeks to do, I knew the *Road Runner* so well that I could do a *Road Runner* in *three* weeks. So the two pictures together would come out at ten weeks. And the front office never knew the difference, because I had everybody cheat on their time cards'" (Maltin, *Of Mice* 267).

7. In his brief history of Warner Bros. animation, Barry Putterman terms Bosco simply "a blatant rip-off of Mickey Mouse" (30), whereas Michael Barrier more kindly describes him as "very much of the same cartoon family as Mickey Mouse and Felix the Cat" (155–56).

8. Toontown Spaces and the New Hybrid World

1. Among similar hybrid films in this period we might note such titles as *Evil Toons* (1992), *Rampo* (1994), and *Space Jam* (1996).

2. For a discussion of classical film narrative and its realist imperatives, see Bordwell, Staiger, and Thompson, *The Classical Hollywood Cinema*, esp. 19–21.

3. Following the success of *Who Framed Roger Rabbit*, three cartoon shorts were created and released: *Tummy Trouble* (1989), directed by Rob Minkoff and released theatrically with Disney's *Honey, I Shrunk the Kids*; *Rollercoaster Rabbit* (1990), directed by Minkoff and released with *Dick Tracy*; and *Trail Mix-Up* (1993), directed by Barry Cook and shown with the feature *A Far Off Place*. All were done as coproductions of the two principal partners in the feature film, Amblin Entertainment and Walt Disney Pictures.

4. The post–World War II, film noirish elements of both films are worth underscoring here. In an earlier study of film noir, I argue that, given its mannered style and frequent narrative experimentation, we should read noir symptomatically, that is, as a symptom of a felt inadequacy in the forms of classical film practice. In adopting a noir context in order to reflect on both the possibilities and failings of contemporary animation, both *Who Framed Roger Rabbit* and *Cool World* reach for a similarly symptomatic atmosphere, evoking that moment of cultural and aesthetic crisis or dissatisfaction to suggest a possible crisis in animation, particularly in its ability to adequately address the "lost," "hidden," or "compressed" dimensions of the postmodern world. See Telotte, *Voices in the Dark*, 220–21.

9. The Pixar Reality

1. As its developers note, they designed RenderMan with a photographic reality in mind, aiming to produce images "virtually indistinguishable from live action motion picture photography" and "as visually rich as real scenes" (R. Cook et al. 95).

2. *Toy Story*'s supervising layout artist, Craig Good, is quite emphatic on

the policy at Pixar for avoiding some of the more irritating freedoms that come with the digital animation process. As he explains, "What bugs me most—and most of us here—are the computer graphics camera moves that take you flying precipitously. . . . The camera twists and rolls all over the place, until the whole audience wants to reach for an air-sickness bag" (Street 84).

3. For a discussion of classic live-action cinema's treatment of depth, see Bordwell, Staiger, and Thompson, *The Classical Hollywood Cinema*, esp. 50–53.

4. It is worth noting that this sense of a dialogue or negotiation between different systems was also fundamental to the styling of the film, owing to the very variety of the monster figures. As the director Peter Docter explains, though the monsters are wildly diverse in size and shape, "*all* have to be able to reach a doorknob and walk through a door. How do you do that? We used multiple doorknobs on the doors. We also designed flexible headsets for phones, so characters with their mouths way down here and their ears way up there could still talk on the same receiver" (Duncan, *Monsters* 113).

5. The model for these amazing shifts in space and orientation is certainly one of the most amazing of live-action comedies, a film that also suggests a level on which our experience of reality is always a kind of trick, Buster Keaton's *Sherlock, Jr.* (1923). In that film Buster, a movie projectionist, imagines himself within a movie and is, consequently, subjected to the vicissitudes of film editing, as his location keeps shifting, depending entirely on the logic—or illogic—of the film's narrative.

6. Technical Director Rick Sayre describes how the production team, from the start, understood the difficulties they faced: "The hardest thing about *The Incredibles* was there was no hardest thing. . . . Brad [Bird] ordered a heaping helping of everything on the menu. We've got it all: fire, water, air, smoke, steam, explosions, and, by the way, humans. . . . Getting hair to work at all and to move and clothing and then doing it with a big ensemble cast. It's a Pixar compendium" (Price 223–24).

7. I take this term from recent architectural theory, wherein "folding" refers to a contemporary effort at what Greg Lynn terms "complexity in both composition and construction" (9). It speaks to efforts by figures like Frank Gehry, Robert Venturi, and Denise Scott Brown to introduce to the architectural field a new "fusion of disparate elements into continuity" (9). Fittingly, that "fusion" would be especially enabled by the emergence of new digital technologies that have helped architects fully envision that unconventional complexity and work out the calculus fundamental to it.

10. Digital Effects Animation and the New Hybrid Cinema

1. On the simplest level, the digital intermediate process (or DI) involves converting filmed images to digital elements so that they can be combined with other digitally created components, and lighting, color, and other visual effects

can be manipulated or adjusted. Once this intermediate process is completed within a computer workstation, the result is then usually transferred to film stock for final processing. For a discussion of the way in which the DI affects contemporary film narrative, see Aylish Wood, "Pixel Visions."

2. John Van Vliet, a former Disney animator and now a visual effects supervisor, has suggested that this "menu" approach is one of the chief problems facing the new digital cinema. As he states, "Everything is menu-driven, a multiple-choice thing" that ultimately stands in the way of creativity and marks what he terms "the end of the age of wizards," especially in the field of effects animation (Duncan et al., "State" 26).

3. We might note that the six-minute short film Conran created to showcase his approach and entice potential investors was set up precisely as a serial, its title screen noting that it was "Chapter One—Mechanical Monsters" of an "O'Conran Brothers Serial." That title also points up the film's indebtedness to period animation, for the title card, with its constructed metal design, is directly copied from the Fleischer brothers' 1941 Superman cartoon of the same name.

4. As Joe Fordham recounts, the production amazingly "averaged 25 first-unit setups a day" while shooting principal photography at Elstree Studios ("Brave" 23).

5. This deleted scene is available as one of the "Special Features" on the Special Collector's Edition DVD of Sky Captain and the World of Tomorrow.

6. Motion capture, or mocap, as it is often abbreviated, refers to the broad category of recording a character's or thing's motion and then translating that recording into a digital figure's movements. Performance capture is essentially a more detailed application of the same principle, involving the tracking of gesture and facial movement to fix the elements of character interpretation so that they can later be mapped onto a digital figure.

7. In Zelig (1983) Woody Allen was obviously doing similar things but working photographically and chemically, just as the Soviets did in the 1930s and 1940s with figures who had fallen out of political favor and were removed from films and thus from the historical-cinematic record. This sort of erasure has a long history in the cinema, but here we are considering only the possibilities of digital manipulation or "image future."

8. That tendency to stand outside the narrative as a kind of "filmmaker/designer" rather than as a true participant is particularly emphasized once Beowulf ascends to the throne and must rule over a constantly expanding kingdom. When challenged by a Frisian warrior, Beowulf's lieutenants twice remind him that "the king must never engage in direct battle."

Conclusion

1. In his Poetics 1448b Aristotle argues that "the instinct for imitation" is "rooted in human nature," as is also "the instinct to enjoy works of imitation" (35).

2. Though the late modernist shift in Disney's work is seldom credited or discussed, Paul Wells offers an important lead in this direction as he observes how, in the immediate postwar period, the Disney studio "sought to be more progressive in its work only to have this received with disappointment and criticism," and that Disney effectively became a prisoner of its own "brand" (128).

3. Jeffrey Katzenberg, one of the founders of Dreamworks and the former head of production at Disney, has announced that his studio will be shifting all feature animation production to a 3-D format: "*Madagascar 2* was the last 2D film made at the studio. Virtually the whole studio has been converted. It has changed virtually every aspect of the filmmaking process, from pre-production to special effects." This move is at least a sign of the extreme good health of the animation field—that Dreamworks must keep up with Disney and its use of 3-D in an animation marketplace that is becoming more crowded and competitive—but it is also an acknowledgment that digital animation is opening up new aesthetic possibilities that can and will be exploited.

BIBLIOGRAPHY

Adamson, Joe. "A Talk with Dick Huemer." *The American Animated Cartoon: A Critical Anthology.* Ed. Gerald Peary and Danny Peary. New York: Dutton, 1980. 29–36.

Adorno, Theodor W., and Max Horkheimer. *The Dialectic of Enlightenment.* London: Verso, 1989.

Amidi, Amid. *Cartoon Modern: Style and Design in Fifties Animation.* San Francisco: Chronicle, 2006.

Aristotle. "On the Art of Poetry." *Classical Literary Criticism.* Trans. T. R. Dorsch. Baltimore: Penguin, 1965.

Barrier, Michael. *Hollywood Cartoons: American Animation in Its Golden Age.* Oxford: Oxford University Press, 1999.

Baudrillard, Jean. *Selected Writings.* Trans. Mark Poster. Stanford: Stanford University Press, 1988.

Bazin, André. *What Is Cinema?* Vol. 1. Trans. Hugh Gray. Berkeley: University of California Press, 1967.

Belton, John. *Widescreen Cinema.* Cambridge: Harvard University Press, 1992.

Benjamin, Walter. "The Work of Art in the Age of Mechanical Reproduction." *Illuminations.* Trans. Harry Zohn. New York: Schocken, 1969. 217–51.

Blackton, J. Stuart. "Early History." *Hollywood Directors, 1914–1940.* Ed. Richard Koszarski. New York: Oxford University Press, 1976. 13–23.

Bordwell, David, Janet Staiger, and Kristin Thompson. *The Classical Hollywood Cinema: Film Style and Mode of Production to 1960.* New York: Columbia University Press, 1985.

Brophy, Philip. "The Animation of Sound." *The Illusion of Life: Essays on Animation.* Ed. Alan Cholodenko. Sydney: Power Publications, 1991. 67–112.

Brown, John Mason. "Mr. Disney's Caballeros." *Saturday Review,* Feb. 24, 1945, 22–24.

Bukatman, Scott. "Comics and the Critique of Chronophotography, or 'He Never Knew When It Was Coming!'" *Animation: An Interdisciplinary Journal* 1.1 (2006): 83–103.

———. *Matters of Gravity: Special Effects and Supermen in the 20th Century.* Durham: Duke University Press, 2003.

Cabarga, Leslie. *The Fleischer Story.* New York: Nostalgia Press, 1976.

Canemaker, John. *The Art and Flair of Mary Blair: An Appreciation.* New York: Disney Editions, 2003.

Cholodenko, Alan. "Introduction." *The Illusion of Life: Essays on Animation.* Ed. Cholodenko. Sydney: Power Publications, 1991. 9–36.

———. "*Who Framed Roger Rabbit,* or The Framing of Animation." *The Illusion of Life: Essays on Animation.* Ed. Cholodenko. Sydney: Power Publications, 1991. 209–42.

Cook, David A. *A History of Narrative Film.* 3rd ed. New York: Norton, 1996.

Cook, Robert L., Loren Carpenter, and Edwin Catmull. "The REYES Rendering Architecture." *Computer Graphics* 21.4 (1987): 95–102.

Crafton, Donald. *Before Mickey: The Animated Film, 1898–1928.* Cambridge: MIT Press, 1982.

Deming, Barbara. "The Artlessness of Walt Disney." *Partisan Review,* Spring 1945, 226–31.

Denslow, Philip Kelly. "What Is Animation and Who Needs to Know?" *A Reader in Animation Studies.* Ed. Jayne Pilling. London: John Libbey, 1997. 1–4.

De Roos, Robert. "The Magic Worlds of Walt Disney" (1963). *Disney Discourse: Producing the Magic Kingdom.* Ed. Eric Smoodin. London: Routledge, 1994. 48–68.

"Disney with No Improvements." *New Yorker,* Oct. 4, 1947, 21.

Duncan, Jody. "All the Way." *Cinefex* 112 (2008): 45–59.

———. "*Monsters, Inc.:* Monsters in the Closet." *Cinefex* 88 (2002): 15–26, 113–14.

Duncan, Jody, Don Shay, and Joe Fordham. "State of the Art: A *Cinefex* 25th Anniversary Forum." *Cinefex* 100 (2005): 17–107.

Ebert, Roger. "*Beowulf.*" *Chicago Sun-Times,* Nov. 15, 2007, http://rogerebert .suntimes.com/apps/pbcs.dll/article?AID=/20071114/REVIEWS/ 71115001/1023 (accessed Dec. 3, 2008).

———. "*Sky Captain and the World of Tomorrow.*" *Chicago Sun-Times,* Sept. 17, 2004, http://rogerebert.suntimes.com/apps/pbcs.dll/article?AID=/20040917/ REVIEWS/409170301/1023 (accessed Nov. 15, 2008).

Eisenberg, Adam. "Romancing the Rabbit." *Cinefex* 35 (1988): 4–33.

Eisenstein, Sergei. *Eisenstein on Disney.* Ed. Jay Leyda. Trans. Alan Upchurch. London: Methuen, 1988.

———. *Notes of a Film Director.* Trans. X. Danko. New York: Dover, 1970.

Ellis, John. *Visible Fictions: Cinema, Television, Video.* Rev. ed. London: Routledge, 1992.

Farber, Manny. "Saccharine Symphony—*Bambi*" (1942). *The American Animated Cartoon: A Critical Anthology.* Ed. Gerald Peary and Danny Peary. New York: Dutton, 1980. 90–91.

Fleischer, Max. "Art of Making Motion Picture Cartoons." Patent no. 2,054, 414. Nov. 2, 1933.

Fleischer, Richard. *Out of the Inkwell: Max Fleischer and the Animation Revolution.* Lexington: University Press of Kentucky, 2005.

Fordham, Joe. "Brave New World." *Cinefex* 98 (2004): 15–33.

———. "A Dream of Christmas." *Cinefex* 100 (2005): 112–35, 169–70.

Foster, Hal. "Image Building." *Architecture: Between Spectacle and Use.* Ed. Anthony Vidler. New Haven: Yale University Press, 2008. 164–79.

French, Lawrence. "*Toy Story.*" *Cinefantastique* 27.2 (1995): 17–37.

Furniss, Maureen. *Art in Motion: Animation Aesthetics.* Rev. ed. Eastleigh, U.K.: John Libbey, 2007.

———, ed. *Chuck Jones: Conversations.* Jackson: University Press of Mississippi, 2005.

Gabler, Neal. *Walt Disney: The Triumph of the American Imagination.* New York: Knopf, 2006.

Gelernter, David. *1939: The Lost World of the Fair.* New York: Avon, 1995.

Goodall, Jane. "Hybridity and the End of Innocence." *The Illusion of Life II: More Essays on Animation.* Ed. Alan Cholodenko. Sydney: Power Publications, 2007. 152–71.

Gunning, Tom. "An Aesthetic of Astonishment: Early Film and the (In)Credulous Spectator." *Film Theory and Criticism,* 6th ed. Ed. Leo Braudy and Marshall Cohen. London: Oxford University Press, 2004. 862–76.

———. "The Cinema of Attractions: Early Film, Its Spectator and the Avant-Garde." *Wide Angle* 8.3–4 (1986): 63–77.

Harvey, David. *The Condition of Postmodernity: An Enquiry into the Origins of Cultural Change.* Oxford: Blackwell, 1990.

"How Disney Combines Living Actors with His Cartoon Characters." *Popular Science,* Sept. 1944, 106–11.

"An Interview with Ralph Bakshi." IGN.com, http://movies.ign.com/articles/518/518805.p1.html (accessed March 8, 2008).

Iwerks, Leslie, and John Kenworthy. *The Hand behind the Mouse.* New York: Disney Editions, 2001.

Jackson, Rosemary. *Fantasy: The Literature of Subversion.* London: Methuen, 1981.

Jameson, Fredric. *Postmodernism: or, The Cultural Logic of Late Capitalism.* Durham: Duke University Press, 1991.

Jones, Kent. "Beyond Disbelief." *Film Comment* 44.4 (2008): 22–26.

Kanfer, Stefan. *Serious Business: The Art and Commerce of Animation in America from Betty Boop to "Toy Story."* New York: Da Capo Press, 2000.

"Katzenberg Converts Dreamworks to 3D Production." *SciFiPi,* Nov. 20, 2008, http://www.scifitv.com.au/Blog/2008/11/Katzenberg-Converts-Dreamworks-To-3d-Production/ (accessed Nov. 22, 2008).

Kaufman, J. B. "Norm Ferguson and the Latin American Films of Walt Disney."

A Reader in Animation Studies. Ed. Jayne Pilling. London: John Libbey, 1997. 260- 68.

———. *South of the Border with Disney: Walt Disney and the Good Neighbor Program, 1941–1948.* New York: Disney Editions, 2009.

Kermode, Mark. "Bergmanesque Superheroes? Come Off It." *Observer,* Nov. 21, 2004, http://www.guardian.co.uk/theobserver/2004/nov/21/features.review57 (accessed May 24, 2008).

Kern, Stephen. *The Culture of Time and Space, 1880–1918.* Cambridge: Harvard University Press, 1983.

Kittler, Friedrich A. *Gramophone, Film, Typewriter.* Trans. Geoffrey Winthrop-Young and Michael Wutz. Stanford: Stanford University Press, 1999.

Klein, Norman M. *Seven Minutes: The Life and Death of the American Animated Cartoon.* London: Verso, 1993.

Koszarski, Richard. *An Evening's Entertainment: The Age of the Silent Feature Picture, 1915–1928.* Berkeley: University of California Press, 1990.

Kozlenko, William. "The Animated Cartoon and Walt Disney." Rptd. in *The Emergence of Film Art,* 2nd ed. Ed. Lewis Jacobs. New York: Norton, 1979. 246–53.

Kracauer, Siegfried. *"Dumbo." Nation,* Nov. 8, 1941, 463.

———. *Theory of Film: The Redemption of Physical Reality.* London: Oxford University Press, 1960.

Langer, Mark. "The Disney-Fleischer Dilemma: Product Differentiation and Technological Innovation." *Screen* 33.4 (1992): 343–60.

Lefebvre, Henri. *The Production of Space.* Trans. Donald Nicholson-Smith. London: Blackwell, 1991.

Leslie, Esther. *Hollywood Flatlands: Animation, Critical Theory and the Avant-Garde.* London: Verso, 2002.

Lynn, Greg. "Introduction." *Folding in Architecture.* Rev. ed. Ed. Lynn. Chichester: Wiley-Academy, 2004. 9–13.

Lyons, Mike. "Cyber-Cinema: A Brief Look at the (Still On-going) History of CGI Effects." *Cinefantastique* 28.8 (1997): 40–43, 62.

Lyotard, Jean-François. *The Postmodern Condition: A Report on Knowledge.* Trans. Geoff Bennington and Brian Massumi. Minneapolis: University of Minnesota Press, 1984.

Maltin, Leonard. *The Disney Films.* 4th ed. New York: Disney Editions, 2000.

———. *Of Mice and Magic: A History of American Animated Cartoons.* New York: New American Library, 1980.

Manovich, Lev. "Image Future." *Animation: An Interdisciplinary Journal* 1.1 (2006): 25–44.

———. *The Language of New Media.* Cambridge: MIT Press, 2001.

Mast, Gerald. *The Comic Mind.* 2nd ed. Chicago: University of Chicago Press, 1989.

McCarthy, Todd. *"Sky Captain and the World of Tomorrow." Variety,* Sept. 9,

2004, www.variety.com/review/VE1117924839.html?categoryid=31&cs=1& p=0 (accessed Nov. 15, 2008).

McGilligan, Patrick. "A Talk with Ralph Bakshi." *The American Animated Cartoon: A Critical Anthology.* Ed. Gerald Peary and Danny Peary. New York: Dutton, 1980. 269–79.

Merritt, Russell, and J. B. Kaufman. *Walt in Wonderland: The Silent Films of Walt Disney.* Baltimore: Johns Hopkins University Press, 1993.

Official Guide Book of the New York World's Fair. 2nd ed. New York: Exposition Publications, 1939.

O'Pray, Michael. "Eisenstein and Stokes on Disney: Film Animation and Omnipotence." *A Reader in Animation Studies.* Ed. Jayne Pilling. London: John Libbey, 1997. 195–202.

Pierson, Michele. *Special Effects: Still in Search of Wonder.* New York: Columbia University Press, 2002.

Postman, Neil. *Technopoly: The Surrender of Culture to Technology.* New York: Random House, 1992.

Price, David A. *The Pixar Touch: The Making of a Company.* New York: Knopf, 2008.

Purse, Lisa. "Digital Heroes in Contemporary Hollywood: Exertion, Identification, and the Virtual Action Body." *Film Criticism* 32.1 (2007): 5–25.

Putterman, Barry. "A Short Critical History of Warner Bros. Cartoons." *Reading the Rabbit: Explorations in Warner Bros. Animation.* Ed. Kevin S. Sandler. New Brunswick: Rutgers University Press, 1998. 29–37.

Reiniger, Lotte. *Shadow Puppets, Shadow Theatres, and Shadow Films.* Boston: Publishers Plays, 1975.

Sartin, Hank. "From Vaudeville to Hollywood, from Silence to Sound: Warner Bros. Cartoons of the Early Sound Era." *Reading the Rabbit: Explorations in Warner Bros. Animation.* Ed. Kevin S. Sandler. New Brunswick: Rutgers University Press, 1998. 67–85.

Schaffer, William. "Animation 1: The Control-Image." *The Illusion of Life II: More Essays on Animation.* Ed. Alan Cholodenko. Sydney: Power Publications, 2007. 456–85.

Scheffauer, Herman G. "The Vivifying of Space." Rptd. in *Introduction to the Art of the Movies.* Ed. Lewis Jacobs. New York: Noonday Press, 1960. 76–85.

Scivally, Bruce. *Superman on Film, Television, Radio, and Broadway.* Jefferson, N.C.: McFarland, 2008.

Segal, Howard P. *Future Imperfect: The Mixed Blessings of Technology in America.* Amherst: University of Massachusetts Press, 1994.

Seldes, Gilbert. "Disney and Others" (1932). Rptd. in *Introduction to the Art of the Movies.* Ed. Lewis Jacobs. New York: Noonday Press, 1960. 170–72.

Shay, Don. "Willis O'Brien: Creator of the Impossible." *Focus on Film* 16 (1973): 18–48.

Skerry, Philip, with Chris Lambert. "From Panel to Panavision." *Superman at*

Fifty: The Persistence of a Legend. Ed. Dennis Dooley and Gary Engle. Cleveland: Octavia Press, 1987. 62–75.

Sklar, Robert. *Film: An International History of the Medium.* Upper Saddle River, N.J.: Prentice-Hall, 2002.

———. "The Making of Cultural Myths—Walt Disney." *The American Animated Cartoon: A Critical Anthology.* Ed. Gerald Peary and Danny Peary. New York: Dutton, 1980. 58–65.

Smith, Conrad. "The Early History of Animation." *The American Animated Cartoon: A Critical Anthology.* Ed. Gerald Peary and Danny Peary. New York: Dutton, 1980. 3–11.

Smoodin, Eric. *Animating Culture: Hollywood Cartoons from the Sound Era.* Brunswick: Rutgers University Press, 1993.

Solomon, Charles. "Animation: Notes on a Definition." *The Art of the Animated Image: An Anthology.* Ed. Solomon. Los Angeles: American Film Institute, 1987. 9–12.

"*Song of the South.*" *Time,* Nov. 18, 1946, 101.

Sperb, Jason. "Sensing an Intellectual Nemesis." *Film Criticism* 32.1 (2007): 49–71.

Street, Rita. "Toys Will Be Toys." *Cinefex* 64 (1995): 76–91.

Telotte, J. P. "Lindbergh, Film, and Machine Age Dreams." *South Atlantic Review* 64.4 (1999): 68–83.

———. *The Mouse Machine: Disney and Technology.* Urbana: University of Illinois Press, 2008.

———. *Voices in the Dark: The Narrative Patterns of Film Noir.* Urbana: University of Illinois Press, 1989.

Thomas, Frank, and Ollie Johnston. *The Illusion of Life: Disney Animation.* Rev. ed. New York: Disney Editions, 1995.

Thompson, Richard. "Meep-Meep!" *The American Animated Cartoon: A Critical Anthology.* Ed. Gerald Peary and Danny Peary. New York: Dutton, 1980. 217–25.

"*The Three Caballeros.*" *Time,* Feb. 19, 1945, 91–92.

Tichi, Cecelia. *Shifting Gears: Technology, Literature, Culture in Modernist America.* Chapel Hill: University of North Carolina Press, 1987.

Vidler, Anthony. *The Architectural Uncanny: Essays in the Modern Unhomely.* Cambridge: MIT Press, 1992.

———. "The Explosion of Space: Architecture and the Filmic Imaginary." *Film Architecture: From* Metropolis *to* Blade Runner. Ed. Dietrich Neumann. Munich: Prestel, 1999. 13–25.

———. *Warped Space: Art, Architecture, and Anxiety in Modern Culture.* Cambridge: MIT Press, 2000.

Virilio, Paul. *The Aesthetics of Disappearance.* Trans. Philip Beitchman. New York: Semiotext(e), 1991.

———. *Art and Fear.* Trans. Julie Rose. London: Continuum, 2003.

———. *The Lost Dimension*. Trans. Daniel Moshenberg. New York: Semiotext(e), 1991.

———. *The Vision Machine*. Trans. Julie Rose. Bloomington: Indiana University Press, 1994.

Waller, Gregory A. "Mickey, Walt, and Film Criticism from *Steamboat Willie* to *Bambi*." *The American Animated Cartoon: A Critical Anthology*. Ed. Gerald Peary and Danny Peary. New York: Dutton, 1980. 49–57.

Walz, Gene. "Charlie Thorson and the Temporary Disneyfication of Warner Bros. Cartoons." *Reading the Rabbit: Explorations in Warner Bros. Animation*. Ed. Kevin S. Sandler. New Brunswick: Rutgers University Press, 1998. 49–66.

Watts, Steven. *The Magic Kingdom: Walt Disney and the American Way of Life*. Columbia: University of Missouri Press, 1997.

Wells, Paul. *Animation and America*. New Brunswick: Rutgers University Press, 2002.

Whalen, Grover. "We Welcome the World." *Official Guide Book of the New York World's Fair*. 2nd ed. New York: Exposition Publications, 1939. 4–5.

White, Eric Walter. *Walking Shadows: An Essay on Lotte Reiniger's Silhouette Films*. London: Hogarth Press, 1931.

White, Timothy R. "From Disney to Warner Bros.: The Critical Shift." *Film Criticism* 16.3 (1992): 3–16.

Winter, Jessica. "Full Metal Racket." *Village Voice,* Oct. 26, 2004, www.villagevoice.com/film/0444,winter2,58041,20.html (accessed May 15, 2008).

Wood, Aylish. "Pixel Visions: Digital Intermediates and Micromanipulations of the Image." *Film Criticism* 32.1 (2007): 72–94.

INDEX

9 780813 125862